T0355083

The Scribes of Sleep

The Scribes of Sleep

*Insights from the Most Important Dream
Journals in History*

KELLY BULKELEY

OXFORD
UNIVERSITY PRESS

OXFORD
UNIVERSITY PRESS

Oxford University Press is a department of the University of Oxford. It furthers
the University's objective of excellence in research, scholarship, and education
by publishing worldwide. Oxford is a registered trade mark of Oxford University
Press in the UK and certain other countries.

Published in the United States of America by Oxford University Press
198 Madison Avenue, New York, NY 10016, United States of America.

Library of Congress Control Number: 2023936680

ISBN 978–0–19–760960–6

DOI: 10.1093/oso/9780197609606.001.0001

Printed by Sheridan Books, Inc., United States of America

For my parents

When you gaze long into an abyss,
the abyss also gazes into you.
　　　　　　—F. Nietzsche (*Beyond Good and Evil*, 146)

Contents

PART IV: EXPLORING DIMENSIONS OF RELIGIOSITY

Introduction

A dream journal begins with a wager about time. The wager is this: if you record a dream today, it will have more meaning for you in the future. You are betting that the effort of keeping the journal now will be rewarded in days to come with insights beyond those that can be currently perceived. New meanings in earlier dreams will emerge when illuminated by the recurrent themes of your long-term history as a dreamer. *Dreams gain value over time.* That is the promise a dream journal makes to your future self.

In addition to leveraging the power of time, a dream journal also leverages the power of numbers. As much as can be learned from a single dream, even more can be learned from studying multiple dreams. An image in one dream may seem ambiguous or unclear, but the same image appearing in a group of dreams becomes easier to understand. By gathering numerous dreams into a single collection, a journal gives you the ability to see large-scale patterns and evolving trends.

This idea is not new. It has a long and fascinating history, as the following chapters will show. Swiss psychiatrist Carl Jung was one of the first modern psychologists to emphasize the importance of interpreting dreams in a series. In his 1935 work "Individual Dream Symbolism in Relation to Alchemy," he said: "Here we are not dealing with isolated dreams; they form a coherent series in the course of which the meaning gradually unfolds more or less of its own accord. The series is the context which the dreamer himself supplies."[1] For Jung, a collection of dreams over time provides an invaluable resource for understanding the deepest currents of a patient's inner life. The meanings of a particular dream become much easier to recognize when viewed in relation to all the other dreams from the same individual.

Another leader of twentieth-century dream research, the American psychologist Calvin Hall, also called attention to the remarkable insights that can be gained from studying large collections of dreams over time. In "Diagnosing Personality by the Analysis of Dreams" (1947), he described his method as follows: "[T]he dreams of a cycle are perused in order to get the atmosphere of the dreams as a whole and to ascertain which of the dreams are

The Scribes of Sleep. Kelly Bulkeley, Oxford University Press. © Oxford University Press 2023.
DOI: 10.1093/oso/9780197609606.003.0001

especially revealing of inner conflict."[2] For Hall, a series or cycle of dreams has an "atmosphere" that can be perceived only by studying all the dreams together, "as a whole." Once you have that big-picture view of the series, you can better identify specific dreams that reflect a person's emotional conflicts and concerns in waking life.

The same idea guided the research of American anthropologist Dorothy Eggan. She looked to dreams for both psychological and cultural meanings, and she found they emerged most clearly in a series of dreams. In her 1952 article "The Manifest Content of Dreams: A Challenge to Social Science," Eggan described her approach as follows: "We will [discuss] the tendency of dreams to concern themselves with different arrangements of the same theme over a period of months or years, each dream illuminating elements in another until an entire picture is clear."[3] She posed this as a "challenge" because most of her fellow social scientists assumed the surface imagery of a dream (the manifest content) was meaningless; only by delving into the dreamer's personal associations could the hidden real meanings (the latent content) be discovered. Eggan showed that a statistical analysis of the manifest content of multiple dreams can in fact reveal important meanings with direct relevance to the individual's waking life.

Jung, Hall, and Eggan all shared the same basic insight: we can learn more about dreams by looking at large numbers of them recorded for months and years. Later in this book, I will discuss their research findings in more detail, but for now, I can simply highlight their agreement on this key point. *The best way to understand your dreams is to study them in a series over time.* Seen in this light, a dream journal can be appreciated not only as a source of personal discovery but also as a surprisingly illuminating path toward new scientific knowledge.

And yet keeping a dream journal has always been an unusual and somewhat obscure practice. Its many potentials have rarely been actualized. To appreciate the marginal status of dream journals in present-day society, consider the following facts:

- All humans have the innate, neurologically hardwired capacity for dreaming. We are all born with brains that, during the regular course of the sleep cycle, go through phases of intense internal arousal—what French researchers call paradoxical sleep and Americans call rapid eye movement (REM) sleep—in which many of our most vivid dreams occur. This is true for everyone with a normally functioning brain, whether or not you remember upon awakening what happened during those times of heightened neural activation. Thanks to the evolutionary architecture of our brains, we belong to a species of natural dreamers.[4]

- Almost everyone remembers at least some of their dreams. According to survey data in the Sleep and Dream Database (SDDb), an open-access digital archive of dream research, to be discussed in more detail in chapter 8, about half of both men and women in present-day America remember a dream once a week or more often. More than 90 percent of men and women remember a dream at least once every few months. This suggests that recalling dreams is an ordinary part of life for the vast majority of the population. Only 6 percent of the respondents say they never remember their dreams. Additional research focusing on these "non-dreamers" has found the actual number for people who have never remembered their dreams is probably closer to 1 percent.[5]

- Many people not only remember their dreams but also share them with other people, such as friends and family members. Dream-sharing practices appear throughout history in cultures all over the world. The surveys in the SDDb show that in the United States today, about 20 percent of women and 14 percent of men share their dreams with someone once a week or more often. More than 70 percent of both men and women say they share their dreams at least once every few months. About 21 percent of women and 28 percent of men say they never share dreams.

- Dreaming is universal, dream recall is nearly universal, and dream-sharing is widespread. But when it comes to *recording* dreams and tracking them over time, the percentages plummet. According to SDDb figures, only about 8 percent of the population records a dream once a week or more often, another 12 percent at least once every few months. Fully 80 percent of both men and women say they never record their dreams.

With so much dreaming, remembering of dreams, and sharing of dreams, why is there so little recording of dreams? Why do so few people keep a dream journal? For some, it's a matter of time. Dream memories can fade very quickly after waking, which means the ideal approach is to set aside a few quiet moments first thing in the morning for private writing and reflection. However, that can be a difficult practice to sustain for anyone whose mornings are busy and unpredictable. For other people, it's a matter of resources. Keeping a dream journal requires both a means of recording the dreams and a secure, private space in which to preserve and access them over time. These resources are not readily available for everyone. Probably the biggest factor is motivation. Why keep a dream journal? What's the point? Even if you have the time and the resources, what are you trying to learn or accomplish?

The practice is found most often today among two groups of people: those who are involved in therapy, and artists. Both groups have a strong motivation for keeping track of their dreams. People in therapy often find their dreams to be a valuable companion during the healing process. Some therapists actively encourage their clients to record their dreams, as a helpful resource for their work together. For artists, dreams offer a time-honored wellspring of creative inspiration. Keeping a dream journal makes it easier to recognize the spontaneous appearance of new ideas, images, and insights, beyond what the rational mind can generate. As a source of raw material for the creative process, a dream journal has tremendous value for all forms of artistic practice.

In cultures around the world, people have recorded their dreams for these and other reasons as well. The earliest written records about dreams come from ancient Egypt, Greece, India, and China, in the form of dream interpretation manuals. These manuals are not personal diaries, but they do rely on the interpreter's lifelong experience with large numbers of dreams, which makes them a literary cousin of the dream journal. Most of the dream interpretation manuals of antiquity focused on illuminating the future, especially around the perennial uncertainties of human life such as health, love, family, hunting, war, death, wealth, and the elemental forces of nature.

This future-oriented motivation remains alive today for people who keep track of their dreams for possible signs of precognition and prophetic insight. For example, John Dunne's 1927 book *An Experiment with Time* (of which Jorge Luis Borges once said, "I know no title more interesting")[6] included several detailed discussions of his dreams and their curious relationship with events happening in the past, present, and future. Inspired by Dunne, many other people began recording their dreams in the effort to replicate and extend his discoveries. This included the novelist Vladimir Nabokov, who kept a dream journal for several months in 1964, using Dunne's method of identifying temporal anomalies and pondering the metaphysical questions raised by the results of his experiment.[7]

Religious beliefs and practices can provide strong motivation for recording one's dreams. For Protestant Christians in England and the United States from the seventeenth to nineteenth centuries, keeping a diary was a common practice of moral self-scrutiny, divine discernment, and introspective prayer. Including dream reports in these diaries was a way of observing and reflecting on the role of providence in one's life. Going back even further in history, Buddhists have been recording their dreams for many centuries, often in relation to their experiences with meditation. In Buddhist traditions, dreaming offers an opportunity to extend meditation practice beyond the waking state, continuing it into sleep. Recording one's dreams allows for a closer monitoring of this development and a favorable means of observing one's progress. Islam, Judaism, and Hinduism all have teachings about dreams as a source of divine wisdom and guidance, giving their followers spiritual motivation for paying close and ongoing attention to their nocturnal reveries.[8]

In addition to all these motivations for keeping a dream journal, some people are just curious. Inquiring minds want to know. That's the best way to describe how I began my dream journal. As you probably guessed, I have been recording my own dreams for many years. Before going further, it seems fair to share the origin story of my journal-keeping practice.

It was the summer of 1981. I had just finished six weeks of Reserve Officer Training Corps (ROTC) Army basic camp at Fort Knox, Kentucky. In addition to a well-guarded horde of America's gold reserves, Fort Knox housed the world's largest collection of land-based military firepower, including thousands of tanks, armored vehicles, and artillery pieces. Training maneuvers and target practice never stopped, and the concussive sounds of exploding ordnance filled the air day and night. I have written more about this experience in an earlier book, *The Wondering Brain* (2006). Here I will just say that by the end of the camp, I could do a lot of pushups, I was a good shot with an M-16 rifle, and I was deeply sleep-deprived. Soon after the camp ended, I flew to Hawaii to visit a couple of friends from school who lived in Honolulu. Before seeing them on Oahu, I went to Kauai first, hitchhiked around the island to the Na Pali coast, and backpacked from one remote beach to another for a week. I brought no stove or cooking equipment, just a few pounds of nut mix; no sleeping bag, just a blanket and pad; no tent, just a plastic tarp; no official (i.e., required) camping permit, just a large Buck knife and a few organic substances of dubious legality.

This is a long setup for the circumstances in which I read Ann Faraday's 1972 book *Dream Power*. It was one of the three or four books I decided were worth bringing on this trip. I'm not sure why *Dream Power* made it into my backpack when so many other seemingly more necessary items did not make the cut, but it's the only one of the books I now remember. It was a best-seller at the time, with lots of favorable press, and a paperback edition had just come out in 1980. It would have been featured prominently in the musty, slightly weird independent bookstores I found most appealing then (and still do). I had already read a few books by Jung and Sigmund Freud, along with Friedrich Nietzsche and various esoteric philosophers, so I was familiar with ideas about the unconscious, the psychology of religion, and the autonomous energies of the mind. Dreams had never been a focus of interest, however, until this trip. I don't exactly remember why, but I'm guessing the intensity of the Army camp experience (awakened at four a.m. each morning by bellowing sergeants; a long, hot day of military training; lights out at ten p.m.; and every fourth night getting up for a random hour of watch duty) disrupted my sleep so thoroughly that I couldn't help noticing my dreams more than ever before. This, as best as I can reconstruct it, is the chain of events that led to my sitting on a wilderness beach on Kauai, reading *Dream Power*, and starting a dream journal.

The first dreams I recorded were nightmares. Long ones. After writing them down, I was struck by their elaborate complexity. Since early childhood, I had been troubled by dreams of being chased or attacked, but I had never thought about them beyond their negative emotions and strange recurrence. Now that I had transcribed a few of them as fully as possible, with all the details I could remember, I realized they were not just random bursts of nonsense. The dreams had much more coherence, clarity, structure, and even beauty than I was expecting. Back at school that fall, I continued with the dream journal, and it became a source of continual surprise over the following weeks. In addition to the ongoing nightmares, I recorded dreams of magical creatures, otherworldly settings, and mythological symbols, all intertwined with vivid images of my friends, family, home, classes, dorm life, and the rest of my regular waking reality. It truly felt like peering through Alice's looking glass and seeing reflections of my normal world in bizarre yet hyper-meaningful forms.

All of that was amazing to discover, and I learned a lot about myself very quickly in the process. But how long would I keep it going? I was a busy student at the time, with lots happening each day and even more each night. As noted above, keeping a dream journal requires consistency and focus, and my life at the time had little to spare of either. Nobody else I knew paid any attention to dreams. I raised the topic with a few friends, but I found no one else with any real interest. In fact, my own interest was still rather shaky. I was playing a team sport; classes were getting more demanding; my friends in the room next door hosted a rowdy party approximately every other night. So many distractions, so many other things going on. It would have been easy to drop the dream journal once the novelty wore off.

I didn't drop it, though. Every night, I placed an open notebook and a pen by my bedside, and every morning, I tried to give myself a few moments after awakening to write down whatever I could remember. At some point in the weeks and months following my Na Pali beach encounter with *Dream Power*, my attitude toward the journal took a surprising turn. I realized I was not simply documenting my dreams, as if I were keeping track of what I ate each day or how much I exercised. Rather, the journal had become a medium for what felt like a relational dialogue, like an exchange of letters between the waking and sleeping parts of my mind. The journal revealed that over time, my dreams were *changing*, apparently in response to my initial efforts to understand their meanings. I still had frequent nightmares, but they felt different now, with less blind terror and more intriguing, thought-provoking characters and themes. *As I began paying more attention to my dreams, they began paying more attention to me.* That's how it felt, anyway. The journal had taken on a life of its own.

In the years since then, I have met many other people who record and preserve their dreams over time. Their reasons vary, but I have noticed that no matter what motivates them to start recording their dreams, the practice often grows into something *more*, something surprising, illuminating, and inspiring. This book is an exploration of that *more* as it emerges in a dream journal. *The Scribes of Sleep* looks at what kinds of people are drawn to this practice, what they learn from it, and how it influences their waking lives. As the coming chapters will show, dream journals are an excellent source of data for scientific study and a fascinating window onto cultural, social, and historical dynamics. Dream journals are also a powerful source of personal discovery, healing, and growth. Because of this dual value—as a source of individual *and* collective insight—the book will address both academic researchers and general, nonspecialist readers. I don't see any way around it: the book must speak to both if it is truly to serve the needs of either. Researchers cannot understand the deeper dynamics of dream journals without paying close attention to the personal lives of the dreamers, and people who keep dream journals have difficulty recognizing all the meaningful patterns in their dreams without some help and guidance from the community of dream researchers. Perhaps it is the practice itself that dissolves this distinction. Keeping a dream journal means engaging in both a personal quest for self-discovery and a scientist's devotion to systematically gathering and analyzing evidence.

Part I introduces seven figures who kept what I believe are the most important dream journals in history. Each of these individuals has a fascinating life story filled with impressive accomplishments, dramatic events, harrowing dangers, and several experiences of mysterious uncertainty. As a group, they reflect the diversity of people who have been drawn into a deeper engagement with the unfolding dynamics of their dreaming selves:

1. Aelius Aristides (117–181), a Roman speaker and writer whose health crisis in his twenties brought him to seek help at the temples of the healing god Asclepius. Aristides began recording his dreams in response to a direct command from the god.
2. Myōe Shonin (1173–1232), an ascetic Japanese monk who advocated for reforms in the Kegon and Shingon schools of Buddhism. He kept a journal of his dreams, visions, and meditation experiences for forty years.
3. Lucrecia de León (1568–?), an illiterate young woman who grew up in Madrid during the imperial reign of Philip II. Catholic priests recorded a series of her dreams over a period of three years, dreams that accurately foresaw the defeat of the Spanish Armada in 1588.
4. Emanuel Swedenborg (1688–1772), a Swedish scientist and philosopher who recorded his dreams over several years, leading to a spiritual awakening and the founding of a new church of mystical Christianity.
5. Benjamin Banneker (1731–1806), a free African American scientist, inventor, surveyor, and author of impressively accurate almanacs. One of the most brilliant minds of his time, Banneker kept a regular dream journal through his adult life, only fragments of which still exist.
6. Anna Kingsford (1846–1888), a crusading English doctor, antivivisectionist, theosophist, and women's rights advocate. She wrote a journal of her dreams from her early twenties to her death at age forty-one.
7. Wolfgang Pauli (1900–1958), a Austrian theoretical physicist whose original work on quantum theory won him the Nobel Prize in Physics

in 1945. He was a therapy patient of Jung's, and for many years, he kept a dream journal and shared its contents with Jung for analysis and interpretation.

Learning about the lives of these seven historical figures and their dream journal practices will set the stage for the main question of the book: *what kinds of insight can be gained from keeping a dream journal?* The chapters that follow will present three methods for answering that central question: a digital analytics approach, a depth psychological approach, and a religious studies approach.

Part II of the book shows how new digital technologies can reveal meaningful patterns in large collections of dreams. Digital methods of data analysis can be used to compare the contents of different series of dreams, revealing both common features and strange anomalies. Part III brings depth psychology into the discussion, with a closer look at what Freud, Jung, and psychological anthropologists such as Eggan have to say about the interpretation of dream series over time. Also included here are contemporary psychologists whose work integrates classical theories with new findings in neuroscience and evolutionary biology. Part IV uses the methods of religious studies to highlight aspects of dream journaling practice that the individuals themselves describe as religious, spiritual, and/or metaphysical in significance. Although not everyone has spiritual interests at the beginning, the practice often leads in this direction as the interaction between dreaming and waking unfolds over time. *The Scribes of Sleep* proposes that keeping a long-term dream journal has the effect of cultivating three specific qualities of religious temperament. On the whole, the figures described in this book tend to be *individualists*, following a personalized path of spirituality; *mystics*, exploring altered modes of consciousness; and *pluralists*, embracing multiple ways of being religious. These are the features that best characterize the existential outlook of people who are most avid about their dream journaling practice. They can be described as *free spirits* whose openness toward dreaming develops into a broader openness toward new metaphysical horizons. They represent a type of religiosity that seems rare but may in fact be latent in everyone, just waiting for the right conditions to emerge.

The Scribes of Sleep proposes that dream journals, and the free spirits who keep them, can best be understood within an interdisciplinary framework that combines digital analysis, depth psychology, and religious studies. Applying these methods to individual dream journals yields valuable insights into the dreamers' personal lives and cultural environments. Previous researchers have experimented with one or another of these methods; this is the first book to use all three in a coordinated, systematic fashion. *The Scribes of Sleep* will also make an additional, complementary argument. In the process of closely studying dream journals, we can discover new potentials in these three methods and thus new ways to discern meaningful patterns not only in dreams but in other phenomena, too. Ultimately, the analysis moves in both directions. The methods shed light on the dream journals, and the dream journals shed light on the methods. This reciprocal dynamic between exploring dreams and being explored *by* dreams is the greatest gift of a dream journal. It is a gift that benefits not only each individual dreamer but the future of dream science as well.

PART I

SEVEN DREAMERS AND THEIR JOURNALS

The chapters in this part introduce the lives of seven historical figures whose dream journal practices are the central case studies of this book. They are the leading characters in the story going forward. Other people, both historical and contemporary, also appear as supporting cast, but these seven remarkable individuals are the stars of the show. We begin with chapters that describe their family backgrounds, their growth from childhood into adulthood, the cultural and religious influences on their development, and the emergence of their interest in dreaming. A few of their dreams are presented here; more will appear in later chapters. All the dreams discussed in this book are available for readers to study in the Sleep and Dream Database, an online archive of dream reports and other material relating to sleep and dreaming.[1]

Why have I chosen these seven people? Why offer them as the most important representatives of the history of dream journals? Several principles guided the selection process, all shaping this final group of seven. To begin, I wanted to make sure the sources presented here are accessible to readers so they can examine the primary evidence for themselves. Each of these seven individuals has been studied to some extent by other scholars and biographers, which allows readers to check my claims in relation to other secondary sources. By the end of the book, I will be making rather large claims on behalf of their journals, so I do not want any concerns about data transparency to detract from those bigger claims. A second principle of selection here is temporal range and the desire to include the oldest, best-documented, and most historically consequential dream journals. This yielded a group of individuals from the second, twelfth, sixteenth, seventeenth, eighteenth, nineteenth, and twentieth centuries. Although there are big gaps in that chronology, it does cover a wide range of time, giving a sense of how people from different historical eras have thought about the patterns of their dreams. The third principle of selection tried to correct for implicit biases in dream research itself, by looking for historical figures who kept dream journals but have attracted relatively little interest from mainstream scholars. Not *no* interest (because of the first principle) but much less interest than the richness of their dream journals deserves. Who has been understudied and underappreciated by the modern community of dream researchers?

By holding all three selection principles in tension and scanning the available biographical resources, I settled on this group of individuals: a male literary artist from the eastern Mediterranean during the Roman Empire, a male Buddhist monk from medieval Japan, a young working-class female from Siglo de Oro Spain, a male engineer and mystic from early Enlightenment-era Sweden, a male African American surveyor in Maryland during Revolutionary times, a female writer and physician in Victorian England, and a male quantum physicist from Austria just before World War II. This group of seven is not perfectly representative of all dreamers from all times, of course. But each of these seven individuals made a dedicated, passionate effort to record their dreams over time, and their journals made a tangible impact on the course of their lives and the world around them.

1

Aelius Aristides

Devotee of the Healing God

We begin with what may be the oldest surviving dream journal, that of
Aelius Aristides, a highly literate man living in the Roman Empire early in
the second century CE.[1] It seems likely that other people prior to Aristides
recorded their dreams in some fashion, but his collection currently stands as
the oldest and most detailed dream journal in history. Aristides had a very
strong motive for keeping his journal: a god appeared to him in a dream and
told him to do so, to write a book about his dreams. Aristides said, "Straight
from the beginning the god ordered me to write down my dreams. And this
was the first of his commands. I made a copy of my dreams, dictating them
whenever I was unable to write myself."[2] Born in 117 CE, Aristides grew up
in Smyrna, a rural province of the Roman Empire on the eastern coast of
the Mediterranean Sea, in present-day Turkey. He came from a wealthy and
socially prominent family with extensive landholdings, which enabled him
to receive an elite education specializing in philosophy, literature, and the
practical speaking skills of rhetoric and oratory. To give a beautiful speech
in front of a large audience, to recite from memory an emotionally moving
poem, to engage in spirited public debates about the great issues of the day—
these were the goals of Aristides's education, and he devoted years of effort
and training to these pursuits.

Through childhood and adolescence, he lived a fairly conventional life for
a young male of his time and place. The Roman Empire had reached its maximum territorial spread during the reign of Trajan, who died in 117, the year
of Aristides's birth. Political infighting and military overreach would eventually lead to the empire's decline and fall, but during Aristides's life, the power
of Rome was near its peak, with military dominance throughout southern
Europe, northern Africa, and Asia Minor. Total control of travel and commerce in and around the Mediterranean enabled the Romans to establish a
widespread system of laws, practices of governance, and religious ceremonies that held the empire together for several centuries. It would have been

The Scribes of Sleep. Kelly Bulkeley, Oxford University Press. © Oxford University Press 2023.
DOI: 10.1093/oso/9780197609606.003.0002

a brutal time to live if you were a conscript soldier, peasant, slave, and/or woman, but it would have afforded tremendous benefits for people with the social power to enjoy the opportunities of a wealthy cosmopolitan life. People like Aristides.

As he grew older, Aristides traveled to Italy, Greece, and Egypt to study with special tutors and practice his skills in public speaking. The ultimate marker of success would be a journey to Rome, the capital city, to give speeches to the citizens and leaders there. Finally, in 144, when he was in his mid-twenties, Aristides felt sufficiently prepared, and he arranged for the long sea voyage from Smyrna to Rome. The ship set out in the middle of winter, and Aristides was already feeling mildly ill before he came on board. His condition worsened along the way, and by the time he reached Rome, he was suffering from fever, earaches, and trouble breathing. These ailments became so bad that it was no longer possible for him to appear in public. Deeply disappointed, he turned around and made the arduous journey back to Smyrna, hoping for a quiet time of recovery and recuperation once he returned to his home.

This was not the first time that an illness had knocked him back. Aristides apparently struggled with health problems from the beginning of his life. According to one source, he suffered from a "shuddering of the muscles" since early childhood, an ailment that today might be diagnosed as epilepsy or some other kind of seizure disorder.[3] Aristides was clearly no stranger to physical pain, but what was different now, as he returned from Rome to Smyrna, was that his bodily ailments had become a major obstacle to his chosen path in life and a threat to his basic sense of identity. For many years, he had trained his mind to do something that his body was now incapable of sustaining. Worse, once he reached his home, the local medical healers in Smyrna had no idea what was afflicting him. They could offer him no help.

It was at this point—feeling lost and alone, suffering both physically and mentally, ridden with fever, and having terrible difficulty breathing—that Aristides received his first dream of the god Asclepius. Thus began a life of religious devotion and therapeutic practice that became a new organizing center of Aristides's existence. His worship of the god not only brought Aristides relief from his sufferings but also inspired him to new creative heights.

Aristides was hardly the only person who turned to the deity in search of medical help. For hundreds of years, Asclepius had served the ancient Greeks and Romans as a powerful god of healing, with numerous temples throughout the Mediterranean world devoted to his worship. His father was the god Apollo, his mother a human woman, Coronis. When Apollo discovered that Coronis was romantically involved with a human man, the god in his jealousy struck her dead. As she lay on the funeral pyre, Apollo rescued the living child—Asclepius—from her womb before the flames consumed them both. Apollo gave the infant to a centaur named Chiron to raise, and Chiron taught Asclepius the arts of medicine. Asclepius learned well and quickly gained fame as a healer. His skills grew so mighty that he found he could even bring the dead back to life. This was too much for Zeus, the greatest of Olympian gods, and he punished Asclepius with a fatal bolt of lightning. However, in recognition of the love for Asclepius among all humans, Zeus transformed him into a god and elevated him to an eternal place in the heavens. Asclepius thus became a divine archetype of the wounded healer.

The worship of Asclepius seems to have begun at a local shrine in the ancient Greek town of Tricca and spread from there. Especially popular was the temple in Epidaurus, where visitors seeking a cure for their ills were welcomed and treated over a period of more than a thousand years.[4] The temples of the god were usually situated away from the active areas of city life, in a sacred grove of trees near a natural source of water (spring, stream, lake, or seashore). A visitor would begin in the outer sanctum with bathing, prayers, and other purifying practices, waiting for a sign that the time was right to enter the inner sanctum, the *abaton* or divine space at the symbolic center of the temple. During this waiting time, the visitor was a kind of prisoner, held in an anxious state of liminal uncertainty. When finally allowed entry to the *abaton*, the visitor found an array of ritual beds, or *kline*, for sleeping and hopefully receiving a divine healing dream. Slithering freely on the floor of the *abaton* were numerous non-poisonous snakes, one of the god's favorite animals. New Asclepian temples in other parts of the Mediterranean were consecrated by the arrival of a snake brought from the great temple at Epidaurus.

Ideally, while sleeping in the *abaton*, the visitor would have a clear dream of Asclepius curing the illness, directly and immediately. Sometimes the visitor would have an opaque and indirect dream that required help from the temple priests to interpret for its medical significance. Either way, from a direct divine message or a priestly interpretation, the visitor received healing energy, therapeutic information, and religious reassurance. If a cure was finally achieved, the visitor was encouraged to write a testimonial to the god's healing power, including a description of their illness, the prayers and purifications they performed, the dream in which the god appeared, and expressions of gratitude. These testimonials were inscribed on the wall of the temple's outer sanctum, to inspire new visitors at the beginning of their own therapeutic journeys.

None of this happened quickly. Most cases required weeks or months of effort. In some cases, like that of Aristides, the treatment stretched out over several years. The Asclepian temples combined the elements of hospital, health spa, and spiritual retreat, which accounts for both their popularity around the ancient world and their remarkable longevity. An unfortunate sign of people's devotion to Asclepius is how vigorously the Christian authorities, once they gained religious supremacy in the late Roman Empire, destroyed the god's temples and turned them into churches or shrines to local saints. As a half-human, half-divine healer who was unjustly killed and then reborn, Asclepius was inevitably seen as a direct competitor to the Christian Savior.

By the time Aristides reached the Asclepian temple in Pergamum, not far from his home in Smyrna, his primary physical problem centered on his digestive system. He had difficulty maintaining a regular intake of food, and he suffered a great deal of stomach and abdominal pain. Nausea and vomiting were constant features of his life. One of his first dreams while there set the pattern for much of the rest to come:

> He [Asclepius] ordered me to go forth unshod. And I cried out in my dream, as if in a waking state, and after I had accomplished the orders of the dream: "Great is Asclepius! The order is accomplished." I seemed to cry out these things, while I went forth.[5]

This dream came in winter, when walking around in bare feet would normally be an unhealthy and inadvisable thing to do and irrelevant, in any case, to his intestinal pains. But this was a recurrent theme in Aristides's waking life and dreams: the failure of human doctors to help him and the true healing power of the god. The surprising nature of the command to go forth unshod highlighted this crucial distinction. Whenever he followed the human doctors rather than the god, his condition worsened; whenever he listened to Asclepius and did as he bade, no matter how strange it sounded, his condition improved. Many other dreams of divine prescriptions came after this, with this same counterintuitive quality of being contrary to the medical advice he was getting from other sources. In obedience to the orders of his dreams, Aristides fasted, bathed, ran circles around the temple, purged himself, rubbed mud all over his body, and performed a variety of rituals and sacrifices. Nor was Asclepius a jealous god; in several dreams, Aristides was encouraged to seek the aid of other deities from Greek, Roman, and Egyptian pantheons. Here is an example of a dream of reassurance he received from the goddess Athena at a time when he had fallen ill from a plague (probably smallpox), beyond the help of the doctors who had given him up for dead:

> Athena appeared with her aegis and the beauty and the whole form of the Athena of Phidias in Athens. There was also a scent from the aegis as sweet as could be, and it was like wax, and it too was marvelous in beauty and magnitude. She appeared to me alone, standing before me, even from where I would behold her as well as possible. She reminded me of *The Odyssey* and said that these were not idle tales, but that this could be judged even by the present circumstances. It was necessary to persevere. I myself was indeed both Odysseus and Telemachus, and she must help me. . . . Thus the goddess appeared and consoled me, and saved me, while I was in my sick bed and nothing was wanting for my death.[6]

The results of his various healing dreams were usually favorable, though never very long-lasting. If one set of symptoms went away, another source of suffering seemed to arise. Again, we do not know enough about his condition to determine if Aristides suffered from a chronic bodily illness or if his problems were primarily emotional, with the physical symptoms appearing as psychosomatic byproducts. The temple practices did not immediately cure him of his ills, but Aristides certainly found great comfort and meaning in the worship of Asclepius, and over time, he became a passionate devotee of the god. Even still, the question remains about the effectiveness of the dream treatments he received at the Asclepian temple. If the goal was to eliminate his physical and emotional suffering, the treatments did not produce a definitive cure. They had mildly positive effects over short periods of time, which was better than nothing, but not a miraculous restoration of perfect health.

Aristides himself, however, considered his time at the Asclepian temple to be a tremendous success. His ailments may not have disappeared, but they no longer overwhelmed him or made it impossible to live his life. Indeed, it seems likely that at some point, he stayed at the temple not because of physical or mental problems but because he enjoyed it and found deep meaning in the worship of Asclepius. He may have originally gone to the temple seeking a cure for his ills, but he soon found much more than mere pain relief.

Inspired by the god's benevolent presence in his life, Aristides began looking to his dreams not only for healing information but also for creative insights to guide him in his career as an orator. He said his experiences with dream incubation were as helpful to his education as any of his classes and tutors:

> Indeed the greatest and most valuable part of my training was my access to and communion with these dreams. For I heard many things which excelled in purity of style and were gloriously beyond my models [of rhetoric], and I dreamed that I myself said many things better than my wont, and things of which I had never thought.[7]

Eventually, Aristides regained enough good health to resume his career pursuits of speaking, writing, teaching, and traveling. By the time of his death in 181, he had become a widely known and well-respected literary figure during an especially prosperous period of Roman imperial history. Even as his public fame and accomplishments grew, he always maintained a strong reverence for Asclepius and gave credit to the god for everything he had done. Toward the end of his life, a strong earthquake destroyed much of Smyrna and the surrounding towns. When the emperor at that time, Marcus Aurelius, visited Smyrna to survey the damage, Aristides gave such an eloquent and passionate speech on behalf of the suffering local residents that the emperor was persuaded to provide the region with extensive rebuilding funds from Rome. Aristides's strongest rhetorical energies were stimulated when he spoke not on his own behalf, not for his own personal honor, but on behalf of the people of his community and the god who saved his life.

The following dreams from Aristides's *Sacred Tales* give a sense of the intermixing of Aristides's personal life concerns with religious and cultural elements from Roman society. His deep familiarity with classical Greek literature comes through in these dreams, and so does his comfort with the worship of deities from Egypt and other great Mediterranean civilizations:

> I dreamed that I saw Plato himself standing in my room, directly across from my bed. He happened to be working on his letter to Dionysus, and was very angry. He glanced at me and said, "How suited do I appear to you for letter writing? No worse than Celer?"—meaning the Imperial Secretary. And I said, "Hush! Remember who you are!" And not much later, he disappeared, and I was held in meditation. But someone present said, "This

man who spoke with you just now as Plato is your Hermes,"—meaning my guardian deity. "But," he said, "he likened himself to Plato."[8]

For I thought that while I stood by the very altar of Zeus in the market place, and was asking him to give me a sign if it were better to sacrifice, a shining star darted through the market place and sanctioned the sacrifice.[9]

I dreamed that I prayed to the Gods, some things in common, to those to whom I am wont to pray, and again privately to Zeus and Ares, and the Gods who hold Syria. And the habitations there appeared nearly the same as those at home. And after this, there was a procession to the Emperor. But I took part in the procession to the Emperor, who was then in Syria. And it turned out well.[10]

There was also a light from Isis and other unspeakable things which pertained to my salvation. Sarapis also appeared on the same night, both he himself and Asclepius. They were marvelous in beauty and magnitude, and in some way like one another.[11]

By his own admission, Aristides suffered for years from a variety of illnesses and ailments, so it would be unfair to criticize his writings for including elements of heightened emotionality, linguistic bizarreness, and psychological disturbance. Although he used all his skills as a rhetorician in its composition, the *Sacred Tales* was a sincere attempt to articulate his actual experiences as a devotee of Asclepius. He was writing the text as a therapeutic practice in obedience to a divine mandate, not as a literary exercise or in rote conformity to temple customs. To sleep in the temple of Asclepius, dream, record those dreams, apply their insights in waking life, and then sleep in the temple again—that was the healing rhythm to which Aristides devoted himself and in which he discovered a deeper purpose for his life than merely giving pretty speeches. As a chronicle of dreams, perhaps the oldest survivor in history, the *Sacred Tales* helps us understand both the complex personal journey of Aristides and the ancient therapeutic culture of the Asclepian temples, where dream incubation served as a foundational practice of medical caregiving.

2

Myōe Shonin

Extreme Visionary

At first sight, it might seem that Myōe Shonin, a twelfth-century Buddhist monk from Japan, would be a strange figure to present as a role model for dream journaling or for anything else.[1] He was strictly celibate, constantly at war with his body, suicidal and self-mutilating, and frequently involved in angry disputes with other Buddhist teachers over subtle issues of doctrine and practice. And yet Myōe also devoted the best energies of his life to cultivating his mind's capacity for imaginative creativity and spiritual insight. All of his teachings and practices were devoted to the goal of generating powerful religious visions. Meditation was the chief means toward this goal, but Myōe actively cultivated dreaming as another authentic source of visionary insight. His dream journal, which he kept from the ages of nineteen to fifty-eight, just before his death, illuminates this compelling motivation for Myōe to keep track of his dreams over time. In other texts, he mentions dreams from younger ages, so it is clear that he was a big dreamer from early in life.

Myōe was born in 1173 in a rural village in southern Japan. His mother had prayed fervently for a son, reciting the Lotus Sutra throughout her pregnancy. His father was a warrior who planned for his son to follow in his martial footsteps. But starting in early childhood, Myōe wanted to become a monk. At one point, he decided to burn and injure himself with heated metal tongs so that he couldn't become a warrior and would only be fit for the priesthood. His fear of the hot tongs prevented him from actually carrying out the plan, but this incident was the first of a lifelong series of self-imposed physical torments in religiously charged situations. When Myōe directed his spiritual energy toward a specific aim, he seemed willing and even eager to risk his body for the higher cause of his chosen goal.

Both of his parents died within a few months of each other, his father in battle and his mother of unknown causes, leaving Myōe an orphan at the age of eight. Under the care of an uncle, Myōe was brought to a temple near Kyoto to be educated. He took his studies seriously and continued to follow

The Scribes of Sleep. Kelly Bulkeley, Oxford University Press. © Oxford University Press 2023.
DOI: 10.1093/oso/9780197609606.003.0003

his yearning to become a priest. He pondered the Buddha's example of compassion for all beings, thinking about how to apply this principle in his own life. One night when he was thirteen, inspired by a story that in a previous life the Buddha had offered himself to hungry beasts, Myōe went to a charnel field where dead bodies were left in the open to decompose. He stayed there the whole night in meditation, hoping a wolf would come to eat him. He left the next morning, whole and disappointed. At sixteen, he took formal vows of renunciation as a monk, which led to more intense studies, more elaborate ritual practices, and more physically risky efforts to model his own life on that of the Buddha. He tried another night in the charnel field, to no avail. He went to offer himself to a leper, but the leper had already died. He chose as his personal deity the Mother of all Buddhas, "Butsugen-butsumo," whose wisdom is symbolized by the all-seeing eye. To prove his devotion to her and to repudiate the secret pride he felt about his monastic humility, he sat in front of a painting of this deity and cut off his right ear. He wanted to emulate the life of the Buddha directly, literally, and completely, and he thus felt the need to eliminate anything, including his own body, that blocked his progress toward his ultimate goal.

Myōe's ascetic practices deliberately took him away from society and separated him from the mainstream of his community, but ironically, the power and wisdom of his teachings drew an increasingly large group of followers, along with more onerous responsibilities for temple administration and more rancorous debates with other teachers from rival schools of Buddhism. He was a victim of his own success, in the sense that his principled rejection of the spiritual corruption of the contemporary world made him more influential and eventually led him back to greater engagement with that world. Myōe happened to live during a time of major transformation in Japan's political and religious institutions. In 1185, after many years of vicious warfare, the samurai warrior class wrested control from the imperial aristocracy and its supporters among the major monastic orders, initiating Japan's feudal era, known as the Kamakura period. Countless temples and shrines were destroyed in the fighting, and in their place, a variety of new schools of Buddhism emerged to offer their own special paths to enlightenment. In this time of social upheaval and religious innovation, Myōe was a traditionalist who rejected the simplistic and misleading claims of the new schools. He did not necessarily question their practices, some of which could be quite effective in stimulating revelatory dreams and visions. What Myōe criticized was their naive suggestions that achieving enlightenment could be reached by means of one easy method, meaning that everything else—the ethical precepts, the time-honored rituals, the historical traditions—was irrelevant and could be ignored. Instead of promoting spiritual growth, Myōe believed these new schools were dangerous forces of cultural destruction that merely appealed to people's short-term desire for an enhanced sense of social rank and status.

The massive shift in Japanese social life during this period intensified Myōe's feeling that he was living during an evil age, that earlier times had been better, but those times were now gone, leaving him trapped in the degraded, declining reality of the present. His religious touchstone was the life of the Buddha, and Myōe clearly wished more than anything that he could have been alive at that time, when he could have learned about enlightenment directly from the Buddha himself. The Kegon school of Japanese Buddhism that Myōe helped develop was focused on the sermon the Buddha gave on the first morning after his enlightenment (known as the "Great and Vast Buddha Flower Garland Sutra"). Myōe's efforts in meditation, dreams, and visions were all oriented by this basic desire to be near the Buddha at the very moment when he had just been enlightened. The pure, original teachings from that time of primal religious power have become corrupted, diluted, and untrustworthy, in Myōe's view, but through a highly trained and cultivated imagination, one can overcome the illusory boundary of time and reconnect with the true living essence of the Buddha. Hence Myōe's lifelong pursuit of dreams and visions, which he rarely interpreted for their symbolic meanings or relevance to the concerns of his waking life. He saw his dreams not as hidden messages to be unraveled but rather as direct spiritual experiences to be appreciated, savored, and integrated into his ever-deepening relationship with the Buddha.

Myōe also practiced a form of esoteric Buddhism known as Shingon, a lineage that taught an array of secret visionary practices. Although he is generally recognized as a leader of both the Kegon and the Shingon traditions of Japanese Buddhism, during his life Myōe denied that any tradition had authority over him or his spiritual pursuits, which he ultimately grounded in the life of the Buddha, not in any human-made institution. Still, he promoted Kegon and Shingon teachings and considered himself a worthy advocate for their ideals. As an adult, Myōe told his followers about a dream his mother's sister had before his birth about two sweet fruits that someone had placed on a plate, a dream that he now felt had foretold the course of his life: "It seems that because I am now at the end of the Kegon and Shingon lineages, someone gave those two large, sweet fruits."[2] In short autobiographical texts, Myōe mentioned other dreams from his childhood and adolescence, not included in the diary he later began at the age of nineteen. Here is Hayao Kawai's rendering of the earliest dream Myōe mentioned in these texts:

> The first dream comes at 9 years of age when Myōe enters the temple. In the dream his late nurse is dismembered with the parts of her body scattered around. She suffered extraordinary pain. Although he knows she had been a sinful woman, he feels especially sad. He thinks he must become a good priest in order to rescue her in life after death.[3]

As noted earlier, Myōe's parents died when he was eight years old, so this dream came not long after that. He had lost another adult caregiver, in an especially gruesome fashion. An acute, reality-based sense of vulnerability comes through in this highly memorable childhood dream. At another level, the dream foreshadows the course of his future life, motivated by a deep compassion toward the suffering of others, even those who have not led religiously upright lives. His ambivalence between moral judgment and personal sympathy toward his nurse anticipates the later tension between the severity of his ascetic practices and the interpersonal connections he formed with other people.

Another early dream, from between the ages of sixteen and nineteen, also anticipates what would become central themes in his mature religious practices:

> In the dream, Myōe goes into a room in a temple where he sees the famous priest, Kukai, sleeping. Kukai's two eyes looked like crystals, and they are lying beside a pillow. Kukai gives them to Myōe who places them in a sleeve of his robe.[4]

Here the theme is not a reflection of vulnerability from the past but rather a look forward to the emergence of strange and valuable new powers. In Myōe's cultural context, it would not be surprising for a young and ambitious monk to dream of entering the presence of a venerable religious elder; that was a familiar means of transmitting spiritual knowledge and guidance in Buddhist traditions. What is surprising about this dream is that Myōe appears as the more powerful of the two, a striking reversal of their ordinary relationship. In the dream, Myōe is awake, while the priest is asleep; he can see, while the priest has removed his eyes; the priest gives his jewel-like eyes to Myōe, who receives the crystal orbs and immediately puts them out of sight in a hidden place known only to him. This is less of a standard sharing of knowledge from one generation to another and more of a radical transformation of that knowledge beyond its usual appearance into something much more powerful and precious, and thus in much more need of careful protection. For a teenage monk, this would be a bold vision of future responsibility for the most sacred wisdom of the Buddhist tradition.

Once he began his journal of dreams, Myōe settled into a lifelong practice of systematically stimulating and training his imagination to envision as realistically as possible the life of the Buddha. Several times, he made arrangements to travel to India for a pilgrimage to the various sites of the Buddha's life, but between his tenuous health and numerous temple responsibilities, he never actually made the journey. Unable to connect with the Buddha through physical space and geographic location, Myōe turned all his spiritual energies inward, trying to learn as much as possible of the Buddha's teachings from increasingly powerful inner experiences of revelation and insight. The following are some of the dreams that Myōe recorded in his journal:

> I dreamed that I had constructed a pond which was about a half or three-quarters of an acre [in size]. There was hardly any water in it. Suddenly there was a downpour and the water filled up. The water was pure and clear. Next to it was another large pond that seemed to be an old river. When the small pond was filled with water, it was separated from the large pond by about a foot. If it rained just a bit more, it would merge with the large pond. I thought that upon the merger [of the waters], fish, turtles, and so forth could traverse to the small pond. Then it seemed that it was the fifth day of the second month. Tonight, I thought, the moon will rise over this pond and it surely will be splendid.[5]

> In a dream . . . there was a jewel that was receiving the sun's light. The jewel in turn radiated light. The light of the jewel reached a good friend, and he became frightened beyond limit. When I saw this, I wondered what it was about the light that frightened him so powerfully.[6]

> During my sleep after sitting in meditation . . . I dreamed that the late Precepts Master Gyoi was in seclusion for a while with the great master's

Brahmajalasutrai at Takao, and he said to me, "Read this commentary." I accepted it, and when I took it and looked at it, it [turned out] to be a mysterious book. This book in my dream said something which I thought to be the Sanskrit word for *boji* [enlightenment], and when I looked in it, there were the Sanskrit letters. Furthermore, wherever there was a bodhisattva's name, there was a picture. The likes of Fudo [a deity who protects the faithful against impurities] and so forth were in the midst of huge flames. The color of the fire was dark blue. I wondered whether this book might have been mistaken in this way for the marrow of the Shingon teachings. I think there are books for verifying cases like this. The covers were faintly scented; the writing style was in a skillful hand.[7]

In a dream . . . there was a single, large monkey who had become used to me. I taught it to practice Zen meditation. The monkey followed my instructions, learned the meditation method, formed mudras, and sat in lotus position. However, his sitting posture was not quite straight. Then I went out into a large street in the capital. I was alone, however, and there was no one attending me. Since I did not know the road, I guessed my way and intended to go [somewhere]. The place I arrived at was Kiyomizudera [an important temple in Kyoto]. I looked about and realized that I should have known [the way] after all. Then there was a large mansion with a pond in front of it. The water was low and filthy. There were tiny worms in it. A house was built over the water like a fishing pavilion, but it was shaky and unfinished.[8]

These dreams give an initial sense of the concerns and conflicts that occupy his mind in sleep: how to connect teachings and practices from different lineages (the small pond and the big pond), how to persuade those who resist spiritual change to welcome its transcendent value (the friend scared of the sunlit jewel), how to look beyond the written words of ancient texts to see their living reality (reading the master's commentary), how to develop the most effective practices to purify and strengthen the ancient traditions of Buddhism in Japan (the mansion with the filthy water). It is unclear if the curious image of teaching a monkey to meditate appears to Myōe as a mocking critique of all his priestly efforts or if it is rather an eye-opening encouragement to spread the teachings even more widely than he had assumed they could be spread. He briefly commented on the dream, relating it to his efforts to continue practicing "esoteric ritual methods," which require going beyond sitting meditation to include more active techniques for stimulating visions and heightened states of consciousness. Seen in this light, the meditating monkey provided Myōe with a novel image of the developmental limits of this particular method, suggesting the need to seek alternatives that are more appropriate and effective for his current spiritual condition and needs.

Years of extreme dietary asceticism (frequently eating nothing but raw vegetables) finally caught up with him, and in 1230, Myōe became so ill that he had to give up teaching and lecturing. He went to a secluded temple and began making preparations for the end of his life. He had a final dream, in which "he became one with the ocean," which he recognized as an omen of death, anticipating the ultimate dissolution of his personal identity and the long-sought release from the bounds of his physical body.

Although he was always a fiercely independent practitioner, Myōe also actively cared for the spiritual welfare of numerous monks, disciples, students, and laypeople who valued his combination of traditional Buddhist principles with new methods and techniques of stimulating the visionary imagination in everyone. According to his biographer George Tanabe, "In a time of severe sectarian contention, Myōe remained an upholder of the tradition of being open to all traditions."[9]

3

Lucrecia de León

Prophet of an Empire's Doom

The introduction discussed the primary conditions required for keeping a dream journal: time, resources, and motivation. Not included on that list was literacy, the ability to read and write. This might seem a strange omission, since writing is required to record one's dreams, and reading is required to understand the written reports over time. And yet a dreamer's illiteracy is not an obstacle to keeping a journal or gaining insights from their dreams. The brief but dramatic life history of Lucrecia de León, a young woman from medieval Spain during the imperial reign of King Philip II, proves this to be the case.[1] Although uneducated and barely able to write her own name, Lucrecia's remarkable dreams attracted the attention of powerful officials in the Catholic Church hierarchy. They helped record her dreams, preserve them, and analyze their symbolic meanings. And when the national disaster long foretold in her dreams finally occurred, threatening people's faith in their king, Lucrecia's dream journal became the prime piece of evidence used against her by the Spanish Inquisition in her trial for sedition and heresy.

Born in 1568 in Madrid, the oldest child of a minor banking official at the royal court, Lucrecia grew up in the center of an imperial capital filled with travelers, diplomats, soldiers, merchants, and Church officials from all over the world. She lived in a densely populated neighborhood known as the Barrio de las Musas, so named because of the many artists who lived there, including the playwright Lope de Vega, just a few years her senior, and Miguel de Cervantes, the future author of *Don Quixote*. Lucrecia was by all accounts a vivid dreamer from early in childhood, and although she had no formal education, her dreams frequently referred to the most important religious and political issues being discussed at her home, in her neighborhood, and throughout the city. For example, when she was twelve years old, she told her family a dream about a royal funeral. Three weeks later, the queen died (Philip ended up outliving four of his wives and seven of his eleven children). This might seem like a minor coincidence, but in a culture where deviations

The Scribes of Sleep. Kelly Bulkeley, Oxford University Press. © Oxford University Press 2023.
DOI: 10.1093/oso/9780197609606.003.0004

from religious orthodoxy and political obedience were punished with swift and savage brutality, any hint of strange powers or prophetic dreaming was an immediate danger not only to Lucrecia but to her whole family. In her later testimony to the Inquisition, she acknowledged that when she was a child, her parents would physically beat her to make her stop dreaming, for fear that the Inquisitors would suspect her of witchcraft and sorcery.

Nevertheless, despite these threats and warnings, Lucrecia continued to dream and share her dreams with others. One day, a cousin of hers, who worked as a high-level secretary for the Church, came to the family's home for a visit (her family lived on the ground floor of a building near the corner of Calle de Atocha, across from the Church of San Sebastian, half a kilometer from the Plaza Mayor). During the conversation, Lucrecia mentioned to her cousin a dream she had about the infamous "street prophet" Piedrola, whose apocalyptic warnings were a topic of great interest and controversy throughout the city. Her cousin later recounted the dream to his superior, Don Alonso de Mendoza, a powerful Church leader from the nearby city of Toledo. Don Alonso was keenly interested in omens and prophecies, and in the fall of 1587, he arranged to meet with Lucrecia, accompanied by her mother as chaperone, to learn more about her dreams. Impressed by what he heard, Don Alonso arranged for another priest in Madrid to come to Lucrecia's house each morning to record what she experienced the previous night. Lucrecia and her mother were naturally concerned about the danger of exposing her to the wrath of the Inquisition, but Don Alonso reassured them that the dream recording would occur as a part of the sacrament of confession and thus would always remain theologically safe. Lucrecia's father was opposed to the whole thing, but since he frequently traveled abroad for long periods of time on court business, he could not prevent the dream-recording experiment from proceeding.

The process got off to a bumpy start. One of Lucrecia's dreams included what were apparently accurate and intimate details about the interior chamber of the monastic cell where the priest who was recording her dreams slept each night. He immediately destroyed all the transcriptions he had made so far and threatened to quit, terrified at the idea of pursuing such uncanny dreams any further. Don Alonso urgently persuaded the priest to reconsider; these kinds of visionary dreams were exactly what they wanted to study, and they should redouble their efforts to document this young woman's strange abilities. The priest finally complied, and the dream-recording process went forward.

At this point, we should bring in some historical information about medieval Spain to provide more cultural context for Lucrecia's dreams. She lived during the "Siglo de Oro," the golden era between roughly 1550 and 1650 that marked the zenith of Spain's power, wealth, and cultural creativity. After Cristóbal Colón (Christopher Columbus) crossed the Atlantic Ocean in 1492 and launched the European colonial conquest of the Americas, Colón's sponsors, Queen Isabella and King Ferdinand of Spain, built an empire that eventually became the largest the world had ever known up to that time, more than twice the size of the Roman Empire at its peak. In 1560, their great-grandson, Philip II, known as "the most Catholic king" for his aggressive defense of the Church, decided to create a grand new capital for his world-spanning empire to rival the other great cities of Europe. He chose Madrid, which was at the time a quiet inland town at approximately the geographic center of the country, and he initiated a rapid, large-scale construction project to build as many palaces, plazas, boulevards, and cathedrals as necessary for a proper imperial capital.

Lucrecia was born just a few years after this ambitious process of civic expansion began, and during her childhood, the population of Madrid grew from ten thousand people to one hundred thousand or more. This rapid urbanization was necessary to service the increasingly complex needs of Philip's far-flung imperial holdings and numerous military conflicts. In addition to defending his colonial territories in the Americas and encouraging his conquistadores to plunder as much gold and silver as possible, Philip also had to contend with Muslim invaders attacking Spain from the south, Ottoman Empire armies pushing into Europe from the east, and Protestant rebels in the north who were stubbornly resisting the vicious mercenary soldiers hired by the king to punish them for their religious disobedience.

More than anything, Philip coveted the throne of England, which he had held for four years (1554–1558) by marriage to the Catholic but childless Queen Mary and then lost after Mary's death to her Protestant half-sister, Queen Elizabeth I. Ever since, Philip had been plotting with his military advisers to invade England, using the most powerful weapon in the world at that time: the Spanish Armada, a mighty fleet of more than one hundred warships, filled with thousands of battle-hardened soldiers who would easily overwhelm the meager English defenses and march straight to London. The invasion of England was the key to Philip's vision for a unified Catholic Europe, the goal toward which he devoted all his imperial resources.

For almost a year before the Armada set sail, Lucrecia began dreaming that the invasion would fail. Here is the most direct example, from December 14, 1587:

> I saw two strong fleets fighting a fierce battle. Because I had seen them fight before, I knew that one was the fleet of the Marquis of Santa Cruz, the other of Drake. This battle was the fiercest and loudest of all those I had seen in other dreams. Previously, I had seen them fighting in a port; this one was on the high seas and lasted all afternoon because before it began I heard a clock strike one; it lasted three hours, until sunset. Once the sun was down, I saw the defeated fleet of the Marquis of Santa Cruz fleeing toward the north, having lost many of its ships and men, and I saw Drake's fleet returning to England to take on more troops. I saw Drake writing letters, asking for more men. He also wanted to forward a request for troops to the Great Turk, but one of his knights said, "Do not send it, the men we have are enough to secure victory." And with this I woke up.[2]

The Marquis of Santa Cruz was a famous Spanish naval hero and admiral of the Armada; Francis Drake was a "privateer" ("ruthless pirate" would be another term for it) and the leading captain of the much smaller English fleet. The Great Turk was the ruler of the Ottoman Empire to the east, not an ally of the English in waking life but a shared enemy of Spain. If it seems strange for an uneducated girl to dream of geopolitical military strategy like this, recall that Lucrecia grew up in the capital city of the empire, surrounded by people who worked in and around the royal court. The Marquis of Santa Cruz, Drake, the Great Turk—these were familiar characters in the many conversations Lucrecia heard from her father and other family members and from neighbors, visitors, priests, and street prophets like Piedrola. For several months, Lucrecia herself worked in the king's palace as a nursery maid for one of his children. This insider's position gave her an especially intimate view of the royal family and its leadership capacities. Clearly, whatever she witnessed did not inspire confidence, as her dreams expressed relentless criticism of Philip, his religious failures, and his inability to defend Spain against its many adversaries. She also dreamed several times that the Marquis de Santa Cruz would not be able to lead the Armada in battle against the English.

It was only a matter of time before local religious officials began investigating the rumors that people in the Barrio de las Musas were talking openly about a girl's dreams of Spain's perilous future. Once they took a closer look, they realized the situation was even worse than they feared. The vicar of Madrid, the senior religious authority within the city government, ordered the arrest of Lucrecia in February 1588 (she was nineteen at this point) and held her in confinement for ten days while a panel of theologians gathered testimony from neighbors, studied her dreams, and debated the appropriate punishment. The prospects would not seem good for a poor young woman who was openly spreading stories that undermined the religious authority of the king. A death sentence could be handed down at any moment.

The proceedings took an unexpected turn, however, when two things happened. First, Don Alonso finally reached Madrid from Toledo, and he took charge of defending Lucrecia's case and appealing to higher authorities for help. Second, news reached the court that the Marquis of Santa Cruz had suddenly taken ill and would soon die. This shocking turn of events gave fresh evidence in favor of Don Alonso's argument that Lucrecia's dreams had prophetic qualities and should be studied, not persecuted. Over the vicar's vehement objections, high-level Church officials agreed with Don Alonso, and they ordered the vicar to release Lucrecia back to her family residence, where she was to remain under Don Alonso's supervision.

Lucrecia's mother seemed to support her dreaming activities, but her father absolutely did not. He was a proud "old Christian," a Spaniard of pure blood, and the last thing he would tolerate was a child of his causing trouble with the Church. When she returned home from the vicar's custody, Lucrecia's father furiously condemned her for dishonoring the family name. He left her with no doubt about the harsh consequences of any further diso- bedience: "Daughter, in my family nobody has ever believed in superstitions, because dreams are only dreams [*porque los sueños eso son*], and if you be- lieve in them I will give the order to have you killed."[3]

After this, Lucrecia kept a much lower profile. A few weeks following her confinement by the vicar, she fell ill, and for several months, she stopped re- porting her dreams. But there was no hiding once the shocking news reached Madrid in early September 1588 that, despite all odds, the "invincible" Armada had been defeated by the English. The Spanish people were stunned, frightened, and deeply disillusioned, and the humiliated king retreated into seclusion and fell into a profound depression.

If Lucrecia posed a danger to the king before the defeat of the Armada, she was a much greater threat to him afterward. Her reputation as an inspired prophet had soared, and the social elite of Madrid flocked to hear what her latest dreams foretold for Spain's future. This was too much for the king to tolerate. Despite the fact that her dreams had been proven true in the most dramatic fashion possible, in May 1590, Philip ordered the agents of the Inquisition to arrest Lucrecia on charges of heresy and treason. She was taken to a secret prison in Toledo, the ancient spiritual capital of the country, where she was repeatedly interrogated and tortured by inquisitors who insisted that she confess to being a liar or a witch or insane, anything other than a prophetic dreamer.

We will return to Lucrecia's story in later chapters. For now, let's focus on the basic characteristics of her dream journal. As noted, the process involved a priest coming to her home each morning to write down her verbal report of whatever dreams she experienced the night before. She did not always have a dream to report, but when she did, it was often quite lengthy and detailed. From a researcher's perspective, this approach has several advantages for gathering high-quality dream reports. Lucrecia was sleeping at home, in a familiar setting, with minimal external disruptions. A professional scribe came to her soon after she awoke, while her recall was fresh, to record as many details as she could remember. The reports were collected and preserved in Church archives in Madrid, where they have remained safe and intact for more than four hundred years. Apart from their explosive political and theological content, the collection of Lucrecia's dreams represents one of the best-documented dream journals from an earlier historical figure.

The process used to gather Lucrecia's dreams also had several disadvantages. There was a drastic imbalance of power between her and the priests who were avidly gathering her dreams and undoubtedly some degree of pressure on her to provide them with enough dreams to satisfy their expectations. Her involvement in the project made Lucrecia, by many accounts a beautiful young woman, increasingly vulnerable to the intrusive attentions of a stream of older, ostensibly celibate men. Don Alonso treated Lucrecia well enough, but ultimately, he regarded her as a means to the end of gaining greater insight into God's plan for Spain's future. And despite his assurances that sharing her dreams in the context of confession would protect them from the Inquisition, not only was Lucrecia arrested by order of the king in May 1590, but so was Don Alonso himself, along with several of the scribes who had helped in recording her dreams.

When the inquisitors arrested Don Alonso, they seized his collection of Lucrecia's dreams, and these documents became evidence against them all in the trials that followed. At first sight, it would seem the Inquisition had everything it needed to reach a swift verdict. Numerous witnesses confirmed that

Lucrecia, Don Alonso, and the others had engaged in activities that openly criticized the king and undermined his authority. They had made public claims about God's plans for Spain that were plainly heretical and contrary to the teachings of the Church. Some of Lucrecia's followers had even built a secret bunker filled with weapons and food to protect her when disaster finally struck, after which she would emerge to lead Spain into a better future—a brazenly treasonous plot of armed rebellion, with Lucrecia at the very center. The Inquisition had sent thousands of people to their deaths on far less evidence than this. And yet in Lucrecia's case, they hesitated. For nearly five years, they held her in confinement while the legal proceedings dragged on, one of the longest Inquisition trials on record. Part of this was due to Don Alonso's high social status and political connections, which he desperately and cleverly used to defend their innocence. The Inquisition's uncertainty about how to proceed was also due to Lucrecia's dreams themselves, which were overflowing with vivid imagery and dramatic religious symbolism, much more than could be properly interpreted by someone without specialized training. Here is an example, a dream that came about a month after the one quoted earlier:

> The twelfth of January of this year [1588] the Ordinary Man came to me and I saw that he was bringing a Cross in his hand; he carried the Cross to the palace and placed it in a tower with a view, and I said to him: "Why are you placing the Cross in this part?" He answered me: "Because his death is close." And I saw a blood river, coming from the area of the stables; this river was surrounding the Palace, flowing with serpents and snakes—that I have seen in other visions—and with lots of crows, squawking with their beaks in blood. Three men came out of this river and looted the place and cut many children's and old people's heads off. When I saw this, it hurt me so much that I started to cry aloud. The Ordinary Man said to me: "Do not be sad, do not cry because these things that God does, he does them to teach us a life lesson, so you should not be in sorrow."[4]

Many of Lucrecia's dreams featured a character she called *el hombre ordinario*, which is literally translated as "the ordinary man," but which in her context seems to mean something more like "the usual guy," a man who regularly shows up in her dreams. The palace in the dream is the royal residence, and the king is clearly the one whose death the Ordinary Man is foretelling (Philip himself appears as a character in several of Lucrecia's dreams). The serpents, crows, and river of blood were familiar religious symbols in the apocalyptic visions of other prophets, and so was the message of a wrathful God deliberately causing worldly suffering for the purpose of revealing higher spiritual truths. None of this was heretical or unorthodox per se; the inquisitors could not easily identify any of the typical signs of a false prophet in Lucrecia's dreams or her behavior. The most obvious problem in her dreams was the harsh criticism of the king's leadership, but this was also the most obvious point on which Lucrecia's dreams had been proven true by Philip's own behavior. It's hard not to imagine that at least some of the inquisitors, looking at her case as a whole, found it difficult to rule out the possibility that Lucrecia was not a fraud, a witch, or a lunatic but a genuine prophet. The collection of her dreams was both the most damning piece of evidence against Lucrecia *and* the most persuasive piece of evidence in favor of her honesty and innocence.

4

Emanuel Swedenborg

Mystical Scientist

Chapter 3 introduced the idea that a dream journal could become not just a personal document for insight and growth but also a target of external attack and persecution by others. The journal to be discussed in this chapter also elicited hostile reactions from religious, political, and cultural authorities who found the dreams threatening to their view of the world. In this case, however, the dreamer was not a poor, uneducated young woman but a prominent and prosperous middle-aged man. Emanuel Swedenborg's collection of dreams from 1743 to 1745 inspired his dramatic transformation from scientist to mystic, from a widely respected expert in engineering to a radical, visionary interpreter of Christian scripture.[1] His theological teachings gave rise to an organized group, the "New Church," which today still has several thousand members in England, the United States, and elsewhere around the world. However, Swedenborg and his dream journal are often best known as the catalyst for Immanuel Kant's mocking critique, *Dreams of a Spirit-Seer* (1766). This early work by Kant, one of the most influential philosophers of the Enlightenment, portrayed Swedenborg as a befuddled fool whose devotion to visions and trances represented a shameful abandonment of the core tenets of science. Dreams, in the view of Kant and many other philosophers at the time, are completely irrational and purely subjective in nature, thus incapable of serving as a valid source of scientific reasoning. Because he recorded his dreams, reflected on their meanings, and shared them with others, Swedenborg became the most infamous example of what Enlightenment-era philosophers were taught *not* to do.

He was born on January 29, 1688, in Stockholm to Jesper Swedberg, an ambitious chaplain in the Church of Sweden (a Protestant branch of Christianity based on Lutheran theology and politically aligned with the Swedish monarchy), and Sara Behm, an heiress from a wealthy upper-class family with extensive mining interests. When Swedenborg was two, his father was

The Scribes of Sleep. Kelly Bulkeley, Oxford University Press. © Oxford University Press 2023.
DOI: 10.1093/oso/9780197609606.003.0005

appointed professor of theology at Uppsala University, requiring the family to move to Uppsala, where Swedenborg lived for the better part of his childhood and early education. His father continued to rise in the national church hierarchy and eventually became a bishop, even though some of his beliefs in angels, spirits, and communion with God veered dangerously close to heresy. By almost all accounts, Jesper Swedberg had an imperious personality and felt extremely confident in expressing his views about the truths of religion, not just in church settings but at home with the family, too. He focused his children's education on himself as an exemplary model of someone who was following a virtuous, God-fearing path through life. When Swedenborg reached adulthood, he never explicitly rejected his father's beliefs, but he did not abide by his intellectual boundaries, either. As he grew older, and especially after his midlife dreaming conversion, he became increasingly comfortable exploring spiritual realms far beyond what his father or the Church of Sweden would deem acceptable.

Swedenborg's mother died when he was eight, and an older sibling died soon after; his father remarried a year later. These family losses and transitions were painful, but Swedenborg's new stepmother was evidently kind to him, and he otherwise enjoyed a stable, healthy childhood. As might be expected from the child of a theology professor, he thought deeply about religious questions from an early age. Later in life, he recollected, "from my 4th to 10th year, I was constantly in thought about God, salvation, and man's spiritual suffering. Several times I disclosed things that amazed my father and mother, who thought that angels must be speaking through me."[2] His father's rise to the position of bishop required him and the rest of the family to move to a new city, but they decided that Swedenborg, now fourteen, should stay in Uppsala, where he had been a student at the university for several years already, and continue with his education. No longer under the immediate control of his father, he took increasing interest in science, technology, and philosophical inquiry. A lifelong stutter prevented him from public speaking, but it did nothing to slow his intellectual development. He finished school at twenty-one and set off on a series of travels throughout Europe, meeting as many scientists, engineers, and inventors as possible. He found London especially appealing and lived there for several years, before returning to Sweden in 1715, where he developed a wide range of scientific activities and research projects. His work in the following years included important contributions to metallurgy, chemistry, anatomy, cosmology, and aeronautics.

Swedenborg also gave valuable assistance to the Swedish king, Charles XII, on several technical projects that helped the country's military during a time of constant warfare with Russia, Denmark, Norway, and other neighboring lands. Swedenborg met the king in 1716, and the two men quickly found mutual interests in mathematics and practical engineering. Soon thereafter, the king appointed him as a special member of the Royal Board of Mines, a position that had little power of its own but gave Swedenborg a governmental title he could use when carrying out plans on the king's behalf. The appointment prompted sharp dissent among other members of the board, but the relentlessly bellicose Charles XII ignored them, because he needed Swedenborg's help with the desperate battles he was fighting on several fronts. These were the waning years of what Swedes called Stormakstiden, or "The Era of Great Power," when they ruled an empire that stretched over most of northern Europe, with colonial outposts in the Americas and Africa. Charles XII had become king at the age of fifteen, and he had been fighting wars ever since. For a while, Swedenborg seemed to derive genuine meaning and satisfaction from being of "practical use to the fatherland," as he wrote to a friend at the time.[3] He worked at the king's behest on building dams, canals, and dry docks; developing domestic salt mines; and, in his most impressive feat, moving the king's naval forces *over land* from a harbor the enemy was about to attack to another harbor sixteen miles away, where the ships would be easier to defend. Just two years later, however, the king was shot and killed in the Siege of Fredriksten (with rumors that the bullet was fired from the Swedish side). His death effectively the ended the Great Northern War, which meant, among other things, that the Swedish royal government abruptly abandoned several engineering projects that Swedenborg had been laboring to develop for the king's military needs. The Stormakstiden came to an inglorious end soon thereafter, with peace treaties formalizing the loss of nearly all of Sweden's imperial territories in 1721.

After his father died in 1735, Swedenborg's focus shifted from large-scale engineering projects toward a close study of the physiology of the brain, with the goal of identifying an anatomical region where he could directly observe the operations of the soul. In the course of these investigations, he was the first scientist to identify neurons as the constituent elements of the brain and to recognize that their interactions, especially in the frontal lobes of the brain, are directly related to the experience of consciousness. His father would find this kind of pursuit irrelevant at best and blasphemous at worst, but for Swedenborg, inquiries like this became the central quest of his life. Like many other philosophers and scientists of early modern Europe, he tried to interpret the latest findings of empirical science in relation to the deepest truths of religion. Unlike most of his other contemporaries, however, Swedenborg also turned his analytic gaze inward, to explore the connections between soul and body as they manifested in a variety of internal conscious states and experiences.

Whenever he traveled, Swedenborg kept a regular journal of his activities and reflections. In 1743, he embarked on a trip to Amsterdam to work on his latest scientific treatise, titled *Animal Kingdom*. His journal started with ordinary travel observations, but then he suddenly added several undated entries involving dreams, which he enumerated as follows:

1. Dreamed of my youth and the Gustavian family.
2. In Venice, of the beautiful palace.
3. In Sweden, of the white expanse of heaven.
4. In Leipsic, of one that lay in boiling water.
5. Of one that tumbled with a chain down into the deep.
6. Of the king that gave away so precious a thing in a peasant's cabin.
7. Of the man servant that wished me to go away on my travels.[4]

It is unclear why Swedenborg would take such a keen interest in his dreams now, at the age of fifty-five, on this particular trip. Why did he suddenly turn all of his formidable mental powers toward the unfolding path that beckoned him in each night's dreams? There is no simple answer. Several factors seem to have come together at this moment: conflicts with the church, disputes with other scientists, uncertainties about his future, and struggles with his powerful ambitions. With so many difficulties pressing on him from all sides, it perhaps makes more sense that Swedenborg would turn within for help. The descriptions of his initial dreams are fragmentary and elliptical, more like notes to himself than anything he ever planned to publish. Perhaps for that reason, a raw immediacy comes through in many of the reports, emphasizing their spiritual urgency more than their documentary details. Here are the next dreams recorded in the journal:

How I set myself against the power of the Holy Spirit, what happened thereupon; how I saw hideous spectres, without life horribly shrouded and moving in their shrouds; together with a beast that attacked me, but not the child.[5]

It seemed I lay on a mountain with a gulf under it: there were knolls upon it; I lay there and tried to help myself up, holding by a knoll, without foothold; a gulf was below.[6]

How a woman lay down by my side, just as if I was waking. I wished to know who it was. She spoke slowly; said that she was pure, but that I smelled ill.[7]

Among the many scandalous aspects of Swedenborg's dreams were their explicit portrayals of sexuality. He never married, but it seems likely he had an active sex life, at least during the time of his various travels abroad. He regarded sexual experience as an important part of human life, not just physically as a means of biological reproduction but spiritually, too, as a potent source of transcendent images, symbols, and metaphors to help us apprehend higher religious truths. Even if other people found such ideas too much to bear (the early editors of his dream journal either removed the sex dreams or translated them into Latin), for Swedenborg they were the natural consequence of an honest, open-minded analysis of his dreams. As he continues with the journal, he begins dating the dreams and adding increasingly thoughtful and self-reflective comments about them. Here is an example, one of his dreams from April 10–11, 1744:

When I came out, I saw a great many people sitting in a gallery, and lo! A mighty stream of water came down through the roof; it was so mighty that it broke through all that it met. There were some that barred the opening or hole. Some also that went aside so that the water should not hit them. Some that dissipated it into drops. Some that diverted its course so that it turned away from the stand. This, I suppose, was the power of the Holy Spirit that flowed into the body and the thoughts, and which in part I impeded; in part I went out of its way; in part, I slanted it from me. For the people I saw represent my thoughts and will.[8]

As his dream journal grows in length and sophistication, Swedenborg can be seen developing the early foundations of his method for interpreting the spiritual meaning of the Bible. As a scientist and a child of the Enlightenment, Swedenborg agreed with critics of religion who rejected naive, literalistic readings of scripture, but he also agreed with religious believers that scripture truly does have a higher meaning, if it can be properly elucidated and understood. To explore and systematically map those hidden realms of higher meaning became Swedenborg's mission, starting in his dream journal and continuing onward for the rest of his life. He told several friends about a dream he experienced in mid-April 1745 (not recorded in his journal) that proved decisive in his turn toward mystical theology. He was in London, staying at an inn and eating a late, hearty dinner, when the light in the room suddenly dimmed, and he thought he saw the floor teeming with snakes, frogs, and other loathsome reptiles; then the reptiles were gone, and he saw a man sitting in the corner, who said in a frightening voice, "Eat not so much." Then the images passed, and Swedenborg found himself alone once again. He quickly left the dining table and went to his room to sleep:

> And during the night the same man revealed himself to me again, but I was not frightened now. He then said that he was the Lord God, the Creator of the world, and the Redeemer, and that He had chosen me to explain to men the spiritual sense of Scripture, and that He Himself would explain to me what I should write on this subject. . . . From that day I gave up the study of all worldly science, and labored in spiritual things, according as the Lord had commanded me to write.[9]

For the next twenty years of his life, Swedenborg obeyed the holy mandate of this dream as he wrote a series of religious books and commentaries on the Bible. Generally considered his greatest work of this period is the *Arcana Celestia*, or *Secrets of Heaven* (1749). Other books he wrote delve into the divine nature of the soul, explore the visionary landscape of heaven and hell, and examine in surprising detail what happens to the sexual dynamics between husbands and wives in the afterlife. In all these writings, Swedenborg relies on his capacity for visionary consciousness as a primary source of theological reflection. The powerful dreams of 1743 to 1745 had launched him in this direction, and as time went on, he found he could intentionally enter dreamlike states while still partly awake by using a variety of techniques: controlled breathing, waking trances, and sustained periods of hypnogogic imagery. In these states, Swedenborg not only gained new insights into the meaning of particular verses of Bible, but, more controversially, he also wrote about his experiences of speaking with the dead, visiting the spirits who live on other planets, and learning to speak the language of angels. He also displayed an ability in waking life to perceive events and gain knowledge at a distance, most remarkably when he told a group of people about a major fire happening at that moment in Stockholm, more than two hundred miles away; several days later, the messengers arrived to report news of the Stockholm fire, at exactly the time Swedenborg had spoken of it to his friends.

The wonder is not that Swedenborg was criticized but that he somehow escaped even more aggressive persecution by the religious authorities. His claims of divine knowledge and special access to spiritual truths went far beyond what Lucrecia de León said about her dreams. Had Swedenborg been a woman, it is difficult to imagine making the same public assertions—about personally traveling to hell, speaking to the dead, and enjoying the heavenly delights of spiritualized sex—without immediately being arrested and harshly punished for witchcraft. As it was, he had to distribute his writings through publishers in Amsterdam and London because of concerns about censorship by Church officials in Sweden. And in 1768, just a few years before his death, a trial was convened to determine if Swedenborg's followers were guilty of heresy by distributing his writings. Although he died in 1772 before a final resolution of the case was reached, the teaching of his ideas was officially forbidden as inconsistent with orthodox Church teachings.

In addition to his theological critics, Swedenborg also had to contend with the scorn of his philosophical critics. They did not bother to examine the symbolic details of his visions and dreams, as the religious officials did. Rather, the philosophers and natural scientists rejected his dream-inspired method as invalid for any kind of rational pursuit of the truth. They saw Swedenborg himself as obviously insane and/or a fraud, a "spook hunter," in Kant's memorably belittling words. Curiously, Kant published *Dreams of a Spirit-Seer* anonymously. Did he not want to be associated with Swedenborg in any way, even as the author of an unsparing attack? Did he want the freedom to write a more biting satire than would be allowed in a conventional philosophical text? There is evidence that in the preceding years, Kant was familiar with Swedenborg's writings and held a more favorable view of his impressive intelligence.[10] Yet in *Dreams of a Spirit-Seer*, the critique ultimately focused on Swedenborg's claims to know things that simply cannot be known in the way he says he knows them. Kant accused Swedenborg of violating the philosopher's ancient dictum that knowledge begins with an admission of what we do not know; only after we make this crucial admission can we build up our knowledge on sure foundations.

Swedenborg and his followers responded to this charge with more precisely detailed explanations of his theory of symbolic correspondences between the natural world and the spiritual realm. But it was too late; the damage was done. *Dreams of a Spirit-Seer* appeared at the end of Swedenborg's life and at the beginning of Kant's rise as the preeminent voice of Enlightenment philosophy. After Swedenborg was gone, Kant's portrait of him as a fuzzy mystic quickly hardened into a general opinion among European intellectuals.[11] As a result, for the next two hundred years, all discussions about Swedenborg—his writings, theories, visions, and dreams—were effectively banished to a philosophical limbo, lost in the shadows cast by Kant's unsigned critique.

5

Benjamin Banneker

Mapping the Heavens

This chapter presents the least-known keeper of a dream journal discussed
in this book, the one from whom we have the least amount of surviving evidence about his life and dreams.[1] During his funeral a few days after he died
in 1806, an arsonist burned his cabin to the ground, along with nearly all his
remaining possessions and journals. Not everything was destroyed, however.
One volume of his personal writings was spared the flames, a volume that included a handful of dream reports. We will see that, although these dreams
are few in number, they provide a rich source of insights into the challenging
life, impressive works, and historical significance of one of the most brilliant
minds of his time.

Benjamin Banneker was born on November 9, 1731, in the tidewater region of Baltimore County in what was then the British colony of Maryland.
His parents were free blacks who owned and worked a tobacco farm in the
remote hills at the upper reaches of the Patapsco River. His father had been
captured in his African homeland of Guinea, shipped to America, and sold
into slavery to a white farmer at a port near Baltimore. At some point, he
converted to Christianity, adopted the name Robert, and was granted his
freedom. When he wed Banneker's mother, Mary, in 1730, he took her surname of Banneky and joined her extended family. Mary Banneky was the
daughter of a poor white woman from England, Molly Welsh, who had been
shipped to Maryland to serve a seven-year period of indentured servitude
working as a farmhand—her alternative punishment for a theft she had committed that otherwise would have resulted in her execution. When she finished her work obligations and gained her freedom, she purchased a small
patch of land just north of the Patapsco River. She also purchased two recently arrived African slaves to help her work and build her farm. At some
point, she freed both of them and married one, whose African name was
Banneka. A tall, quiet man, he was an indifferent worker but carried himself with a noble bearing and natural dignity. He came from a royal family,

The Scribes of Sleep. Kelly Bulkeley, Oxford University Press. © Oxford University Press 2023.
DOI: 10.1093/oso/9780197609606.003.0006

perhaps from the Dogon people of Mali, and it seems likely that he shared traditional African teachings and wisdom with his wife and their four daughters, including knowledge about weather, astronomy, agriculture, and dreaming. How much of this was passed down to his grandson is unclear, but there is no doubt that Banneker's adult interests in these topics were deeply rooted in his childhood experiences and early education. His grandmother played a vital role in stimulating his precocious intellectual interests and guiding them in religiously responsible directions. According to one of Banneker's biographers:

> Much of Benjamin's free time as a small boy was spent at his grandmother's farm, where she taught him to read and write. She was particularly concerned that he should become a religious man. Partly to practice his reading and partly to learn its contents, on every Sabbath day she had Benjamin read to her from her copy of the Bible. She had sent to England for it, and it was described by her grandchildren as being a volume of large size. It was one of Molly's few treasures, which she enjoyed sharing with her young grandson.[2]

In this vignette, we can see the emergence of the central themes of Banneker's later life: the rhythms of farming life, reading and writing, following the moral teachings of the Bible, and sharing knowledge in books. While he was a child, his grandmother apparently arranged for him to go to a one-room school in a nearby settlement, which he attended for several years until he was physically mature enough to work for his father on the farm. Beyond that, he received no formal education. He continued teaching himself, however, driven by the sheer force of his curiosity and innate intellectual ability, especially in mathematics. The first great example of his innovative talents came when he saw a pocket watch for the first time and had an opportunity to study its inner mechanical workings. Banneker went back to his cabin (where he lived virtually his entire life) to draw diagrams of what he remembered, and after much tinkering, he eventually succeeded in building a working clock using the only materials available to him: pieces of handcrafted wood, with a few small bits of metal. He was twenty-two years old at the time, and the marvel of his wooden timepiece gave him a reputation as a man of remarkable intelligence and ability.

His father died a few years later, and now Banneker was the principal owner and caretaker of the family farm. He seems to have gone through a period of depression during the following years, perhaps due to his father's death or a failed romance (he never married) or the ugly threats from racist neighbors that continually plagued him and his family. He continued working the farm, on which he grew tobacco as a cash crop, like nearly all the other farmers in his area, white or black. Of the few writings of his that remain from this period, there are three "dream stories," long first-person accounts of dreams describing a variety of adventures, spiritual discoveries, and moral dilemmas. Here is an excerpt from one of the stories:

> I thought I was dead and beheld my body lay like a corpse, there seemed to be a person in the appearance of a man, his raiment somewhat of a sheep skin or bright fawn color, who said follow me. He ascended a hill on the top of which was a large building. . . . The farther we went in, the brighter it appeared, and more like the reflection of the sun. . . . There appeared a sweetness & composure in every countenance, far beyond what I ever seen in any person while in the body. . . . I looked to see if I could distinguish men from women but could not. . . . I then asked my guide what is this place. He answered Heaven. . . . I had but just time to take a view of this fine place before a number of persons richly dressed passed us who smelled so strong of brimstone, that I seemed almost suffocated. All of them were talking to themselves, and before they came to us they looked well, but when they came near, there appeared a blackness on their lips and [they] seemed to mutter to themselves. . . . I was seized with horror and asked my guide what is this place and what are these. He answered this place is Hell and them are Miserable forever. . . . Then I awoke, but the horror and distress I felt on my mind I am not capable of expressing. I seem as if I fetched my breath in a room where sulfur and brimstone were burning.[3]

A narrative like this might seem too long and coherent to be an actual dream. By now, however, we are familiar enough with the creative capacities of the dreaming imagination to avoid making that assumption. Some actual dreams do indeed have contents that are extremely long and coherent. Of course, those dreams are less common than shorter, more fragmentary dreams, but they do occur, and their existence prevents us from concluding that a long and coherent dream report cannot be authentic solely because "real" dreams are never like that. With Banneker's dream stories, it seems likely they do have their roots in his actual dream experiences, both because he explicitly named them as such and because their complex spiritual themes correspond with the actual dreams he recorded several years later in his journal.

An important development in Banneker's life was the arrival in Maryland of the Ellicotts, a prosperous family who had moved from Pennsylvania and bought property near a large waterfall on the Patapsco River for building a gristmill. The Ellicotts belonged to the Religious Society of Friends, also known as the Quakers, a tradition of Protestant Christianity whose members had been persecuted in England, prompting many of them to travel across the Atlantic in search of a place to live in religious freedom. Compared with other early colonists, they tended to be more tolerant of religious and racial differences and more strongly opposed to slavery. Their overriding belief in the direct inner connection of every individual to God's divine light gave them a reputation for spiritual intensity, for trembling and "quaking" with religious feeling. Banneker soon befriended the Ellicotts, who welcomed his interest in the mechanics of the mill. Over time, they loaned him academic books and scientific instruments, including those used in astronomy and land surveying. In 1791, Andrew Ellicott was asked by Thomas Jefferson, then the U.S. secretary of state, to survey and define the territory that would become the capital of the new federal government, Washington, D.C. Straddling the Potomac River, this land had been ceded to the government by the two states of Virginia and Maryland, with a proposed district of ten miles on each side, one hundred square miles in total. It was Ellicott's job to determine the official boundaries by making precise measurements and establishing clear markers that both states would regard as fair. He enlisted Banneker's help in the project, which meant trekking through densely wooded brushlands with a heavy load of equipment, determining exact base points, and making astronomical observations at carefully timed moments. President George Washington himself visited the surveying site several times during the process, and it seems likely that at some point, he met Banneker and knew of his contributions.

As important as this work was on behalf of the new American government, Banneker left the survey project after a few months to return to his home near Ellicott's mills. He needed to tend to his farm, which had been neglected for too long, and he also needed time to complete a personal project that had been gestating for many years: an almanac and ephemeris. In this era of American history, almanacs played a central role in the economic and cultural lives of rural communities. Their primary service was providing information that would be useful for farmers, to help them determine the most favorable times for planting and harvesting their crops. To this end, the almanacs contained details about the rising and setting of the sun, the phases of the moon, high and low tides, and seasonal weather patterns. Eclipses and planetary conjunctions were also noted, along with dates of religious holidays and governmental meetings. In addition to its value as a repository of factual information, the almanac also conveyed a wealth of cultural information in the forms of brief essays, poems, proverbs, and spiritual reflections. To write an almanac, one had to calculate accurately all of the astronomical predictions for the coming year *and* intimately understand the practical daily concerns of farmers *and* generate a variety of literary content with a distinctive, pleasant, broadly accessible tone. Few people in the early American republic possessed that combination of skills, even at the highest levels of academic achievement. Despite having barely more than a grade-school education, Banneker succeeded in publishing his first almanac and ephemeris in 1792, and its positive reception encouraged him to produce a new edition each of the next five years. No longer just a local prodigy, he and his intellectual talents now reached the attention of a wider public throughout the new nation.

The only surviving reports of his dreams come from this late phase of his life, when he was already in his sixties. He had been keeping a journal all his life as a kind of personal almanac, in which he recorded his observations of the weather, agricultural yields, and the movements of the planets and stars, along with personal essays, drafts of letters, and his dreams. We know that dreams had been at the front of his mind years earlier, with the writing of his "dream stories," but no other evidence of his actual dream experiences remains beyond the following four reports. They are presented here with the original spelling and punctuation:

December 5, 1791. On the night of the fifth of December 1791, Being a deep Sleep, I dreamed that I was in a public Company, one of them demanded of me the limits of Rasannah Crandolph's Soul had to display itself in, after it departed from her Body and taken its flight. In answer I desired that he show me the place of Beginning "thinking it like making a Survey of the Land." He replied I cannot inform you but there is a man about three days journey from Hence that is able to satisfy your demand, I forthwith went to the man and requested of him to inform me place of beginning of the limits that Rasannah Crandolph's soul had to display itself in, after the Seperation from her Body; who gave me answer, the Vernal Equinox, When I returned

I found the Company together and I was able to Solve their Doubts by giving them the following answer Quincunx.

December 13, 1797. I Dreamed I saw some thing passing by my door to and fro, and when I attempted to go to the door, it would vanish and reapted [?] it twice or thrice, at length I let in the infernal Spirit and he told me that he had been concerned with a woman by the name of Beckey Freeman (I never heard the name as I remember) by some means we fell into a Skirmish, and I threw him behind the fire and endeavored to burn him up but all in vain—I know not what became of him but he was an ill formed being—Some part of him in Shape of a man, but hairy as a beast, his feet was circular or rather globular and did not exceed an inch and a half in diameter, but while I held him in the fire he said something respecting he was able to stand it, but I forget his words.

April 24, 1802. I dreamed I had a fawn or young deer; whose hair was white and like unto lamb's wool, and all parts about it beautiful to behold. Then I said to myself I will set this little captive at liberty, but I will first clip the tips of his ear that I may know him if I should see him again. Then taking a pair of shears and cutting off the tip of one ear, and he cried like unto a child hath the pain which grieved him very much altho then I did not attempt to cut the other but was very sorry for that I had done I got him at liberty and he ran a considerable distance then he stopped and he looked back at me I advanced toward him, and he came and met me and I took a lock of wool from my garment and wiped the blood of wound which I had made on him (which sorely affected me) I took him in my arms and brought him home and hold him on my knees, he asked the Woman if she had any trust and she answered him in the affirmative and gave him Some, which he began to eat and then asked for milk in a cup She said the dog had got the cup with milk in it under the house but there is milk in the cupboard. My dream left me.

April 24, 1802. Being weary holing for corn, I laid down on my bed and fell into a deep sleep and dreamed I had a child in my arms and was viewing the back part of its head where it had been sore, and I found it was healed with a hole through the skin and Skull bone and came out at forehead, that I could see very distinctly through the child's head the hole being large enough to receive an ordinary finger—I called some woman to see the strange sight, and she put her spectacles on and Saw it, and she asked me if I had previously lanced that place in the Child's head, I answered in the affirmative. N.B. the Child is well as any other.[4]

The chapters to come will explore the significance of these dreams from multiple angles. Here we can start by considering the remarkable fact that Banneker kept track of his dreams at all, that he felt his dreams were worthy of being recorded along with the other natural phenomena he was observing, tabulating, and analyzing in his journal. His goal in recording the movements of the stars and planets was to use this systematically gathered information to reach higher levels of knowledge, understanding, and insight. By extending his data-collection process to his dreams, he seemed to be following a similar intuition about the potential for discovering new dimensions of knowledge in dreaming by using the same empirical methods of analysis.

Indeed, there may have been a direct connection between Banneker's astronomical and oneirological interests. For much of his adult life, he spent his nights alone outside, looking up at the sky and taking measurements of the various objects that crossed above him. We can imagine that, being in a remote rural location with no artificial lights to diminish his view, Banneker would have enjoyed a spectacular window onto the heavens. Following these late nights of quiet, solitary reflection on the celestial realms, he often slept far into the morning, before waking up to start the day's work on his farm. This wake-sleep pattern enabled him to make regular, precise observations of astronomical phenomena; it also enhanced his efforts to keep a dream journal, as we can now appreciate thanks to new findings about the sleep cycle. Current scientific research on brain activities during sleep have shown that the longest phase of neural activation occurs at the end of the sleep cycle, right before waking. These periods of high brain arousal correlate with highly energetic dreaming. When people wake up before the natural conclusion of their sleep cycle, for example, because of an early alarm clock, they lose that final intense phase of dreaming. On top of that, an early and abrupt awakening makes it nearly impossible to remember any dreams that might have come from earlier in the sleep cycle. By contrast, a practice of sleeping late into the morning has the double benefit of allowing the end-of-sleep dreaming process to runs its course *and* enhancing the chances of consciously remembering those dreams upon awakening. Seen in this light, Banneker's lifelong routine of stargazing and late, deep sleeping can be recognized as a highly effective means of cultivating the power of his dreaming imagination and amplifying its impact on his waking awareness. His nightly astronomical observations became a personalized form of dream incubation, with the starry skies above as his divine temple and his journal as the systematic recording of both what he saw high above and what he saw deep within.

6

Anna Kingsford

Spiritual Dynamo

In her brief but highly productive life, Anna Kingsford achieved amazing success in many roles—as author, editor, public speaker, physician, animal rights advocate, feminist, theosophist, visionary—and yet her pioneering insights and accomplishments have been largely forgotten.[1] After her death in 1888, little was done to explore or analyze her life and works. Edward Maitland, Kingsford's close friend and collaborator, wrote an admiring but strangely digressive biography of her in 1908, and since then, few scholarly efforts have been directed toward her many writings of fiction, medical science, occult mysticism, and political advocacy. The present chapter does not address the full range of Kingsford's various activities and pursuits but rather focuses on one particular interest: dreams. She was a vivid dreamer from early in life, and over the years, she recorded two dozen of her most memorable dreams in a journal that she authorized for publication just before she died. This text also includes several "dream-stories," pieces of fiction with a basis in her dreams that she wrote and published at various points during the course of her life. A close study of Kingsford's dreams can illuminate the core ideals and passions that animated her remarkably energetic existence.

She was born Anna Bonus on September 16, 1846, to a merchant family living near London, during the peak years of imperial Great Britain. The shipping business of her father likely involved him in the commerce of colonial exploitation of foreign lands and peoples, fueling the empire and enabling London to become one of the wealthiest cities in the world. Kingsford grew up in this time of imperial power and prosperity, and she certainly benefited from it, even as she spent much of her life criticizing Britain's failings and tirelessly pushing for radical reform. From an early age, she was marked by a vivid imagination, active both by day and at night in her dreams. Doctors examined her in childhood, and they dismissed her dreams as mere fancies and warned her about the dangers of an "over-excited" brain.[2] From this and other early experiences, Kingsford developed a lifelong distrust of doctors

The Scribes of Sleep. Kelly Bulkeley, Oxford University Press. © Oxford University Press 2023.
DOI: 10.1093/oso/9780197609606.003.0007

and a determination to follow her own intuitions and inner knowledge no matter what other people told her.

Although she did not receive the same educational training as her older brothers, Kingsford was an early reader and a precociously creative writer. Her brothers were all between seven and eighteen years older than she, so she effectively grew up as an only child. Her greatest enjoyment lay in composing poems and stories, trying to express in written form the vivid ideas and images bubbling up from her imagination. She continued with this passion after her marriage to her cousin, Algernon G. Kingsford, in 1867 and after the birth of her daughter, Eadith, in 1868. When her father died a couple of years later and left her a stipend of seven hundred pounds a year, she suddenly gained a degree of financial independence that was truly life-changing. She now had what Virginia Woolf famously advised her female listeners in 1928 to seek: "a woman must have money and a room of her own if she is to write fiction."[3] Actually, Woolf considered five hundred pounds a year an adequate amount for literary self-determination, so Kingsford, with her seven hundred per annum, found herself in an especially fortunate position.

In 1872, at the age of twenty-six, she converted to Roman Catholicism, despite her husband's profession as an Anglican priest. We do not know if this created any marital problems between them. It seems not, especially since she always maintained an active and involved presence in their daughter's life and upbringing. Apparently, he was fine with her conversion away from his faith and the official faith of the nation. She clearly felt the Church of England was an inadequate vessel for her unique spiritual journey, and she certainly did not want to play the homely role of an English vicar's wife. Over time, her interests expanded beyond traditional Catholic theology, too, as she sought out non-Christian, non-Western religious concepts and theories to articulate the insights arising from her personal visionary experiences.

Also in 1872, she purchased and became editor of *The Lady's Own Paper*, a periodical devoted to women's ideas, issues, and concerns. In the course of her editorial work, Kingsford learned about the brutal practices of animal cruelty underlying the British medical system, which critics termed "vivisection." To study the science of physiology, aspiring doctors were taught to experiment on and dissect live animals, often without giving the creatures any anesthetic. Kingsford soon joined other antivivisectionists in expressing outrage at this horrible mistreatment of animals. Defenders of the system said doctors had no other way of learning the anatomical information and practicing the surgical skills they needed to ease the suffering of humans, which should be the primary moral concern. Kingsford, her empathetic imagination highly engaged with the plight of the animals being sacrificed, refused to accept this conclusion. To prove her case, she moved to Paris to attend medical school and become a doctor and to do so without any reliance on killing animals for experimental study. It took six years, but she finally succeeded, and she returned to London as a professional physician and a powerful advocate for animal rights, vegetarianism, and women's educational opportunities.

Around the time of her conversion to Roman Catholicism and her purchase of *The Lady's Own Paper*, Kingsford became close friends with English widower Maitland, who was twenty-two years her senior. They shared interests in literature, esoteric religion, and politics, and he accompanied her on most of her travels over the coming years. Apparently, this unconventional arrangement was acceptable to Kingsford's husband, and Maitland soon became a close confidant and collaborator. With his encouragement, she expanded her writing and speaking activities to include spiritual teachings derived from her copious visionary experiences. For many years, Kingsford had been drawn to the ideas of theosophy, a nineteenth-century spiritual movement in Europe and North America that blended ancient beliefs from Egypt, Greece, and India with mystical traditions in Judaism and Christianity. Kingsford's dreams and visions were filled with profound religious symbolism and allegorical wisdom, and now she began using her literary skills to share her own spiritual insights, using theosophical concepts to help frame and elucidate their significance for her contemporary readers. She and Maitland collaborated on numerous articles and pamphlets in which she envisioned a transcendent harmony among the world's many religious traditions, a harmony in which all forms of life, both animal and human, were recognized as true members of God's creation. In 1883, she was elected president of the London Lodge of the Theosophical Society, a great honor and a clear indication of the high esteem in which she was held by other esoteric thinkers and writers of the time. However, a year later, Kingsford left to form her own organization with Maitland, the Hermetic Society. Once again, she needed a new, more expansive vessel in which to journey forward. As president of the Hermetic Society, she continued energetically writing, speaking, and traveling abroad to promote her many causes, until ill health forced her to return to London in 1887. She died a few months later, at the age of forty-one. According to her brother, Kingsford succumbed to pneumonia first contracted while standing in a cold winter's rain for several hours outside a medical laboratory in Paris, protesting the vivisection practices of Louis Pasteur.[4]

In the months before her death, Kingsford began organizing her collection of dreams and stories based on dreams for publication as a book. She passed away before it could be finished, so Maitland took over and completed the text in 1888. He added a preface in which Kingsford briefly describes her general experiences as a dreamer. As noted, her oneiric aptitude manifested itself early in childhood. She confessed to feeling highly unusual in this aspect of her life: "So far, I have not yet met with anyone in whom the dreaming faculty appears to be either so strongly or so strangely developed as in myself."[5] According to one of her contemporaries, "Since the time of Joseph it is doubtful whether anyone ever deserved so emphatically to be called 'the dreamer' as Mrs. Anna Kingsford."[6]

Not all of her dreams had deep meaning or spiritual significance. She acknowledged that many of them were so lacking in clarity and coherence that they should be considered merely "the product of incomplete and disjointed cerebral function."[7] Other dreams, however, such as the ones she had been writing down throughout her life, had a superabundance of both clarity and coherence, rivaling waking life itself for experiential realism. These were the dreams she found so powerful and influential in her life, and although she offered no general theory of dreaming, she rejected explanations that reduced her dreams to a trivial kind of mental disorder:

> I am tolerably well acquainted with most of the propositions regarding un-conscious cerebration, which have been put forward by men of science, but none of these propositions can, by any process of reasonable expansion or modification, be made to fit my case. . . . The singular coherence and sustained dramatic unity observable in these dreams, as well as the poetic beauty and tender subtlety of the instructions and suggestions conveyed in them, do not comport with the conditions characteristic of nervous disease.[8]

She added that she was a vegetarian; abstained from alcohol, tobacco, and other intoxicants; and had spent much of her adult life devoted to literary and scientific activities "demanding accurate judgement and complete self-possession and rectitude of mind."[9] Nothing else in her life indicated that her mind was disordered or that she suffered from a pathology of the brain. Her dreams, as vivid and hyperrealistic as they sometimes became, never diminished her capacity to recognize the difference between dreaming and waking life:

> On the contrary, the priceless insights and illuminations I have acquired by means of my dreams have gone far to elucidate for me many difficulties and enigmas of life, and even of religion, which might otherwise have remained dark to me, and to throw upon the events and vicissitudes of a career filled with bewildering situations, a light which, like sunshine, has penetrated to the very causes and springs of circumstance, and has given meaning and fitness to much in my life that would else have appeared to me incoherent or inconsistent.[10]

One of the reasons Kingsford did not feel the need to offer a general theory of dreaming was that her most vivid dreams tended to have an allegorical quality, which made them relatively easy to interpret and understand at multiple levels of meaning. It also made them easy to translate into poems and stories for others to read, something she did with several of her dreams. The second half of her book presents five "dream-verses" and eight "dream-stories" that she directly attributed to specific dream experiences. These verses and stories do indeed share many features of tone, language, theme, and character with the twenty-four dream reports presented in the first half of the book. She did not attribute the literary creativity of her dreams to visits from supernatural beings, as another of her contemporaries, Robert Louis Stevenson, did with the Scottish trickster-elves known as "Brownies" who came in his sleep and gave him ideas for stories. Rather, Kingsford regarded her creative writings, her dreams in sleep, and her visions in waking (also collected posthumously by Maitland and published in the book *Clothed with the Sun* in 1912) as all arising from the same source in the depths of her imagination, a source that could be explained, at least in part, as the product of unusually intensified brain functioning. As a scientifically trained physician, Kingsford felt comfortable associating her dreaming faculty with the activation of a special kind of "cerebral state" having the "necessary magnetic or psychic tension" required to generate such powerful experiences. What she disputed was the assumption that dreams like hers must derive from a brain operating at a lower, degraded level of functioning. Kingsford presented her collection of dreams as direct evidence against that dismissive idea. She argued that some dreams cannot be explained in that way, and in fact, these unusual dreams seem to reflect the brain's operation at a higher, more refined level of functioning. This is the possibility that

Kingsford wanted her readers and all empirically minded people to keep in mind as they considered the series of dreams collected in her book.

The first dream presented, "The Doomed Train," could hardly be more dramatic or ominous. She originally recorded it in a letter to Maitland at the end of 1876. It begins with Kingsford finding herself among a group of people who have been summarily sentenced to death by the authorities of a new regime:

> It was night, dark and starless, and I found myself, together with the whole company of doomed men and women who knew that they were soon to die, but not how or where, in a railway train hurrying through the darkness to some unknown destination. I sat in a seat, and was leaning out of the open window, peering into the darkness, when, suddenly, a voice, which seemed to speak out of the air, said to me in a low, distinct, intense tone, the mere recollection of which makes me shudder,—"The sentence is being carried out even now. You are all of you lost. Ahead of the train is a frightful precipice of monstrous height, and at its base beats a fathomless sea. The railway ends only with the abyss. Over that will the train hurl itself into annihilation. *There is no one on the engine!*"[11]

No one else hears the awful voice, only Kingsford. She is looking around the carriage at the people's blank faces, unsure what to do, when she hears the voice speaking again. It tells her the only way to save herself is to leap from the train immediately:

> In frantic haste I pushed open the carriage door and stepped out on the footboard. The train was going at a terrific pace, swaying to and fro as with the passion of its speed; and the mighty wind of its passage beat my hair about my face and tore at my garments.[12]

Then another figure appears in the dream, whom a footnote identifies as Maitland himself. Kingsford sees him on the train and cries for him to join her in jumping for safety. He, however, persuades her not to jump but to try stopping the train instead. She reluctantly agrees, and together they creep toward the front of the train:

> Presently we reached the last carriage, and saw by the lurid light of the furnace that the voice had spoken truly, and that there was no one on

the engine. You [Maitland] continued to move onwards. "Impossible! Impossible!" I cried; "it cannot be done. O, pray, come away!" Then you knelt upon the footboard, and said,—"You are right. It cannot be done in that way; but we can save the train. Help me to get these irons asunder."[13]

Together, with enormous effort, they manage to unhook the irons connecting the engine to the rest of the train. Suddenly, "with a mighty leap as of some mad supernatural monster, the engine sped on its way alone, shooting back as it went a great flaming trail of sparks, and was lost in the darkness."[14] The remaining cars of the train gradually slow and come to a stop. Kingsford and Maitland hurry back to the people to deliver the miraculous news: "Saved! saved! and then amid the confusion of opening the doors and descending and eager talking, my dream ended, leaving me shattered and palpitating with the horror of it."[15]

Dreams for Kingsford had experiential qualities rivaling those of the most intense moments of waking life. They conveyed spiritual insights beyond anything she found in the dogma or ceremonies of the Church. They spoke in an enchanting allegorical language of vivid imagery that she tried her best to understand and actualize in the waking world. Here is a dream she had at a time when she and Maitland were considering whether to share their metaphysical discoveries with a group of academic authorities in Paris. She titled it "The Treasure in the Lighted House":

I saw a house built in the midst of a forest. It was night, and all the rooms of the house were brilliantly illuminated by lamps. But the strange thing was that the windows were without shutters, and reached to the ground. In one of the rooms sat an old man counting money and jewels on a table before him. I stood in the spirit beside him, and presently heard outside the windows a sound of footsteps and of men's voices talking together in hushed tones. Then a face peered in at the lighted room, and I became aware that there were many persons assembled without in the darkness, watching the old man and his treasure. He also heard them, and rose from his seat in alarm, clutching his gold and gems and endeavoring to hide them. "Who are they?" I asked him. He answered, his face white with terror; "They are robbers and assassins. This forest is their haunt. They will murder me, and seize my treasure." "If this be so," said I, "why did you build your house in the midst of this forest, and why are there no shutters to the windows? Are you mad, or a fool, that you do not know everyone can see from without into your lighted rooms?" He looked at me with stupid despair. "I never thought of the shutters," said he. As we stood talking, the robbers outside congregated in great numbers, and the old man fled from the room with his treasure bags into another apartment. But this also was brilliantly illuminated within, and the windows were shutterless. The robbers followed his movements easily, and so pursued him from room to room all round the house. Nowhere had he any shelter. Then came the sound of gouge and mallet and saw, and I knew the assassins were breaking into the house, and that before long, the owner would have met the death his folly had invited, and his treasure would pass into the hands of the robbers.[16]

According to Maitland, this dream was enough to dissuade Kingsford from allowing unguarded access to the inner treasures of her spiritual insights. To be clear, the dream did not tell her to shut herself off from the world and abstain from all conversation about her experiences. On the contrary, she was always willing to share her thoughts and discoveries in public, in the hope of helping and enlightening others, and this dream did nothing to discourage those efforts. Rather, the dream seemed to be suggesting that, as a precondition for being able to share her jewels of wisdom with others, she needed first to take responsibility for protecting the jewels in a private space, safeguarding them from those who would steal her treasure and debase its value. This is what Kingsford took from the dream—it was too late for the old man, but she still had time to defend herself better and to share the wealth of her ideas on her own terms, by her own initiative. Throughout her life, she navigated through difficult situations like this by relying on her dreams and visions, trusting the dynamic conversation between the conscious and unconscious forces of her mind to guide her along the best path forward.

7

Wolfgang Pauli

Quantum Physicist, Depth Psychologist

The last of the seven journal keepers to be introduced is Wolfgang Pauli, an Austrian scientist and pioneer of quantum physics. In addition to his pre-eminence in the physical sciences, Pauli also had an enormous influence on the psychology of Carl Jung, in both open and covert ways.[1] Over the course of a relationship lasting nearly thirty years, Pauli was a client, friend, object of study, thought partner, and sly critic of Jung. Jung used Pauli's dreams and visions in anonymous form as the central evidence in his 1935 lecture "Dream Symbols of the Process of Individuation," and he referred to Pauli's dreams numerous times throughout his career. Pauli himself wrote extensively about quantum physics in relation to philosophy and psychology, and he freely cited his own dreams to illustrate his most important points and explain nuances of his arguments. Pauli did not consider dreaming to be the opposite of rationality or a threat to a scientific view of the universe. On the contrary, his intense and long-lasting engagement with his dreams had the effect of stimulating his scientific creativity and catapulting his mind far beyond the bounds of conventional thought.

Wolfgang Ernst Friedrich Pauli was born on April 25, 1900, in Vienna, the first child in his family. His sister Hertha was born six years later. His father, Wolfgang Joseph Pascheles, had come to Vienna from Prague, where his Jewish family had lived for many generations. After medical training in Prague, Pascheles had joined the faculty of the University of Vienna, eventually rising to the position of professor of chemistry. There he became close friends with Ernst Mach, a professor of experimental physics and one of the great scientific authorities of the age. As a way of integrating himself more fully into his newly adopted home city, Pascheles changed his religious faith from Judaism to Catholicism, the predominant religion of Vienna. He changed his surname, too, from Pascheles to Pauli. In 1899, he married Bertha Camilla Schütz, and when their son was born about a year later, they gave him his father's first name and a middle name from his godfather, Mach.

The Scribes of Sleep. Kelly Bulkeley, Oxford University Press. © Oxford University Press 2023.
DOI: 10.1093/oso/9780197609606.003.0008

This circumstance held great meaning for Pauli, as he later related in a letter of March 31, 1953, to Jung:

> He [Mach] had thus graciously agreed to assume the role of my godfa-
> ther. . . . He evidently was a stronger personality than the Catholic priest,
> and the result seems to be that in this way I am baptized "antimetaphysical"
> instead of Catholic. . . . In spite of my larger spiritual transformations in later
> years it remains a label which I myself carry, namely: "of antimetaphysical
> descent."[2]

All of that was to come later. As a child, Pauli was raised Catholic and attended Catholic schools. Early in his schooling, it became clear that he had tremendous aptitude for mathematical thinking. Thanks to his father's university resources, young Pauli received the best educational support and tutoring available, all of which encouraged him to push his talents as far as they could go. He also received a great deal of care and attention from his mother, a professional writer, and her mother, his grandmother, a former opera singer and musical bon vivant. This may be part of the reason Pauli, in addition to math and science, took interest from an early age in history, philosophy, and classical culture. It also helped his educational development that Pauli grew up in Vienna during a golden era of creative vitality in music, art, philosophy, and science, all with a strong trend toward vigorous modernism. Indeed, Pauli was born just a few months after one of the most important events of this era, the publication of Sigmund Freud's *The Interpretation of Dreams* in November 1899. The brilliance and fervor of the city's cultural environment stimulated Pauli's intellectual development and encouraged his willingness to question traditional scientific theories of reality and experiment with new models and modes of perception.

Pauli began making significant scientific contributions while still a teenager, and he earned his Ph.D. at the age twenty-one. Soon thereafter, he wrote a two-hundred-page encyclopedia article on Albert Einstein's theory of relativity, endorsed by Einstein himself, which became a standard reference work in the field. Over the next few years, Pauli spent time at the University of Hamburg, the University of Göttingen, and the famous Institute for Theoretical Physics in Copenhagen, collaborating with Niels Bohr, Werner Heisenberg, and other young leaders of the emerging field of quantum physics. Among this group, Pauli was known as a bold and brilliantly forward-looking thinker who held everyone in their field, himself included, to the highest standards of scientific reasoning—hence they referred to him as "the conscience of physics." He gained special notice for his "exclusion principle," which clarified the behavior and location of electrons around their nuclei. By all accounts, this was a revolutionary discovery and an epochal advance in human knowledge. Pauli, still in his twenties, had worked out the mathematical laws that govern the basic structure of matter, from the micro level of atoms to the macro level of the everyday world.

He emphasized, however, that these laws only work as statistical probabilities for large groupings of subatomic particles. The laws cannot predict the behavior of any individual particle because the act of observation inescapably influences the selected particle's behavior in ways that conform to the observer's perceptual tools. This factor of "quantum indeterminacy" directly challenges the classic Western model of physics that has held since Isaac Newton, refuting the idea that we can develop a complete causal explanation for the material world. According to Pauli, that kind of explanation is no longer possible. To advance the scientific analysis of matter into the subatomic realm, we need to cast aside many of our assumptions from ordinary reality and open ourselves to the possibility that what initially seems irrational and bizarre may lead to a higher rationality and greater insight.

In 1928, Pauli became a professor of physics at the Eidgenössische Technische Hochschule (ETH), the Swiss Federal School of Technology, in Zurich. This is where he became acquainted with Jung, an eminent psychologist by this point who also taught at the ETH and who personally knew other leading scientists of the day, including Einstein. Pauli first reached out to Jung as a potential client, seeking help for emotional problems he was suffering due to difficulties in his personal life. A year earlier, in 1927, Pauli's mother had died in tragic circumstances, possibly of suicide. Soon after, Pauli's father, whose infidelity had caused many of his mother's woes, married again, this time to a much younger woman. Although he was able to function well enough at work, Pauli fell into a deep depression and began drinking heavily and getting into fights at bars. In 1929, he finally left the Catholic Church, and in a moment of exuberance, he married Luise Deppner, a cabaret dancer in Berlin. She left him just a few weeks after the wedding, and they divorced less than a year later. Jung, upon hearing Pauli's story, referred him to Dr. Erna Rosenbaum, a recent trainee in Jungian psychotherapy with a private practice in Zurich. Rosenbaum had regular sessions with Pauli for several months, during which she asked him to share any dreams that seemed significant. He obliged by providing her with a torrential outpouring of dreams and visions that, with his permission, she shared with Jung. The process quickly grew beyond just therapy for Pauli, to become an experimental study of the symbols of the individuation process. Here is how Jung described it in the introduction to "Individual Dream Symbolism in Relation to Alchemy":

> The material consists of over a thousand dreams and visual impressions coming from a young man of excellent scientific education. . . . In order to avoid all personal influence, I asked one of my pupils, a woman doctor, who was then a beginner, to undertake the observation of the process. . . . Except for a short interview at the very beginning, before the commencement of the observation, I did not see the dreamer at all during the first eight months. . . . Hence conditions were really ideal for unprejudiced observation and recording.[3]

For Jung, this was an ideal opportunity to demonstrate his method of analyzing dreams and interpreting their archetypal meanings. He later developed the original lecture into a case study of nearly two hundred pages. Nowhere else in his writings does Jung devote as much focused attention to a single individual (other than himself), and the text now serves as a model for depth psychologists in the interpretation of dreams at the level of the collective unconscious, or the "objective psyche," as Jung sometimes called it.

For Pauli, the experience seems to have been mostly positive and perhaps even transformative. He clearly felt honored by the attention of Jung, nineteen years his senior and already recognized as one of the great psychologists of the age. The essential findings of the analysis—that Pauli had an overdeveloped intellect, an underdeveloped feeling function, a tendency to project negativity onto other men, and an unconscious anima complex that made it difficult to relate to women—helped him make practical and positive changes in his life. His emotional troubles diminished in severity, he resumed his academic pursuits, and he eventually found a woman with whom he could form an intimate, mature, loving relationship. In April 1934, Pauli was married again, to Franziska Bertram, with whom he remained wed for the rest of his life. In a brief note dated April 28, 1934, Jung said to him, "My best congratulations on your marriage. I am very pleased that you have arrived at this conclusion."[4]

This and other letters between Pauli and Jung provide a primary source for insight into Pauli's dreams. In the collection of their correspondence between

1932 and 1958, available in English translation as *Atom and Archetype* (2001), Pauli described several additional dreams not included in the initial set that Jung studied in 1935. Pauli also tried to explain to Jung the peculiar features of his dreams, which frequently used concepts and analogies from physics to express psychological feelings and experiences. For Pauli, the concepts of physics did not merely symbolize aspects of his inner life. Rather, he felt that his dreams were striving, *through* the concepts of physics, to apprehend bigger truths at a level where physical and psychological languages could be united. He agreed with Jung that the medieval discipline of alchemy, long scorned as superstitious pseudoscience, actually held the right idea in seeking a transcendent union of physical transformation and mystical insight. Indeed, Pauli himself can truly be said to have solved the great alchemical mystery of the "philosopher's stone." His exclusion principle revealed for the first time the unique structural identity of each element and thus showed exactly which subatomic particles needed to move where to transform one element into another—telling us how, for example, to turn lead (Pb, atomic number 82) into gold (Au, atomic number 79).

Jung encouraged Pauli to record and share only those dreams that seemed significant, not ordinary dreams having to do with transient events of daily life.[5] An explicit screening process was thus applied to Pauli's engagement with his dream life, both narrowing and intensifying his focus on certain kinds of dreams. Here are the first three dreams (undated) of Pauli's that Jung presents in "Individual Dream Symbolism in Relation to Alchemy":

> The dreamer is at a social gathering. On leaving, he puts on a stranger's hat instead of his own.
>
> The dreamer is going on a railway journey, and by standing in front of the window, he blocks the view for his fellow passengers. He must get out of their way.
>
> The dreamer is surrounded by a throng of vague female forms. A voice within him says, "First I must get away from Father."[6]

These dreams, although brief, include themes that recur in many of Pauli's other dreams. In the first dream, the mysterious stranger appears, a figure who brings difference, conflict, and tension into his dreams; in a letter to Jung's wife, Emma, Pauli considers the recurrent stranger as an embodiment of the archetype of the magician.[7] The second dream has recurrent elements of movement, light, perspective, and balance, all of which directly relate to the chief concerns of his scientific theorizing. For Pauli, dream symbols can be imaginal versions of mathematical symbols, and vice versa. The third dream is a variation on the theme of powerful, threatening women; these were among the most vivid and intense dreams Pauli ever experienced, eliciting a great deal of self-reflection on the role of feminine energies (Jung's anima archetype) in his life.

At the same time as Jung promoted special attention to dreams with time-less themes, he also encouraged Pauli to note any possible parallels between his personal life and the collective social and political dynamics of the world at large. In a letter of May 24, 1934, Pauli wrote to Jung that he feared his psychological problems were about to break out among all the people of Europe:

> The specific threat to my life has been the fact that in the second half of life I swing from one extreme to the other [*enantiodriomia*]. . . . This abrupt swing into the opposite is a danger not just for me but for our whole civi-lization. . . . In this moment everything can turn into primitive barbarism, unless Tao and individuation step in. This is why my personal problem is also a collective one, and, conversely, the danger that I personally was faced with was greatly heightened by a disposition that was forced upon me by the collective unconscious.[8]

Like Jung with his own dreams and visions in the years preceding the out-break of World War I, Pauli felt his recent dreams had an ominously anticipa-tory quality at a level of significance beyond his own personal life. Here is his dream from January 23, 1938:

> At the top there is a window, to the right of it a clock. In the dream I draw an oscillation process beneath the window—actually two oscillations, one beneath the other. By turning to the right from the curves, I try to see the time on the clock. But the clock is too high, so that doesn't work. Then the dream continues. The "dark unknown woman" appears. She is crying be-cause she wants to write a book but cannot find a publisher for it. In this book there is apparently a great deal of material on time symbolism—e.g., how a period of time is constituted when certain symbols appear in it. And at the end of one page of the book there are the following words, read aloud by the "voice": "The definite hours have to be paid for with the definite life, the indefinite hours have to be paid for with the indefinite life."[9]

More will be said in later chapters about Pauli's departure from Europe at the start of World War II, his time in the United States, his winning of the Nobel Prize, and his eventual return to Zurich, where he worked on developing the philosophical implications of his thinking about the interaction between psyche and physics. I finish here by noting a curious biographical fact. According to several colleagues, odd things happened around Pauli, so much so that everyone began to expect bizarre misfortunes when interacting with him. One of his closest collaborators, Markus Fierz, described the situation as follows:

> Even quite practical experimental physicists were convinced that strange effects emanated from Pauli. It was believed, e.g., that his mere presence in a laboratory produced all sorts of experimental mishaps, he so to speak tricked the objects. This was the "Pauli Effect." For this reason, his friend Otto Stern, the famous artist of molecular beams, never let him enter his laboratory. This is not a legend, I knew Pauli and Stern both very well! Pauli himself thoroughly believed in his effect. He once told me that he sensed the mischief already before as a disagreeable tension, and when the suspected misfortune then actually hit—another one!—he felt strangely liberated and lightened.[10]

Pauli himself clearly took great delight in his reputation as a paranormal scientific trickster. In a letter to Jung from June 16, 1948, he starts by mentioning the latest instance of "that amusing 'Pauli effect,'" the inexplicable overturning of a vase during a talk he attended at the founding of the Jung Institute a few weeks earlier.[11] By acknowledging the reality of such phenomena, Pauli did not abandon science or rationality, no more than he did when he explored the archetypal dimensions of dreams. On the contrary, he believed that more attention to dreams, the "Pauli effect," and other spontaneous creations from the unconscious mind could enrich science and expand rationality—and, incidentally, bring greater health and wholeness to individual lives. He knew this was a controversial point of view among both scientists and the general public, where such claims appeared superstitious, bizarrely speculative, and possibly dangerous in calling into question the credibility and authority of science. However, this was not an unfamiliar position for Pauli. In 1932, during the worst depths of his emotional crisis and therapeutic work, he proposed the existence of a new subatomic particle, the "neutrino." He had no observations or experimental evidence to support his claim, only his intuitive insight that certain anomalies in the process of radioactive decay could best be explained by the existence of a subatomic particle with neither positive nor negative charge—a neutral particle, or a neutrino. More than twenty years later, evidence finally emerged that Pauli was right. The clincher came in 1956, when the first atomic bomb tests in Los Alamos, New Mexico, yielded clear observations of neutrinos in the blast radius. "All things come to those who are patient" was his reply upon hearing the confirming news.

PART II

DISCOVERING PATTERNS
OF CONTENT

Now that we have taken an initial look at seven people's dreams and their journaling practices, what can we learn from them as a group? How do we start trying to make sense of all this information? Some of the dreams seem to have obvious meanings, while others seem devoid of any significance. They have a degree of chronological connectivity—one dream often leads thematically into a following dream—but many of the dreams have no obvious temporal relationship to other dreams or anything happening in the individual's waking life. Where to begin, then? Choosing one dream, or one type of dream, as the starting point of the analysis seems arbitrary and misleading. The same goes with choosing a single theory of dreaming as the initial framework for studying a collection of dreams like this. Any theory is going to highlight some dreams and downplay others, when what we need at the outset is a way to identify the basic patterns and contours of *all* the dreams as a collection, in relation to one another and to dreams from other sources.

The three chapters in this part of the book use new digital methods of dream content analysis to provide this kind of overview. The results of this analysis will not provide specific interpretations of the dreams, but they will give us a broad perspective on all the dreams included in the journals, their typical and atypical contents, and their most frequently recurring themes and images. The results of these digital methods of analysis can help set reasonable boundaries and expectations about the various interpretations we will consider in the chapters of parts III and IV. For instance, an interpretation that focused on the symbolism of flying dreams could be interesting in theory, but if a digital analysis showed that a set of dreams had references to flying in only 2 percent of the reports, we would see that the interpretation is an incomplete assessment of the set as a whole. Likewise, if a digital analysis showed that a set of dreams had references to animals in 50 percent of the reports, then we would expect an interpretation of the whole set to take this into account and make something of it, and we would reject a reading of the dreams that ignored or dismissed the high frequency of animals. The digital analysis does not say what the dreams mean, but the results it provides about their basic patterns can be tremendously helpful as we begin the process of distinguishing better from worse interpretations.

8

Digital Methods of Analyzing Dreams

As the earlier chapters have shown, a single person's dream journal can generate huge amounts of complex information. If you keep a dream journal, you probably know the pregnant feeling of *knowing* there are multitudes of important meanings in the text but *not* knowing how to access or understand them. Until recently, it required truly Herculean efforts to analyze so much dream material. We may sense deeper layers of meaning in a large collection of dreams, and we may even get intuitive flashes of insight into these meanings, but it is dauntingly difficult to confirm our insights by systematically analyzing all the dreams.

Still, intrepid scholars have applied themselves to this task. For hundreds of years, the basic method has been the same, from the quill-and-ink charts Don Alonso made to compare Lucrecia de León's dreams with biblical omens, to Dorothy Eggan's pencil-and-graph-paper tabulations of cultural and psychological themes in the dreams of her Hopi informants, to the content analysis spreadsheets created by Calvin Hall and Robert Van de Castle to analyze the dreams of American college students. In each case, the first step is for the researcher to establish a set of content categories that can be expected to appear in the dreams. Second is creating a two-dimensional grid, with the categories along one axis and the number, date, or title for each dream report on the other. The third step is reading through all the dreams and marking down on the grid which ones have instances of the preselected categories. This can be done in two different ways: either by reading one dream and coding it for all the categories, then reading a second dream to code for all the categories, and so on, or by reading all the dreams to code for a single category, then reading all the dreams again to code for a second category, and so on.

This basic approach combines the analytic power of the human mind with the technical power of the handwritten two-dimensional chart. Wherever such a method has been used, it has provided researchers with new perspectives and insights that can be verified by the tabulated evidence of the chart. In this way, it is a fundamentally empirical method, grounded in

The Scribes of Sleep. Kelly Bulkeley, Oxford University Press. © Oxford University Press 2023.
DOI: 10.1093/oso/9780197609606.003.0009

openly available data that can be examined and verified by others. It is also a method that expands the human mind's capacity to process and apprehend the meaningfulness of dreaming over time, far beyond what can be learned from ordinary approaches to single dreams in isolation from one another.

Thanks to this approach to empirical dream analysis, our knowledge about dream content grew tremendously in the twentieth century. It should be noted, too, that this method also has serious disadvantages. It is tedious, time-consuming, and labor-intensive. Developing a reliable set of categories is a difficult process, and so is training people to code the dreams and use the categories in a consistent and accurate way. The quality of the results depends on the skill and judgment of the people doing the coding, which can be quite variable and problematically influenced by their personal biases, consciously and/or unconsciously. Someone else could theoretically re-examine a set of dreams and test the original categories or try new ones of their own, but in practical terms, the validation process is prohibitively difficult for anyone other than professional scholars.

This chapter looks beyond the handwritten chart to introduce the next generation of digital tools for studying dream journals and other large collections of dreams.[1] These new tools have limits of their own, but they also have enormous benefits and advantages, foremost of which is their accessibility. The emergence of digital archives, databases, and search engines for dream research has made tools once restricted to academic specialists available to anyone with a computer and an internet connection. The Sleep and Dream Database (SDDb), discussed in more detail later in this chapter, is one such online resource. Everything presented in this book has its empirical grounding in the SDDb's collection of dreams. This means that everything here is available to be tested, inspected, and evaluated by you, the reader. You are the lucky beneficiary of a radical democratization of dream research. You have the potential, therefore, to become a co-creator of the future of the field.

Several questions naturally arise about whether digital tools can be legitimately applied to dream journals at all. It is worth taking these skeptical questions seriously from the outset. They can help us gain a better understanding of what we can and cannot learn about dreams from these methods. Before going any further, let's consider a few basic questions.

First, are dreams legitimate data for this kind of analysis? This is a key concern that must be addressed before any further steps in the digital direction may be taken. From a skeptic's view, it seems that a dream journal, or any collection of dreams, is essentially a group of first-person, retrospective accounts of private experiences that occurred in another state of consciousness and cannot be independently observed or verified. Can computer technologies really give us genuine insights into such intimately subjective phenomena? This question is a new version of the long debate about dreams as valid scientific data. Many researchers make a distinction between a dream *experience* and the individual's *report* of the dream experience, and they point to the vast and apparently unbridgeable gulf between the two, a gulf born of the insufficiency of the report to convey all the multi-sensory perceptions in the experience, along with the surplus of extraneous verbiage that can imperceptibly creep into the waking report and distort the actual details of the experience. What someone reports as "a dream" is always the product of countless *non-dream* forces and influences, too. Factors of memory, recency, motivation, language, self-deception, interpersonal dynamics, and cultural morality all contribute to the final shape of each dream report we receive for analysis.

Does this mean we are forever doomed to study nothing but pale, secondary aftereffects of people's dreams and never the primary experiences themselves? That seems too extreme a view. Dream reports may not be perfect representations of dream experiences, but there is good reason to believe the reports do accurately convey at least some important features of an actual underlying experience. For instance, neuro-imaging studies have shown that during the phases of sleep when most dreaming occurs, several regions of the brain are especially active, including those involved in emotional arousal, instinctive responses, and visual imagination. As coming chapters will explain in more detail, these are all prominent features in the typical dream content of people around the world and throughout history. In other words, modern neuroscience is showing a rough match between what the brain is doing in sleep and what features of content appear most often in dreaming. Physiology and psychology are finding common ground in the study of dreams—a small-scale illustration of E. O. Wilson's notion of "consilience" across multiple scientific domains.[2] This kind of consilient research is expanding rapidly, with the promise of narrowing even further the gap between dream report and dream experience. In light of such trends, we should give due attention to the various influences that shape people's reports of their dreams and *also* acknowledge that their reports can provide us with accurate descriptions of real, authentic experiences.

To be clear, the danger always remains that people are being less than fully honest or forthcoming when they report their dreams. Indeed, it cannot be ruled out that some people are simply fabricating everything they say.

Dream research is not a risk-free enterprise. It requires putting a high degree of trust in introspective data. The risks in working with such sources cannot be eliminated, although they can be mitigated if we focus on broad patterns in large collections of high-quality data. The neuroscientist Antonio Damasio has defended the importance of first-person reports of inner psychological feelings as a legitimate source of evidence for the scientific study of the brain, and he has said the goal for researchers should be to illuminate "the external consistency of many internal subjectivities."[3] Collecting a host of introspective reports from multiple individuals and sifting through them to identify recurrent themes is, according to Damasio, a valid and productive path in modern neuroscience. I suggest the same is true with dream research. Scholars in this field have always had a wealth of introspective reports to study. What they have lacked are analytic tools with sufficient power to discern the external consistencies among the multiple individuals. Now better and more powerful technologies are emerging, and the prospects are bright for new discoveries and insights in coming years. All in all, dream reports are turning out to be a legitimate and surprisingly fruitful source of data for digital methods of analysis.

A second question accepts the use of digital tools to study the dreams of contemporary people but casts doubt on the idea that such tools can be applied to people from other periods of history and/or to people who record their dreams in languages other than modern English. Because new methods of digital analysis have been developed by modern, mostly English-speaking people, the methods work best in their linguistic and temporal context. But how effectively can the digital tools be used outside that original setting? Is it possible to bridge the vast differences in people's experiences with language, culture, and history? In an absolute sense, the answer is surely no. There will always be aspects of personal meaning that elude the best research tools, even when used among people who are contemporaries and speak the same language. But as a matter of scholarly practice, the answer can be a qualified yes. With modest expectations, the help of high-quality translations, and careful attention to an individual's background and personal circumstances, researchers can legitimately and productively use modern tools of inquiry to identify significant features in the dreams of people from various places and times. The following chapters will demonstrate this pragmatic approach and its value in highlighting relatively clear and straightforward patterns of meaning in people's dreams, the patterns that are most prominent and easiest to observe—the low-hanging fruit, as it were, that digital tools are especially well suited to illuminate, gather, and analyze.

Here is a third question that should be answered before moving forward with the discussion of the seven dream journals. Can we analyze the meanings of a set of dreams without the active participation of the dreamer? We all know from our own dreams how deeply intertwined their contents can be with our private thoughts, recent activities, and current preoccupations. This information seems essential for the valid analysis of anyone's dreams and their significance. If we have no access to the personal details and waking-life context out of which an individual's dreams emerged and if we have no way to get feedback and corrections from that person, how can we avoid misinterpreting what the dreams really mean?

For this reason, Sigmund Freud's method of dream interpretation emphasizes the importance of personal associations as the keys necessary to unlock the dream's symbolic meanings. When talking about a dream, Freud asked his patients to suspend their judging, evaluating, self-critical way of thinking and simply say whatever came into their minds in relation to the various elements of their dreams. He said this would elicit a "a series of associations to each piece, what might be described as the 'background thoughts' of that particular part of the dream."[4] Only with the help of this information from the dreamer, Freud believed, could the interpretation of dreams have a claim to scientific validity and not descend into a superstitious practice of divination.

Personal associations can certainly help to interpret a dream, but are they *essential*? Even Freud ultimately said the answer to that question is a qualified no.[5] Some aspects of meaning *can* be discerned in a dream without any personal associations provided by the dreamer, thanks to the universality of "typical" symbols and themes that appear from time to time in virtually everyone's dreams. As examples, Freud discussed the classic themes of appearing naked in public, a visitation from a loved one who has died, and anxiety about tests and examinations. If we understand the common symbolic meanings of such themes, we have a legitimate basis for offering possible interpretations of dreams in which they appear—not certain or complete interpretations but possible dimensions of meaning that have less to do with personal concerns in waking life and more to do with the collective concerns of humankind and perhaps with the concerns of all life. Freud noted that with many "typical" dreams, people simply don't have any associations from recent daily life to offer, which is itself a sign that the dreams are pointing beyond the personal to the impersonal.[6]

Much more than Freud, Carl Jung developed a psychological framework for exploring the impersonal aspects of dreaming, which he referred to as the archetypes of the collective unconscious. Originally trained as a medical psychiatrist, Jung integrated modern psychology with research from archaeology, anthropology, comparative mythology, and the history of religions to explain the aspects of symbolic meaning in dreams that can be illuminated without personal associations from the dreamer. He accepted the value of "little dreams" as helpful reflections of personal concerns in daily life. But Jung put much greater value on "big dreams" and their impersonal images and symbols, which may not have any obvious connection to the waking world but carry a strong emotional charge that makes a powerful impact on the dreamer.[7]

Psychological anthropologists such as Dorothy Eggan have also developed methods of interpreting dreams in ways that do not require the personal associations of the dreamers. For these researchers, the cultural environment in which each person grows up and lives is replete with stories, symbols, characters, and metaphors holding multiple dimensions of collective significance.[8] When these elements appear in dreams, they probably have a personal range of meanings, but they may also carry cultural meanings that can be observed and analyzed by researchers without reliance on the dreamer's personal associations. The chapters of part III will go into more detail about how to apply Freudian, Jungian, and culturally oriented methods of interpretation to dream journals. Here these approaches help to answer the central question about the necessary role of personal associations in dream analysis. Yes, the dreamer's personal input is valuable, but some dreams may have collective, cultural, or impersonal meanings that the individuals themselves do not understand, suggesting that a sensitive outside interpreter with the right methods might be able to clarify such meanings for the benefit of both the dreamer and the community at large.

If these answers are acceptable—that dream reports are a legitimate source of data, differences of language and history can be partly overcome, and some valid interpretations can be made without personal associations from the dreamer—then the stage is set for the emergence of digital databases for the study of dreams. I believe this represents one of the most important advances in dream research of modern times. These databases gather, preserve, and make accessible huge collections of dream reports, with search tools to analyze the dreams with unprecedented speed and ease. More than neuro-imaging tools, which are expensive, difficult to operate, and extremely limited in their use, digital databases can be free, user-friendly, and open-access. This is enabling a dramatic expansion of new research by people from all over the world, whose findings have already begun to transform the field.

A pioneering effort in this area was the Dreambank.net, created by G. William Domhoff and Adam Schneider of the University of California, Santa Cruz. Begun in the early 1990s, the Dreambank contains dozens of sets and series of dreams and makes them available for study via a system of keyword searches. Domhoff and Schneider combined Hall's extensive collection of dream reports with thousands of new reports, and they developed their digital tools as an extension of his content analysis method. From the beginning, Domhoff and Schneider have been very supportive of my research, and we have collaborated on several studies that I will describe in coming pages.

After more than ten years of working with the Dreambank and learning how to apply its tools to various kinds of dreams, in 2009, I persuaded Kurt Bollacker, a computer scientist in San Francisco, to help me design a new database with several features that are not available in the Dreambank. Highly skilled and philosophically curious, Bollacker had been working as research director for the Long Now Foundation, a group devoted to long-term thinking about human civilization. Much to my benefit, he took on the SDDb as an experimental project and taught me how to build "long now" principles into the architecture of the database. Simplicity, accessibility, transparency, flexibility, portability—these are the cardinal virtues we tried to establish as the deep framework of the SDDb. We wanted the database to be simple to use and accessible to all, with transparent sources of data that can be studied in a variety of ways and easily downloaded for further analysis. Those continued to be the goals as Bollacker passed the technical management of the ever-growing database to Graybox and its Portland, Oregon–based team of programmers and web designers. Now the team of developers of the *Elsewhere* dream journaling app—Daniel Kennedy, Sheldon Juncker, and Gez Quinn—have become the primary technical managers of the SDDb, with the goal of integrating its resources with their public-facing portal for digitally recording and analyzing one's dreams.

The SDDb includes collections of dreams from the seven historical figures introduced in part I—Aelius Aristides, Myōe Shonin, Lucrecia de León, Emanuel Swedenborg, Benjamin Banneker, Anna Kingsford, and Wolfgang Pauli—and from many other people, both historical and contemporary. The database offers tools to search all these dreams by keywords, and it includes a template of forty content categories to help in the study of especially common elements in dreams (such as emotions, perceptions, characters, social interactions, etc.). Keyword searches can quickly reveal the basic contours of a large collection of dreams and thus provide valuable guidance in deciding which aspects of the collection seem most worthy of further detailed study. For example, if you want to study dreams about animals, you can use the "animal" category of characters in the SDDb template to identify all the dreams with at least one mention of an animal. There is no need for you to spend time reading through all the dreams in the database and highlighting the ones with animals in them—the computer can do that task for you. Using those quickly generated results as a springboard, you can focus all your energy and attention on exploring that subset of animal-related dreams. It is this powerful combination of reducing the tedious work of coding and categorizing and thereby increasing your ability to focus on the most valuable results that makes the simple keyword search so useful.

The database also makes it easy to compare the dreams and content frequencies of one person with the dreams and content frequencies of other people. A comparative analysis can reveal many distinctive features of an individual's dream journal, features you might not recognize or appreciate if you did not have the context of other dreams in the database. For example, let's say a word search yields the finding that references to fear appear in 10 percent of a certain person's dreams. You might wonder, is that a high or low figure? Do other people have more references to fear in their dreams or fewer? If you knew the answers to those comparative questions, it would enhance your understanding of the significance and possible meanings of fear in the person's dreams.

The next two chapters show how to use these SDDb tools and resources to highlight the most basic and easily identified patterns of meaning in a collection of dreams. To be clear, these methods are first steps only. They set the empirical stage for other, more advanced and sophisticated modes of interpretation—psychological and cultural in part III and religious and spiritual in part IV.

9

Baseline Patterns in Dream Content

From my earliest reading of Ann Faraday's *Dream Power* until I finished graduate studies ten years later, I held a very skeptical view of quantitative methods of dream research. It seemed like a fool's errand to dissect dreams into little atomized bits, calculate their statistical frequencies, and then claim these frequencies somehow represent the dream's true and objective meaning. How, I wondered, could such a method account for the complex symbolism of the dream's imagery, the subtle threads of meaning that connect one scene to another, the deep personal associations with the dreamer's life, and the experiential gestalt of the dream as a subjectively realized life-world? Quantitative methods seemed to bulldoze over the most vital qualities of dreaming, leaving a flat, arid expanse of numbers in its wake. In my doctoral dissertation and first book, *The Wilderness of Dreams* (1994), I directed lots of critical ire at Calvin Hall and his content analysis approach on these points, especially his claim of scientific objectivity:

> Hall argues that his dream series method provides certain, objective information on what dreams mean, and yet his conclusions simply mirror many of the distinctive cultural values of mid-twentieth century America. For example, Hall is not aware of how his culture's views of male-female relations are coloring his "objective" findings. *The Meaning of Dreams* (Hall 1966) is (from a late-twentieth century perspective) likely the most sexist book on dreams ever written, presenting numerous culturally specific notions about gender as self-evident, objective fact.[1]

I still hold to that critique of Hall's writings. However, I confess that soon after finishing graduate school, I made a 180-degree turn regarding the value of quantitative methods like content analysis. Once an adamant foe, I am now an enthusiastic advocate. Paradoxically, it was the glaring bias of Hall's gender claims that taught me how to distinguish the *tool* from the *user* of the tool. I belatedly realized the problem wasn't the method of content analysis per se, but it was rather users of the method making subjectively biased

The Scribes of Sleep. Kelly Bulkeley, Oxford University Press. © Oxford University Press 2023.
DOI: 10.1093/oso/9780197609606.003.0010

claims under the cloak of objective fact. If those biases could be set aside and if the tool could be applied more modestly and self-reflexively—as one approach among others, always conditioned by the user's personal interests—then maybe, just maybe, something interesting could be done with it. That was what I began thinking, anyway. Around this time, I had a series of conversations with G. William Domhoff and Adam Schneider, who were in the early stages of developing the Dreambank website and experimenting with word-search methods of digital data analysis grounded in Hall's work. In the late 1990s, with Domhoff and Schneider's help and encouragement, I applied their methods to a three-year set of dreams from my journal. I can still remember the jaw-dropping surprise I felt when I first looked at the results. It was a kind of empiricist epiphany. The unmistakable consistency over the three years of my dreaming in terms of characters, emotions, and social interactions was remarkable and strangely startling. *How did I not know this about myself?* Previously, I had always studied my dreams individually and in small thematic series. This was the first time I had ever looked at a large collection of dreams over a long period of time. The quantitative method of content analysis helped me identify new levels of meaning and significance in my dream journal, levels I never even knew existed and certainly could not have reached without technological assistance.

In the years since then, I have found the best way to introduce people to these deeper patterns in dreaming is to start with the twin concepts of *continuity* and *discontinuity*. This chapter considers several dimensions of continuity in dreaming, and the next chapter will look at aspects of discontinuity. Among present-day researchers, the term "continuity" has several overlapping and sometimes conflicting definitions, so I want to be clear about how it will be used in this book. Here we will be exploring four distinct types of continuity in dreaming:

1. *Internal & Personal*: A dream pattern is continuous with the other patterns in the individual's dreaming.
2. *Internal & Collective*: A dream pattern is continuous with the general patterns of other people's dreaming.
3. *External & Personal*: A dream pattern is continuous with the primary emotional concerns of the individual's waking life.
4. *External & Collective*: A dream pattern is continuous with the primary emotional concerns of the individual's waking culture and community.

Let's ease into this by looking at the dream patterns of the seven historical figures we met in part I, starting with Aelius Aristides. Aristides offers a total (by my count) of 121 dream reports in the *Sacred Tales*. This is a good number of reports for quantitative analysis, providing enough content for finely grained methods of analysis to do their work. Domhoff has recommended a set of 100 to 125 dreams as the minimum necessary for a valid analysis of content patterns.[2]

Historical evidence does not always afford us that much material, so we do the best with what we have. Fortunately, what we have can often be more than enough. There are many aspects of dream content that can be clearly and reliably identified in even smaller numbers of reports.

A key point to consider when beginning to analyze a new set of dreams is the length of the reports, that is, the total number of words each report contains. The SDDb calculates these figures automatically, and for Aristides, his shortest dream is 7 words long, and his longest is 898 words in length. The whole set of 121 dreams has a total of 10,724 words, resulting in an average or mean word length per report of 89 words (10,724 divided by 121). However, the median word length of Aristides's dreams is 42 words, meaning half the dreams in his series are longer than 42 words, and half are shorter than 42 words. If we take these two figures together, the mean of 89 and the median of 42, we can see that most of Aristides's dream reports are on the shortish side, but he has several very long dreams, too.

The collection of Aristides's 121 dream reports has been uploaded into the SDDb, where I analyzed them using the forty categories of content in the SDDb word-search template. The forty categories are organized into eight classes: Perception, Emotions, Characters, Social Interactions, Movement, Cognition, Culture, and Elements. (In the following pages, capitalization will be used to designate members of the eight classes and forty categories.) Many of the categories were originally drawn from the Hall and Van de Castle content analysis system, to make it easier to compare results from digital word searches with previous generations of research using their method (i.e., backward compatibility). Each SDDb category consists of a collection of words relating to a particular type of content. If a dream report has one or more instances of any of those words, it is counted as a dream containing that category of content.

Table 9.1 shows the results of applying this method to the dreams of Aristides.

Table 9.1. Word-Search Results for Aelius Aristides

SDDb Categories	Aelius Aristides N = 121 mean 89, median 42	7-898
	Percent	Most-used words
Perception		
Vision	19	saw, see
Hearing	12	heard, ears
Touch	14	hand, hands, held
Smell and Taste	2	sweet
Color	5	white
Emotion		
Fear	3	afraid
Anger	4	angry
Sadness	2	distressed
Wonder	4	wondered
Happiness	6	pleased, glad
Characters		
Family	12	father, son, brother, mother
Animals	10	horse
Fantastic Beings	0	
Male References	65	he, him, his, man
Female References	6	her, mother, she, woman
Social Interactions		
Friendliness	26	friends, praise, honor
Physical Aggression	2	attack, enemies
Sexuality	2	kiss, lover
Movement		
Walking/Running	5	walking, run
Flying	0	
Falling	1	fell
Death	4	dead, death
Cognition		
Thinking	27	thought, think, intended, prepared
Speech	55	said, say, spoke, called
Reading/Writing	14	written, letter, read, wrote

Table 9.1. Continued

SDDb Categories	Aelius Aristides N = 121 mean 89, median 42	7-898
	Percent	Most-used words
Culture		
Architecture	9	home, house, room
Food and Drink	14	eat, drink, wine, bread, eggs
Clothing	3	wore
School	5	teacher
Transportation	4	road, ship, path
Technology	0	
Money and Work	4	bought, coins, rich, work
Weapons	1	daggers
Sports	3	athlete, gymnasium
Art	8	drawing, poet, sang, theater
Religion	50	god, temple, Zeus, priest, sacred
Elements		
Fire	8	sun, burn, fire, star
Air	2	air
Water	12	water, river, sea
Earth	8	mud, earth, land

This is a lot of information to take in, with dimensions of meaning that can only be discerned after further analysis and study. But right away, we can make a few observations about prominent features of the numerical patterns in Aristides's dreams. Among the forty categories of content, the highest frequencies for Aristides are Male references, Speech, and Religion. Knowing this enables us to begin building a profile of Aristides's basic dream patterns and to make some initial claims about the Internal & Personal continuities in his dreams. We could now look at a single dream of Aristides's and determine with empirical precision whether it is continuous with the contents of his other dreams (i.e., has references to males, speaking, and/or religion) or is discontinuous with those basic patterns of content.

However, this level of analysis cannot tell us whether Aristides's frequencies of dream content are higher or lower than anyone else's. How would we know if his frequency of references to Religion, for example, are unusually high, unusually low, or about average compared with religious references in the dreams of other people? This is the Internal & Collective dimension of continuity, and it requires a new tool of measurement—what I call *baselines*—that can be applied after the word-search analysis has been performed. The SDDb Baselines are a specially selected collection of more than five thousand dreams gathered by myself and other researchers from a wide variety of people between the 1950s and the present. I have analyzed these dreams using the SDDb word-search template of forty categories, resulting in a set of general frequencies for each type of dream content, for both men and women. Of course, the SDDb Baselines are not a perfect representation of all dreams from all people. But they do provide a useful measuring stick for highlighting continuities and discontinuities in dreams. Indeed, there is currently no better, more comprehensive set of baseline dreams in use by contemporary researchers. Let's look at Aristides's dream content frequencies once more, this time with the frequencies of the SDDb Male Baselines as a comparison set. See table 9.2.

Again, this is a lot of information to process, so let's take it slowly. The Male Baselines have an average word length of 105 words, compared with the 86-word average of Aristides's dreams. A difference like this will usually lead to slightly lower frequencies in Aristides's dreams compared with the Baselines, since longer dreams have more room for various types of content. However, we can see that in many categories of content, Aristides's dreams have much higher frequencies than the Baselines. These are *discontinuities* at the Internal & Collective level, which we will discuss further in chapter 10. Here let's focus on the ways in which Aristides's dreams seem to be *continuous* with the Baselines. The specific percentages matter less than the patterns and relations among the categories. For example, in the Perception categories, Aristides's dreams have lower raw frequencies than the Baselines but the same relational ranking *between* the categories: Visual references most frequent, followed by Touch and Hearing, with Smell and Taste far behind. This relational ranking of perception in dreams is characteristic not just of the Baselines but of almost all other sets of dreams that contemporary researchers have studied—a strong pattern, indeed. Other instances of Internal & Collective continuity between Aristides's dreams and the Male Baselines include more Friendliness than Physical Aggression or Sexuality and more references to Water than any other element.

These few continuities aside, the most striking feature of Aristides's dreams is their many *discontinuities* with average patterns of dreaming. For instance, it turns out that 50 percent of men's dreams do *not* typically include references to Religion, as is the case with Aristides; the figure in the Baselines

Table 9.2. Word-Search Results with Baselines for Aelius Aristides

SDDb Categories	Baselines Males N = 2,135 mean 105	Aelius Aristides N = 121 mean 89, median 42	7-898
	Percent	Percent	Most-used words
Perception			
Vision	29	19	saw, see
Hearing	9	12	heard, ears
Touch	12	14	hand, hands, held
Smell and Taste	1	2	sweet
Color	12	5	white
Emotion			
Fear	15	3	afraid
Anger	5	4	angry
Sadness	3	2	distressed
Wonder	18	4	wondered
Happiness	6	6	pleased, glad
Characters			
Family	27	12	father, son, brother, mother
Animals	12	10	horse
Fantastic Beings	2	0	
Male References	40	65	he, him, his, man
Female References	35	6	her, mother, she, woman
Social Interactions			
Friendliness	34	26	friends, praise, honor
Physical Aggression	19	2	attack, enemies
Sexuality	6	2	kiss, lover
Movement			
Walking/Running	27	5	walking, run
Flying	6	0	
Falling	8	1	fell
Death	7	4	dead, death
Cognition			
Thinking	38	27	thought, think, intended, prepared
Speech	32	55	said, say, spoke, called

(*continued*)

Table 9.2. Continued

SDDb Categories	Baselines Males N = 2,135 mean 105		Aelius Aristides N = 121 mean 89, median 42	7-898
	Percent		Percent	Most-used words
Reading/Writing	5		14	written, letter, read, wrote
Culture				
Architecture	41		9	home, house, room
Food and Drink	12		14	eat, drink, wine, bread, eggs
Clothing	11		3	wore
School	13		5	teacher
Transportation	28		4	road, ship, path
Technology	8		0	
Money and Work	22		4	bought, coins, rich, work
Weapons	5		1	daggers
Sports	4		3	athlete, gymnasium
Art	7		8	drawing, poet, sang, theater
Religion	6		50	god, temple, Zeus, priest, sacred
Elements				
Fire	4		8	sun, burn, fire, star
Air	5		2	air
Water	12		12	water, river, sea
Earth	10		8	mud, earth, land

is 6 percent. Again, we will explore Internal & Collective discontinuities in more detail in chapter 10. In ordinary practice, the two go together, as we scan the dream patterns for continuities *and* discontinuities. I am separating them here to make it easier to learn how the various stages of this word-search process relate to each other.

Turning to External & Personal continuities, we can see right away that Aristides's frequencies in several categories of dream content accurately reflect the important concerns, activities, and relationships in his waking life. (To identify these External & Personal continuities requires noting a few

Internal & Collective discontinuities—there's only so much simplifying I can do.) We know that he was educated in public speaking and the literary arts, which seems directly continuous with the unusually high frequencies of Speech and Reading/Writing in his dreams and with the somewhat elevated frequency of references to Art. His personal involvement with Religion in waking life comes through very clearly in his dreams.

To identify External & Personal continuities, unusually *low* frequencies can be as revealing as unusually *high* ones. For example, Aristides has very few Female references, which seems continuous with the minimal role that women played in his waking life. He has a very low frequency of Physical Aggression, continuous with his peaceful life as a privileged citizen of the Roman Empire. He has few references to Clothing, Architecture, or Money and Work, corresponding to his apparent indifference to such matters in waking life. Knowing as we do about the chronology of his life, we might expect more references to School and Transportation; knowing about his many illnesses, we might expect higher frequencies of Fear, Falling, and Death. Yet these content frequencies appear quite low in his dreams. Perhaps this represents a limit to these kinds of continuities. Or perhaps the continuities do exist, but the word-search tools are not (yet) subtle enough to identify them. At this stage in the development of digital technologies for dream research, it seems appropriate to proceed with caution whenever we explore possible External & Personal continuities between dreaming and waking life.

The same is true when we try to identify External & Collective continuities. This is the anthropological dimension of dreams, reflecting not just the personal concerns of individuals but also the widely shared concerns of their communities and cultural traditions (to be discussed further in chapter 13). With Aristides, this can be seen in the extreme disparity between Male and Female References in his dreams, continuous not just with his personal life but also with the male-dominated gender structures pervading the social world of late antiquity Rome. It can also be seen in his Religion references, which include several mentions of Zeus, the supreme deity of the classical pantheon, along with other culturally important gods and goddesses. The absence of several types of highly frequent content in modern-day dreams—planes, cars, guns, computers, and so on—makes it easy to identify Aristides as a member of a premodern culture.

This digital word-search method may seem awkward and complicated (as it did to me when I first learned it), but the essential value is the simplicity with which meaningful insights can be gained with a quick visual scan of the

Table 9.3. Word-Search Results with Baselines for Myōe Shonin

SDDb Categories	Baselines Males N = 2,135 mean 105	Myōe Shonin N = 170 mean 88, median 65	4-431
	Percent	Percent	Most-used words
Perception			
Vision	29	25	saw, see
Hearing	9	7	hear
Touch	12	14	hand, hands, held
Smell and Taste	1	2	sweet
Color	12	10	white, black, blue
Emotion			
Fear	15	9	afraid, fear
Anger	5	1	disgusted
Sadness	3	2	depressed
Wonder	18	11	wondered, suddenly
Happiness	6	8	happy, pleased
Characters			
Family	27	6	mother, son
Animals	12	22	horse, fish, bird, dog, snake
Fantastic Beings	2	3	dragon, spirit
Male References	40	48	he, his, him
Female References	35	13	she, her, ladies, lady
Social Interactions			
Friendliness	34	27	visit, friend, honored, visited
Physical Aggression	19	5	killed
Sexuality	6	1	sexual
Movement			
Walking/Running	27	11	stepped, walked, walking
Flying	6	3	flew, flying
Falling	8	8	fell, fall, falling
Death	7	6	dead, die
Cognition			
Thinking	38	51	thought, think, thinking
Speech	32	37	said, saying, called
Reading/Writing	5	15	letter, written, wrote, book
Culture			
Architecture	41	20	house, hall, room
Food and Drink	12	12	ate, eat, food, rice

Table 9.3. Continued

SDDb Categories	Baselines Males N = 2,135 mean 105	Myōe Shonin N = 170 mean 88, median 65	4-431
	Percent	Percent	Most-used words
Clothing	11	11	wearing, robes, clothes
School	13	1	teacher
Transportation	28	8	road, boat, avenue, path
Technology	8	0	
Money and Work	22	4	wealth, work
Weapons	5	2	arrow, sword
Sports	4	0	
Art	7	2	drawing, poem
Religion	6	54	priest, meditation, Buddha, priests, nun
Elements			
Fire	4	5	fire, burn, burning, star
Air	5	2	Air
Water	12	18	water, pond, ocean, river, sea
Earth	10	15	mountain, rock, landed

data, once you know what to look for. Naturally, this takes a little practice. Let's move on from Aristides and see how the process works with other kinds of dreamers.

The dream journal of Myōe Shonin (see table 9.3) includes 170 reports of 4 to 431 words, with a mean length of 88 words, almost identical to the mean length of Aristides's dreams. This means that, as with Aristides, we will expect Myōe's word-usage frequencies to be generally lower than the Baselines, which have a higher average number of words per report. As it turns out, Myōe's frequencies on Perception words are very close to the Male Baselines. He has fewer references to Emotions and far fewer references to Family characters, consistent with the life of an ascetic monk. His social interactions are almost all friendly, and he has high frequencies of Cognition words. His Food and Drink and Clothing references are close to the Baselines, but his other Culture references are much lower. The big exception is his unusually high frequency of references to Religion. Just as we found with Aristides, this represents the clearest point of External & Personal continuity between Myōe's dreams and his waking-life concerns and activities.

Table 9.4. Word-Search Results with Baselines for Lucrecia de León

SDDb Categories	Baselines Females N = 3,110 mean 100	Lucrecia de León N = 45 mean 874, median 842	265-1698
	Percent	Percent	Most-used words
Perception			
Vision	37	100	saw, see, eyes, vision
Hearing	10	82	heard, listen, noise, loudly
Touch	12	84	hand, hands, holding
Smell and Taste	2	31	nose, tongue, smell
Color	17	69	white, black, red, brown, green
Emotion			
Fear	23	58	scared, afraid
Anger	8	22	anger, angry
Sadness	5	18	sad, disappointed
Wonder	18	13	suddenly, surprised
Happiness	9	36	happy, glad, pleased
Characters			
Family	40	53	son, wife, father, mother
Animals	13	89	lion, crows, lions, turkey
Fantastic Beings	2	24	spirit, devil, demon, dragon
Male References	47	100	he, him, man, his, men
Female References	44	80	her, she, woman, women
Social Interactions			
Friendliness	46	76	help, friend, warn, love
Physical Aggression	12	69	enemies, war, fight, battle, killed
Sexuality	4	20	naked
Movement			
Walking/Running	27	60	walking, walked, running
Flying	4	16	flying, flew, floating
Falling	7	42	fell, fall, falling
Death	9	62	dead, die, death
Cognition			
Thinking	39	87	think, thought, aware, pray
Speech	35	100	said, saying, say, called, talk
Reading/Writing	6	51	read, letter, letters, write

Table 9.4. Continued

SDDb Categories	Baselines Females N = 3,110 mean 100	Lucrecia de León N = 45 mean 874, median 842	265-1698
	Percent	Percent	Most-used words
Culture			
Architecture	47	73	house, room, door, floor, home
Food and Drink	14	56	bread, drink, fruits, wheat
Clothing	14	73	dressed, clothes, clothing
School	17	2	educate
Transportation	24	58	street, ships, streets, cart
Technology	7	0	
Money and Work	18	49	work, money, business, rich
Weapons	3	44	weapons, sword, knife, spear
Sports	4	0	
Art	10	22	paintings, painting
Religion	7	91	God, church, saint, priests, prophet
Elements			
Fire	4	47	fire, burning, star, flames, sun
Air	4	24	air, blowing, breath
Water	13	56	water, sea, river
Earth	10	60	land, earth, lands, stone, rock

With Lucrecia de León (table 9.4), we have a challenge at the other end of the word-length spectrum. Her shortest dream is 265 words in length, and her longest is 1,698 words. This means that we should expect her word-usage frequencies to be far higher than the Female Baselines, and this turns out to be mostly true. Her dreams are very high in Perception words, with one of the highest Smell and Taste frequencies of any series I have ever studied. This may be an artifact of the great length of her dreams. It may also reflect an External & Collective continuity with the intense odors in Lucrecia's waking-life environment—a crowded urban neighborhood with no running water or sewage system. Her dreams have many references to Fear, along with high frequencies of Physical Aggression and references to Fantastic Beings, Death, and Weapons. These nightmarish themes seem directly continuous with her personal circumstances, under direct physical threat from many directions. Every one of her dreams has a Male Reference and a reference to Speech, which accurately characterizes the centrality in her waking life of conversations with men, both her supporters and her persecutors. Lucrecia has a high frequency of Female References, too; not as high as her Male References but much closer to a gender balance than we found with Aristides and Myōe. She has more references to Reading/Writing than we would expect from an illiterate person, although she was an active participant in the dream transcriptions, and the quality of her energetic engagement in the process is what seems to come through in the dreams. The descriptive detail of her dreams includes many Culture references, with a reference to Religion in nearly every one of the reports. These details are continuous with Lucrecia's personal concerns and activities and with the general living conditions and cultural environment in late-sixteenth-century Madrid.

The mean (86) and median (61) lengths of Emanuel Swedenborg's 120 dreams (table 9.5) are almost exactly like Myōe's and close to Aristides's, too. Swedenborg's dreams have more references to Vision, Touch, and Color than the SDDb Male Baselines but fewer Emotions of all kinds. He has fewer Family characters and more Animals, a relative proportion we also saw with Lucrecia and Myōe. Since both the Male and Female Baselines have more than twice as many references to Family characters than Animals, this is a curious pattern among our group that we should keep in mind going forward. Swedenborg is generally close to the Baselines on Social Interactions and Movement, with less Walking/Running and more Falling. Unlike the Baselines, he has more references to Speech than to Thinking and more overall references to Reading/Writing. His frequency of Religion references is much higher than the Baselines, consistent with his waking-life interest in mystical Christian theology. Given his innovative work as a scientist and engineer, it is surprising to see virtually no references to Technology in Swedenborg's dreams. This is an instance of an External & Personal discontinuity—something important from the waking world that we expect to see reflected robustly in the dreams but instead find only minimally occurring or completely absent. We will pick up on the question of this non-content in Swedenborg's dreams in chapter 10.

Table 9.5. Word-Search Results with Baselines for Emanuel Swedenborg

SDDb Categories	Baselines Males N = 2,135 mean 105	Emanuel Swedenborg N = 120 mean 86, median 61	7-287
	Percent	Percent	Most-used words
Perception			
Vision	29	41	saw, see
Hearing	9	8	heard
Touch	12	23	hand, hold, hands, held, holding
Smell and Taste	1	5	tongue
Color	12	19	white, black, brown, green
Emotion			
Fear	15	10	afraid, frightened
Anger	5	2	angry
Sadness	3	0	
Wonder	18	9	wondered, wondering
Happiness	6	2	glad
Characters			
Family	27	13	father, brother, married, sister
Animals	12	19	dog, horse, animal, bear
Fantastic Beings	2	6	spirit, dragons
Male References	40	56	he, him, his, man
Female References	35	23	she, woman, her
Social Interactions			
Friendliness	34	24	love, help, friend, helped
Physical Aggression	19	13	bite, attacked, hit
Sexuality	6	5	kissed
Movement			
Walking/Running	27	14	walked, walking, ran, walk
Flying	6	4	flying, flew
Falling	8	11	fell, dropped
Death	7	6	dead, died

(continued)

Table 9.5. Continued

SDDb Categories	Baselines Males N = 2,135 mean 105	Emanuel Swedenborg N = 120 mean 86, median 61	7-287
	Percent	Percent	Most-used words
Cognition			
Thinking	38	30	thought, thoughts, noticed, intended
Speech	32	43	said, spoke, saying
Reading/Writing	5	12	book, written, letter
Culture			
Architecture	41	18	room, house, home, door
Food and Drink	12	13	bread, wine, dinner
Clothing	11	9	dressed, clothes, wearing
School	13	1	library
Transportation	28	10	road, ship, stairway
Technology	8	1	machine
Money and Work	22	15	money, work, buy, costly
Weapons	5	5	sword, cannons
Sports	4	0	
Art	7	3	drawing, sang
Religion	6	24	God, holy, Christ, church
Elements			
Fire	4	2	fire, sun
Air	5	3	air, blows
Water	12	8	water, ice, lake
Earth	10	5	earth, hills

The four dreams that remain from Benjamin Banneker's journal are too few for a full-scale word-search analysis. However, several waking-dreaming continuities can be observed in just these four dreams. Each one has a female character, consistent with the importance of women in his childhood and family background. Each of the dreams has a vivid element of physical aggression or bodily misfortune, which seems continuous with his waking-life feelings of being perpetually threatened by hateful neighbors. Two of the dreams have explicitly religious themes about the soul, the devil, and what happens when we die, theologically consistent with what we know of Banneker's Christian upbringing and adult beliefs. He mentions ordinary objects and activities from his daily life—a cupboard, shears, the front door of his cabin, woodland animals, preparing corn, surveying the land—that ground the dreams in his waking-world realities. Yet each of the dreams has a magical, fantastic, or supernatural element that gestures beyond the continuities with his present life circumstances toward a wider horizon of discontinuities.

The tremendous length of Anna Kingsford's 24 dreams (table 9.6), with a mean of 709 words and a median of 607, is comparable to what we found with Lucrecia's dream series. This might be taken as evidence that women tend to experience, remember, and/or record longer dreams than men do. Whether or not that is true (still an open question among researchers), the gender point seems less significant than what these two cases can tell us about the results of having optimal conditions for big dreamers to record their dreams. For the illiterate but hyper-dreaming Lucrecia, it involved a trained scribe coming to her house each morning soon after she woke up to record her verbal report of whatever she had dreamed. For the hyper-literate and hyper-dreaming Kingsford, her work as a professional writer and editor gave her excellent skills to communicate her experiences within the surreal worlds of her dreams. In both cases, people with naturally vivid dreaming also had ideal resources for recording their dreams as fully as possible. If Lucrecia's and Kingsford's long and highly detailed dreams are evidence of anything, it is that we should be cautious about making artificially low estimates of the average patterns of dream recall before more research has been done with the experiences of people like them who occupy the higher end of the recall spectrum.

Compared with the Female Baselines, Kingsford's dreams have higher frequencies in most categories. Her dreams have lots of perceptual detail and a variety of emotions. It seems notable that she has twice as many references to Sadness than to Happiness, quite an unusual emotional proportion in dreams and possibly continuous with the emotional cost of her deeply empathetic openness to the suffering of others and/or the many personal sacrifices she made during her relentless drive for higher pursuits. Her dreams have

Table 9.6. Word-Search Results with Baselines for Anna Kingsford

SDDb Categories	Baselines Females N = 3,110 mean 100	Anna Kingsford N = 24 mean 709, median 607	123-2,055
	Percent	Percent	Most-used Words
Perception			
Vision	37	84	saw, eyes, see
Hearing	10	72	heard, sound, hearing
Touch	12	80	hand, hands, holding, touch
Smell and Taste	2	8	bitter, delicious
Color	17	68	white, grey, black, red, green
Emotion			
Fear	23	36	anxiety, fearful, guilty, nervous
Anger	8	16	furious, mad
Sadness	5	24	distress, hopeless, miserable
Wonder	18	52	suddenly, sudden, confusion, wondered
Happiness	9	12	happy, cheerful
Characters			
Family	40	28	brother, father, husband, mother
Animals	13	48	animals, bear, horse
Fantastic Beings	2	36	spirit, monster, spirits, devil, dragon
Male References	47	88	him, he, his, man, men
Female References	44	48	her, she, woman, women
Social Interactions			
Friendliness	46	60	friend, help, save, social, visited
Physical Aggression	12	40	shot, hurl, killed, pursuing
Sexuality	4	8	naked
Movement			
Walking/Running	27	48	ran, step, run, walk
Flying	4	20	floating, flying, fly
Falling	7	24	fell, dropping
Death	9	36	death, dead, die
Cognition			
Thinking	39	80	aware, thought, sense, effort
Speech	35	80	said, called, speak, spoke
Reading/Writing	6	44	read, written, book, scroll

Table 9.6. Continued

SDDb Categories	Baselines Females N = 3,110 mean 100	Anna Kingsford N = 24 mean 709, median 607	123-2,055
	Percent	Percent	Most-used Words
Culture			
Architecture	47	56	room, door, house, apartment
Food and Drink	14	24	wine, bread, eaten
Clothing	14	48	dress, wore, attire, robe
School	17	8	education, school, student
Transportation	24	32	path, cart, street, train
Technology	7	8	engine, scientific
Money and Work	18	24	work, bought
Weapons	3	16	arrow, bullets, knives, spear
Sports	4	0	
Art	10	24	drawing, art, artistic, dancing
Religion	7	72	spirit, heaven, Christ, God, religious
Elements			
Fire	4	48	fire, flame, stars, sun
Air	4	36	air, wind
Water	13	56	sea, mist, snow, water
Earth	10	52	earth, crag, mountain, stone, crystal

many more references to Animals than Family characters, more references to Males than Females, and an unusually high frequency of Fantastic Beings. Fully a third of her dreams refer to Death. All categories of Cognition have very high frequencies in her dreams, consistent with her avid intellectual pursuits in the waking world. Most of her dreams have a reference to Religion, while only a few have any reference to the school activities and scientific pursuits that predominated in her life for many years.

With Wolfgang Pauli (table 9.7), we are back to a dreamer of relatively few words. The 58 dreams in the collection presented by Jung in his text on alchemy and individuation have a mean length of 48 words and a median length of just 22 words. Most of Pauli's dreams are very short, just a sentence or two. This means that the frequencies of word usage will likely be much lower than the Baselines, and we do find that to be true in most instances.

Table 9.7. Word-Search Results with Baselines for Wolfgang Pauli

SDDb Categories	Baselines Males N = 2,135 mean 105	Wolfgang Pauli N = 58 mean 48, median 22	5-550
	Percent	Percent	Most-used words
Perception			
Vision	29	7	see
Hearing	9	3	hear, heard
Touch	12	5	hand
Smell and Taste	1	0	
Color	12	16	green, red, yellow, blue
Emotion			
Fear	15	1	regrets
Anger	5	0	
Sadness	3	0	
Wonder	18	3	suddenly
Happiness	6	2	cheerful
Characters			
Family	27	12	father, mother
Animals	12	9	animal, dogs, foxes
Fantastic Beings	2	0	
Male References	40	48	he, his, him, man, father
Female References	35	33	woman, mother, she
Social Interactions			
Friendliness	34	10	friend, party
Physical Aggression	19	17	battle, war, attacked
Sexuality	6	0	
Movement			
Walking/Running	27	19	running, run, walk, runs
Flying	6	2	glide
Falling	8	3	falls
Death	7	0	
Cognition			
Thinking	38	9	concentrate, discover, notice
Speech	32	26	says, say, said
Reading/Writing	5	7	letter, reads, writes

Table 9.7. Continued

SDDb Categories	Baselines Males N = 2,135 mean 105	Wolfgang Pauli N = 58 mean 48, median 22	5-550
	Percent	Percent	Most-used words
Culture			
Architecture	41	9	room, door, house
Food and Drink	12	5	nuts, drunk, wine
Clothing	11	3	hat
School	13	2	students
Transportation	28	7	airplane, car, ship, train
Technology	8	0	
Money and Work	22	5	business, coins, work
Weapons	5	2	guns
Sports	4	0	
Art	7	12	drawing, actor, dance, music
Religion	6	9	ascetic, Catholic, Christ, church
Elements			
Fire	4	10	star, burning, fire
Air	5	0	
Water	12	12	water, fog, river, sea
Earth	10	10	cave, diamond, crystals, mountain

His dreams have very few references to Perceptions, Emotions, Movement, or Culture. Despite the overall low numbers, a few relative proportions among the various categories do stand out as signaling External & Personal continuities. Pauli has higher frequencies of Physical Aggression than Friendliness, which seems consistent with the struggles in his social life that led him to seek Jung's help in the first place. He has more Male than Female References, consistent with his greater difficulty in relationships with women than with men. The low frequency of Thought is puzzling, coming from an individual with such a powerful intellect. Perhaps his reports are too short to include meaningful descriptions of his thought processes; perhaps his dreams are more imagery-driven than conceptual. His Religion frequency is higher than the Baselines, and his frequencies for Fire, Water, and Earth are equal to or above the Baselines. His references to Color are somewhat high and unusual in their distribution. Everyone we have looked at so far and most people whose dreams I have previously studied have white and black in some order at the top of their list of most-used colors. Pauli's list of dream colors, however, has green, red, yellow, and blue at the top. Does his dreaming preference for chromatic over achromatic colors have some kind of connection with his theoretical work as a quantum physicist? I can think of no reason for that; perhaps it is just an arbitrary variation with no further significance. But at the least, future research now has something specific to test and explore. The power of digital analysis comes in creating greater focus and awareness for the follow-up use of more advanced research methods, such as parts III and IV will use.

10

Anomalous Patterns in Dream Content

The first time I used digital methods to explore other people's dreams was in a 2008 article that focused on religious themes in the dream series of "Merri" and "Barb Sanders" in Dreambank.net. This was before I developed the Baselines, when I was still learning what digital tools could and could not do. At this point, my primary question was whether the External & Personal continuity between people's dream patterns and waking-life concerns extended to their religious concerns. Researchers had found strong connections between dreams and people's most important relationships, activities, and beliefs in the waking world. I wanted to know if a similar kind of continuity in dreaming reflected a person's concerns about religion and spirituality. The big challenge with this kind of research—and I knew, because I had been such a sharp critic previously—is persuasively demonstrating that a continuity arises innately from the dream data, rather than being imposed by the subjective biases of the researcher. Was it possible to identify a person's religious concerns in their dreams without the researcher's own views, opinions, and expectations getting in the way?

After I consulted at length with Domhoff and Schneider, we devised a clever solution. "Merri" and "Barb Sanders" were pseudonyms for two contemporary women whose dream journals were available in the Dreambank and with whom Domhoff remained in contact. I did not know the women personally; all I knew was what I read in their dreams (a total of 316 in Merri's series and 3,116 in Barb Sanders's) and what I gleaned from word searches via the Dreambank. I began with a search for instances of the word "God" and followed the results from there with searches for "Jesus," "Christmas," "music," "holy," and "death." Eventually I put together a set of inferences about the role of religion in their waking lives, based on the patterns I found in their dreams, and sent them to Domhoff. He forwarded my inferences to the two women, who were invited to confirm or disconfirm them. Domhoff sent me their responses, and then we all had an open exchange about the accuracy of the inferences. Overall, the predictions derived from Merri's and

The Scribes of Sleep. Kelly Bulkeley, Oxford University Press. © Oxford University Press 2023.
DOI: 10.1093/oso/9780197609606.003.0011

Barb Sanders's dreams were mostly confirmed. Merri was raised as a Baptist but no longer belonged to that tradition and felt negatively toward its coercive forces; religion and music were very strongly related for her. Barb Sanders was not raised in a religious family, but she felt positively toward God and other divine figures.[1]

The research for this article convinced me of the strong continuities between waking and dreaming on topics such as religion and spirituality, beyond what Hall, Domhoff, and other cognitive psychologists had explored so far. The research process also revealed the importance of learning from mistaken inferences, such as the instances when Merri and Barb Sanders told me I was wrong about a prediction I had made based on the numerical patterns in their dreams. With Merri, I had inferred that religion was only moderately important in her life, whereas she said, in fact, she was "very devout" in her unchurched spirituality. I thus realized that for people who consider themselves more spiritual than religious, my word searches would have to look beyond the Religion category to consider their frequencies of Death, Fantastic Beings, and Art. With Barb Sanders, she revealed that when she married her first husband, she had converted to the Episcopalian Church. At first, I thought this was a startling *failure* to make an inference: if I had been looking through her dreams for evidence of religious beliefs and practices, and I missed the fact that during this time she became a religious convert, then my method was not working as it should. But during further discussion with her about this time of her life, she said the conversion was actually a trivial, pro forma affair that she underwent to satisfy familial expectations, with no special personal significance beyond that.

This exchange revealed a vital insight that has remained central to my digital research ever since. The contents of Barb Sanders's dreams were continuous not with the external religious happenings and events of her life but rather with their *meaning* for her, their emotional energy and relevance to her ongoing sense of identity. That suggests that a dream journal is more like a poetry notebook than a newspaper report, more of an emotional collage than a factual documentary. Her conversion to the Episcopalian Church, although it happened in her waking life, did not appear in her series of dreams because it had no intrinsic meaning for her and no significant impact on her actual spiritual beliefs. What I learned, then, was that I would be wrong to infer from her dreams that Barb Sanders had never converted to a religious tradition, but I would be right if I inferred that she never had a meaningful, personally important conversion to a religious tradition. The patterns of dreams accurately track the emotional contours of our lives. They illuminate our greatest cares and concerns and our most important relationships.

These findings about dreams, religion, and spirituality were encouraging, but I knew I was using the Dreambank's word-search method to explore a relatively rare dimension of dream content. To get a better view of that unusual aspect of dreaming, I realized I needed a stronger understanding of normal, average dimensions of dream content. In other words, I needed *baselines*. The Hall and Van de Castle (HVDC) Norm dreams had served this function for many decades, but their demographic limits (two hundred Midwestern college students from the early 1950s) made it difficult to rely on them alone as a measuring stick for everyone else's dreams. The SDDb Baselines integrated the HVDC Norm dreams with several thousand other dreams from a wider variety of people in terms of age, location, education, and race/ethnicity. The frequencies in the Baselines are in most cases backward-compatible with earlier research using predigital methods of content analysis, and they can be used to determine what specifically makes each individual's dreams unique and distinctive and to spotlight unusual features of content that would be virtually impossible to identify in a large collection of dreams without some degree of technological assistance.[2]

I tested the use of the Baselines in several further studies with Domhoff and others.[3] These experiments in "blind analysis" enabled us to refine the process of making inferences about waking-dreaming continuities. The general method was an extension of what we initially did with Merri and Barb Sanders. After Domhoff sent me a set of anonymous dreams, I used the SDDb word-search template to generate a set of statistical frequencies and then made inferences about the dreamer's waking-life concerns, based solely on comparisons with the Baselines, without ever reading the dreams themselves. Domhoff then forwarded my inferences to the dreamer, who told us which of the inferences were correct and which were incorrect. The percentages of correct inferences in these studies ranged between 75 percent and 85 percent. Once the "veil of ignorance" was lifted, the dreamers and I had further exchanges about what they found most significant and meaningful in their dreams.

The results of these experiments taught us several lessons. At the most basic level, they provided strong evidence that dreams are *intrinsically* meaningful, to such an extent that at least some of their meanings can be identified by purely statistical means, without any personal contact with the dreamer. This is important because a common criticism of dream interpretation has been that it involves nothing more than seeing faces in the clouds—a projection of meaning onto essentially random and meaningless phenomena. The more an interpreter knows about the personal life of the dreamer, the easier it is to make these false projections and misattributions of meaning. The blind analysis method shows how that criticism can be overcome, by bracketing out all personal information about the dreamer and imposing an empirical discipline on the interpreter, requiring that inferences of meaning derive from clear and prominent statistical features of the word-usage frequencies. Another way of stating the significance of these studies is that their findings make it much harder to argue that dreaming is nothing but random nonsense. They provide strong evidence for the idea that dreams have intrinsic meanings at many levels, some of which can be identified easily and accurately with simple word-search methods.

The goal of the blind analysis experiments was not only to refute skepticism of that sort. More important, these studies gave us an opportunity to explore in more detail the areas in people's lives where they experienced the strongest continuities between waking and dreaming. We found the most vivid points of continuity appeared in connection with personal relationships, emotional difficulties, work activities, cultural interests, and religious attitudes. These were the strongest signals of meaning, the continuities that jumped out of the data regardless of how little was known about the dreamer's personal life.

As we found in the study with Merri and Barb Sanders, some of the most valuable insights came as a result of *mistaken* inferences, when I was wrong in predicting something about the person's waking life. With "Van," whose dreams (192 in total) Domhoff and I discussed in a 2010 article, I made fourteen inferences, twelve of which he confirmed as correct. One of the incorrect inferences was that he experienced many nightmares, based on high frequencies in his dreams of references to Fear, Physical Aggression, Falling, Animals, and Death. Van said that he did *not* have nightmares, but he did have dreams that related to his frequent and enthusiastic playing of video games, which involved enjoyable adventures of fighting and battling a variety of simulated enemies. What initially looked to me like the dream patterns of a chronic nightmare sufferer turned out to be the dream patterns of an avid gamer. There *was* a waking-dreaming continuity here, just not the one I first predicted.

With the dream series of "Bea" (2012), I made fifteen inferences, eleven of which she confirmed as correct. One of the incorrect inferences was that she had little interest in art, based on her low frequencies of Perception references. In fact, she was an art history major in college who described herself as a highly visual person. She said she could not always include every sensory detail from her dreams when she reported them; it would require an overwhelming amount of time to do so thoroughly. This gave us the useful insight that extra caution is required in making inferences based on Perception references alone. The SDDb word-search template has changed since then, and it now has an Art category that would have immediately highlighted Bea's waking-life interest in art.

With the dream series of "Beverly" (2018), I made twenty-six inferences, and she confirmed twenty-three as correct. One of the three incorrect predictions was that she had been impacted by an earthquake, based on an unusually high frequency of that word in her dreams during a specific period of time (1986). She said she had not been impacted by an actual earthquake, but she added that the religious cult in which she had been a member for many years finally fell apart in that same year of 1986, so the "earthquake" references might have been continuous *metaphorically* rather than literally with that massively disruptive and ground-shaking event in her waking life. I still did not count it as a correct inference, but since then, I have tried to think more carefully about metaphorical continuities and whether they can be identified in patterns of word-usage frequencies. It is entirely possible that the answer here is that digital methods of analysis reach the end of their usefulness when we go beyond literal continuities to consider the appearance in dreams of symbolic, figurative, and metaphorical continuities and discontinuities.

All of this is meant to give you some degree of reassurance that the word-search method being presented here is not a rigid, top-down imposition of meaning onto dreams. If these digital tools of analysis are used cautiously, modestly, and in coordination with other sources of contextual information, they can provide valuable results—even when they seem to get something wrong.

Let's return now to the seven dream journal keepers and look at their word-usage patterns in relation to four types of *discontinuity* that parallel the four types of *continuity* discussed in chapter 9 (see the appendix for a table summarizing all of the word-search results for the journal keepers).

> *Internal & Personal:* A dream pattern is discontinuous with the other patterns in the individual's dreaming.
> *Internal & Collective:* A dream pattern is discontinuous with the general patterns of other people's dreaming.

> *External & Personal:* A dream pattern is discontinuous with the concerns of the individual's waking life.
>
> *External & Collective:* A dream pattern is discontinuous with the concerns of the individual's waking culture and community.

The first of these discontinuities, Internal & Personal, arises when a particular dream in a series has contents that differ greatly from the average patterns of content in that person's dream series. Being able to identify such discontinuities can help in understanding the distinctive meanings of unusual dreams, some of which qualify as "big dreams" in Jung's sense of the term. More about this will be discussed in the chapters of part III.

In chapter 9, we noted several Internal & Collective discontinuities among the group of seven journal keepers. Here we can draw these observations together to form a more distinct understanding of these people and their dreams. Compared with the SDDb Baselines, all of them have unusually high frequencies of references to Religion. Most of them have high frequencies of Animal characters, and all of them have more Animals in relation to Family characters than is found in the Baselines. All of them have comparatively high frequencies of Male References, Reading/ Writing, and most of the Elements (Fire, Air, Water, Earth). The five men in the group all have relatively low frequencies of Emotions in their dreams. Even taking into account the length of their dreams, the two women in the group have very high frequencies of Fantastic Beings, Physical Aggression, Death, Clothing, and Weapons. This is where Internal & Collective discontinuities can yield insights into External & Personal continuities. If we knew nothing else about the seven members of this group other than the discontinuities between their dreams and the SDDb Baselines, we could make several inferences about their waking lives: they are people with special interest in religious themes and issues, they focus more on male than female relationships, they are actively engaged with reading and writing, and they are sensitive to the natural world; the men do not emphasize emotionality in their waking lives, while the women feel threatened by external dangers.

In the blind analysis studies mentioned earlier, my mistaken inferences usually revolved around the inadvertent discovery of the third type of discontinuity, External & Personal. What looked like a continuity between dreaming and waking turned out to be something else. Lucrecia de León, for example, had references to the seashore in two-thirds of her dreams, yet there is no evidence she ever traveled beyond the inland cities of Madrid and Toledo, hundreds of kilometers from the sea. Why then did she dream so much of the seashore? Unlike the blind analysis studies, we do not have the opportunity to ask the dreamer directly, but it seems likely this setting had a metaphorical meaning for her as the liminal boundary between land and sea, Spain and its enemies, this world and the beyond. Discontinuities like this can sometimes be recognized as metaphorical continuities. Another example of this kind of discontinuity is that Wolfgang Pauli's dreams have no references to Technology, even though in waking life, he was a professional scientist and the winner of a Nobel Prize. Why don't his dreams mention any of this? They actually do mention a variety of scientific concepts, ideas, and theories, but not in terms that the SDDb word-search category for Technology can recognize. Pauli mentioned in his work on physics and psychology that his dreams gradually developed a kind of hybrid language of images, words, and symbols to represent his insights into the deeper dynamics of the mind as it relates to physical reality. What looks like a discontinuity between his dreams and his waking-life concerns is revealed upon closer inspection to be a continuity manifesting itself in a creative new form of dream content.

The last type of discontinuity to consider, External & Collective, depends on knowing as much as possible about the circumstances of the dreamer's life as a social being, as a member of a community. If we have this information, we can identify instances in which continuities with personal concerns are at the same time discontinuities with the concerns, activities, and values of the dreamer's community. Anna Kingsford's high frequency of references to Animals and Death, for example, accurately reflects her public advocacy on behalf of the rights of animals, whose suffering was not a widely shared concern among other people in mid-nineteenth-century England. Another example is Myōe Shonin's extremely low frequency of references to Family characters, which was continuous with his personal commitment to an ascetic life as a Buddhist monk but discontinuous with the majority of people for whom family relationships are among the most important concerns in their waking lives.

This is a realm of dream meaning where the SDDb categories (2.0 version) do not work very well, to be honest. Outside the cultural context of modern Western society, several SDDb categories do not make much sense (e.g., Money and Work, Sports, Technology). At this point, the limits of this particular method of digital analysis become clear. The discussion of dreams as reflections of collective conflicts and concerns will continue later in chapter 13, on cultural psychology.

To finish this chapter with one more example, let me share the results of a word-search analysis of a set of my own dreams, from the years 2019 to 2021 (N = 1,095) and briefly consider some of the continuities and discontinuities that emerge. (See table 10.1.)

With a mean word length of 88 and a median of 69, the linguistic shape of my dream series is quite close to Myōe's (88 and 65), Emanuel Swedenborg's (86 and 61), and Aelius Aristides's (89 and 42). Knowing what you now know about digital dream analysis, you can probably make several accurate inferences about my waking-life activities and concerns, for instance, that I am visually sensitive, prone to wonder and confusion, relatively happy, a cat person, more concerned with women than with men, enjoy basketball and theater, and have my closest relationships with my wife and my mother. However, two inferences that seem clear would be incorrect. It might appear that Reading/Writing is *not* especially important to me, looking at how my frequencies are no different from the Baselines, whereas I actually devote most of my waking hours to those activities, much more than the average person. It might also appear that I have no interest in Religion, given how low my frequency is compared with the Baselines, and yet most of my reading and writing is on the topic of religion, and that has been true from college through graduate school and all the way to the present. Amid all the other External & Personal continuities in the patterns of my dreams, these are two glaring discontinuities. What can be learned from these reasonable yet false inferences?

With Reading/Writing, perhaps the dreaming-waking continuity is not with the acts of reading and writing but with the specific contents being communicated through those acts—ideas, feelings, characters, situations, problems, and insights. It would be difficult to quantify, but I have the strong subjective sense that I am constantly dreaming about the *themes* of my reading and writing. I don't dream about those themes in the context of books, papers, computers, and so on, but rather in the open spaces of the imagination.[4]

As for the Religion category, my dreams may be inaccurate reflections of my interest in religion and yet accurate reflections of my lack of partic-ipation in conventional religious practices in waking life. I do not belong to a church or faith tradition, nor do I come from an especially religious family. The low frequency of religion references in my dreams is consistent

Table 10.1. Word-search results with Baselines for the author.

SDDb Categories	Baselines Males N = 2,135 mean 105	KB 2019–2021 N = 1095 mean 88, median 69	10-456
	Percent	Percent	Most-used words
Perception			
Vision	29	47	see, watching, watch
Hearing	9	5	hear, listening
Touch	12	10	hand, holding, hold, hands, touch
Smell and Taste	1	1	nose, disgusting, smell
Color	12	46	white, black, green, blue, brown, red
Emotion			
Fear	15	18	worried, worry, scared, upset, anxious
Anger	5	5	angry, mad, annoying
Sadness	3	3	disappointed, sad
Wonder	18	37	wonder, surprised, suddenly, confused
Happiness	6	13	happy, relieved, pleased, glad
Characters			
Family	27	18	wife, mom, family, dad
Animals	12	17	cat, dog, cats, birds
Fantastic Beings	2	1	alien, monster
Male References	40	41	he, guy, him, his, guys
Female References	35	51	woman, she, her, wife, women
Social Interactions			
Friendliness	34	40	help, helping, party
Physical Aggression	19	12	hit, fight, shoot
Sexuality	6	7	naked, sex, sexual
Movement			
Walking/Running	27	19	walking, walk, running, run
Flying	6	5	flying, floating, fly
Falling	8	6	fall, falling, drop
Death	7	2	dead, dies

(*continued*)

Table 10.1. Continued

SDDb Categories	Baselines Males N = 2,135 mean 105	KB 2019–2021 N = 1095 mean 88, median 69	10-456
	Percent	Percent	Most-used words
Cognition			
Thinking	38	45	realize, think, decide, sense
Speech	32	21	say, says, talking, talk
Reading/Writing	5	5	book, books, letters, write
Culture			
Architecture	41	37	house, room, building, door, floor
Food and Drink	12	9	food, eat, drink, bread
Clothing	11	16	clothes, wearing, shirt, shoes
School	13	4	school, test
Transportation	28	25	car, road, street
Technology	8	9	television, phone, TV, computer
Money and Work	22	15	work, working, job, company
Weapons	5	4	gun, guns, knife
Sports	4	7	basketball, baseball, football
Art	7	9	theater, music, artists, movie
Religion	6	2	church, divinity
Elements			
Fire	4	3	fire, sun, star
Air	5	4	air, wind
Water	12	11	water, ocean, creek, wet
Earth	10	11	dirt, hill, land, rocks

with my low frequency of religious behaviors in the waking world. At the same time, it is also possible that the SDDb category for Religion does not adequately measure the dream contents that would yield a more accurate portrait of my spiritual perspective. I know that is true for people from non-Western societies, and perhaps it is true for people within Western society, too. Another revision of the SDDb word-search template is pending, and the Religion category will be at the top of the list for further refinement.

PART III

INTERPRETING PSYCHOLOGICAL MEANING

In the preceding chapters we identified the basic patterns of dream content for the seven journal keepers. Using the twin concepts of continuity and discontinuity, we found several meaningful connections between their dreams and their waking lives. Just as important, the process of identifying these patterns has helped to orient us within the complex landscape of each dream journal. Knowing this information gives us a basic sense of what's there and what's not there. It sets a few general parameters for our expectations about the dreams, and it directs our attention toward themes and areas of content that may be worthy of special attention. These parameters are not fixed; we continue looking for unusual and anomalous elements in the dreams, and we try not to let our expectations limit our ability to perceive the unexpected. We take advantage of the analytic power of the digital tools as a way of enhancing our practices of interpretation, rather than diminishing or replacing them.

Parts III and IV present methods that go beyond statistical frequencies to highlight additional dimensions of meaning in the dream journals. The chapters here in part III examine methods that can be used to identify psychological meanings in the dreams in relation to the dreamer's personality, family, waking-life activities, emotional temperament, integration of conscious and unconscious aspects of the mind, capacity to surmount difficulties and recover from losses, and creative engagement in cultural activities. Part IV will then consider the dream journals in a more existential framework, showing how they relate to the dreamer's religious upbringing, spiritual experiences, metaphysical beliefs, moral values, and personal answers to ultimate questions. In the study of dreams, the boundary between psychology and religion cannot always be drawn with sharp lines. The distinction between the two can blur, shift, or even disappear, depending on what aspect of dreaming is being discussed. This is why, at several points in the psychology part, we will look ahead to themes that will be discussed more fully in the religion part. Likewise, in the religion part, we will pause to review relevant insights from earlier chapters in the psychology part.

The three chapters here interpret the dream journals from three psychological perspectives: the psychoanalysis of Sigmund Freud, the archetypal psychology of Carl Jung, and the cultural psychology of Dorothy Eggan and other anthropologists. I chose these perspectives for several reasons: their core ideas are straightforward and can be summarized in brief terms; they are "classic" approaches, each with a long history of stimulating important advances in dream research; they recognize the deep interplay of psychological and religious dynamics in people's lives; and, most important, they are *useful*, especially in the study of dream journals—they can illuminate important patterns of meaning that elude other forms of analysis. This emphasis on pragmatic value means the three approaches will not be treated as museum pieces, whose use must be restricted to their original orthodox applications. The following chapters will show how new evidence from sleep laboratory research, neuroscience, and evolutionary biology can be incorporated into the classic approaches to the psychology of dream interpretation, in ways that enhance and amplify the study of long-term dream journals.

11

Psychoanalysis

Sigmund Freud was one of the great pioneers of dream research, but he did not devote any direct attention to the study of dreams in a long-term series. This makes for some tension in using his ideas in our context. Freud believed that, compared with the hidden (or *latent*) meanings revealed by his psychoanalytic method, the surface (or *manifest*) contents of a dream are essentially meaningless. And if the surface contents of one dream are insignificant, why should we believe that aggregating the contents from multiple dreams will lead to anything more? Zero plus zero plus zero still equals zero. This poses a big problem for the word-search approach we used in the previous chapters, which depends on tabulating precisely those details of manifest content that psychoanalytic theory rejects as irrelevant. From a strictly Freudian perspective, nothing could be more pointless. The question naturally arises of whether it is appropriate to apply psychoanalytic ideas to the study of dream journals.

This question could be answered positively by referring to Freud's own flexibility in adjusting his ideas to different conditions. I noted an example of this in chapter 8, during the discussion of the legitimacy of interpreting dreams without the personal associations of the dreamer, a practice that Freud both rejects and allows, depending on the circumstances. The question could also be answered in the affirmative by looking more closely at Freud's case studies and other writings on dreams, which reveal a more nuanced appreciation for the psychological meanings that can emerge from a series of dreams over time. But the best answer to this question, especially for readers who are not experts in psychoanalysis, is a more pragmatic one. Freud's ideas can be validly applied to the study of dream journals because they *work* as tools of interpretation. They help to identify important meanings in the dreams and their relevance to the psychological dynamics of the individual's waking life.

An approach like this starts with a set of psychoanalytic concepts that seem most promising as guides for understanding dreams in a series. This will involve less emphasis on other aspects of Freudian theory, such as the mechanisms of the dreamwork, that are primarily designed for the study of

The Scribes of Sleep. Kelly Bulkeley, Oxford University Press. © Oxford University Press 2023.
DOI: 10.1093/oso/9780197609606.003.0012

single dreams, not dreams in a series. If the goal is to gain insight into the psychological meanings of a large collection of dreams over time, the following five ideas from Freud will be especially helpful.

1. *Conscious-unconscious conflict.* Freud developed psychoanalysis around the idea that ego consciousness is a small fraction of the whole psyche, most of which is unconscious. According to Freud, there is perpetual conflict and tension between these two aspects of the mind. The job of ego consciousness is to adapt to the constraints of physical reality and the obligations of social life while trying to satisfy the urgent instinctual desires (sexual, aggressive, narcissistic) that continually surge forth from the unconscious. In actuality, the task of balancing all these demands is virtually impossible to achieve, and thus most people are destined to suffer from endless inner conflict. The unconscious is generally inaccessible to consciousness, except in special circumstances—such as dreaming.

2. *Childhood experience.* Psychoanalysis is a *developmental* theory that sees human life as an unfolding process with crucial stages in the earliest years of life. More than other psychologists before him, Freud put special emphasis on child development and the formative, lifelong impact of experiences in the family, in school, and in the child's own growing and changing body. Much of Freud's work as a therapist involved tracing adult problems back to their unconscious roots in childhood. The challenge for every human is how to mature and grow forward in a healthy manner, even though all our earlier conflicts and unresolved problems continue to dwell within the unconscious and repeat themselves in various ways throughout our lives.

3. *Mourning.* Freud devoted careful attention to what happens when we experience *loss*—the loss of a family member, a friend, a time of life, a place, an ideal, and so forth. A variety of psychological defenses (e.g., denial, evasion, substitution, projection) typically come forth following a loss, defenses that Freud's therapy tried to overcome because they prevent people from honestly dealing with the reality of their own emotional truths. If these truths can be faced and accepted, the emotional energies generated by the loss can prompt the development of new psychological structures, deeper self-knowledge, and stronger capacities for adaptive resilience.

4. *Sublimation.* This concept is key to the psychoanalytic view of creativity. Sublimation involves the process of transforming an individual's unconscious feelings and instinctual desires into publicly accessible cultural creations. Not everyone can find avenues for sublimating their instincts, but for those who do, a remarkable burst of creative energy and works of inspired originality can be the result. These works include many of the greatest achievements in human civilization, especially in the arts and sciences. In activities like these, the instinctual energies that motivate everything humans do are channeled and guided—sublimated—toward non-instinctual aims. Freud reserves this term for what he views as the most noble and admirable creative works of history.

5. *The uncanny.* A more literal translation of the German word *unheimlich* would be "un-homely." It refers to things that make us feel weird and unsettled, especially things that arouse an eerie sense of encountering a lost secret or hidden knowledge or occult powers—something that feels both familiar and unfamiliar, real and unreal, long gone and yet here right now. For Freud, an experience of the uncanny is a direct portal to the unconscious, revealing aspects of the mind we are rarely able to access in ordinary consciousness. Although he wrote his essay about the uncanny in 1919, Freud seemed to have something like this in mind much earlier, when he wrote in a famous footnote in *The Interpretation of Dreams* (1899) that "in every dream there is a point at which it is unplumbable—a navel, as it were, that is its point of contact with the unknown."[1]

Keeping the statistical patterns from part II in mind as an empirical framework, we can go ahead and try applying these psychoanalytic ideas to the dreams of our group of journal keepers and see how far they take us. Freud launched the psychoanalytic movement with the claim that all humans share a basic system of mental functioning that grows, develops, and takes shape over time—a claim he made after a detailed study of dreams. This chapter tries to extend the reach of Freud's ideas and expand the range of evidence supporting them.

Little is known about the childhood and family background of Aelius Aristides, which makes him seem like a poor candidate for the application of the psychoanalytic concepts I have been discussing. And yet we do know a great deal about the various illnesses and ailments he suffered for years, all without a clear physical diagnosis and yet strangely responsive to "symbolic" healing methods. This is precisely the kind of psychosomatic suffering that Freud's therapeutic approach was designed to address. As long as we stay close to the few well-established biographical facts of Aristides's life, psychoanalysis can be a useful guide here. To begin, it seems clear that whatever else happened to Aristides in childhood, he had a serious developmental crisis in his transition to full adulthood, when he became so sick on his first journey to Rome that he had to abandon his long-planned path toward a career as a public orator. In addition to the physical sufferings he endured during this time, the loss of his public identity seemed to leave him psychologically adrift and unsure what to do with his life.

A purpose in life is just what the god Asclepius gave him. Aristides experienced several dreams in which Asclepius and other divine beings provided him with specific messages, directions, and warnings. Recall the high frequencies of words relating to Speech and Religion in Aristides's dreams; this is a predominant theme that demands his conscious attention and increasingly shapes the behaviors of his waking life. Here are a few brief examples of the god's dreaming directives:

> He ordered me to wash in the river which flows through the city . . . and he predicted that there would be three baths.
>
> He commanded me to put on a small linen tunic and nothing else, but to persevere in this, and going from my bed to wash at the spring without.
>
> He commanded me again to draw blood from my forehead.
>
> He ordered me to take some mud, pour it on myself, and sit in the courtyard of the Sacred Gymnasium, calling on Zeus, the highest and best God.
>
> He commanded me again to use the mud in the same way, and to run in a circle about the Temples three times.[2]

From a psychoanalytic perspective, these dreams suggest that a parent-child type of relationship gradually developed between Aristides and the healing god Asclepius. At a frightening time of unexplained physical suffering and uncertainty about his future, Aristides experienced a series of dreams that drew him into a progressively deeper relationship with Asclepius, who provided him with special care and attention, literally giving him a home in the sacred temple, prescribing treatments for his health, and easing his sleep with reassuring dreams. The weirdly irrational and counterintuitive qualities of the god's directions—their *uncanniness*—appealed to Aristides precisely because they defied everyone else's advice, enabling him to display the depths of his devotion to Asclepius. The god reciprocated with a bounty of divine attention, singling him out for special consideration. There is a regressive quality to Aristides's dreams, an uninhibited return to the thoughts, feelings, and desires of earlier stages of life. Paradoxically, this had the apparent effect of catapulting him forward in his psychological development by forging a new balance of the conscious and unconscious parts of his mind. His relationship with Asclepius gave him an unshakable confidence in the god's benevolent presence in his life, what in Freud's terms could be called an unconscious source of narcissistic support and satisfaction. Although psychoanalysis has become infamous for its emphasis on sexual and aggressive instincts, Freud also believed the egocentric instinct of narcissism has a comparably powerful role in human life and development. Aristides suffered a severe narcissistic blow when he could not complete his educational training and perform as a speaker in front of an appreciative audience in Rome. His illnesses blocked that path toward an adult identity. As he mourned the loss of the plan that had guided his life for so many years, Aristides turned within and found his own unconscious resources for creating a new, more self-integrated identity that enabled him to re-emerge into the world.

The numerous books of religious, literary, and historical reflection that Aristides wrote in his later life testify to a vibrant capacity for sublimation, for channeling his instinctual energies into creative works of culture that have lasted for nearly two thousand years. He never seems to have eliminated entirely his physical maladies, but Freud would not consider that a realistic goal. Aristides found in his devotion to the healing god a path toward more conscious-unconscious balance, deeper acceptance of primal instincts, and the discovery of new creative energy. This path is far from the one generally prescribed by psychoanalysis, but Aristides does seem to have ultimately become a psychologically healthier person, with several of the virtues that Freud found most admirable in a mature person's mental constitution.

Turning to the life and dreams of Myōe Shonin, several observations can be made from a psychoanalytic viewpoint. His determination from early childhood to become a monk, despite his warrior father's insistence that he also become a warrior, indicates a deeply rooted paternal tension, what Freud would likely regard as an Oedipal conflict. According to Freud's developmental theory for boys (things are different for girls and non-conforming boys), fathers and sons have a primal rivalry over the affections of the mothers, which the sons must overcome and outgrow by separating from the family, seeking the affections of mother substitutes, and developing their own distinct identities as men who are independent from their fathers. In this process, the sons mourn this separation from their fathers by internalizing the fathers' values and ideals, which is the original source and commanding power behind the inner voice of conscience, or superego. We know that both of Myōe's parents died when he was eight years old, which put an abrupt end to his nuclear family and quickly launched him into the process of developing a mature, self-reliant identity. Was this double death of his parents a traumatic experience for Myōe? We do not know. He never describes the loss in those terms, but perhaps that represents a defense against painful feelings. From a psychoanalytic perspective, it appears that his later devotion to Butsugen-butsumo, the Mother of All Buddhas, provided him with a powerful symbolic means by which he expressed and satisfied his unconscious needs for maternal connection. It also appears that his strong ethical code and ascetic principles of behavior represent an internalized paternal voice of authority and of occasional violence. Freud would surely consider Myōe's masochistic, self-harming behavior an excessively harsh attempt by his conscience to control his instinctual desires. In effect, Myōe did become a warrior as his father wished—a spiritual warrior fighting a lifelong battle against the enemy of his own body.

And yet in his dreams, these tensions eased somewhat, and Myōe was able to experience feelings and encounter parts of himself that were forbidden to him as an ascetic monk. For example, his strict commitment to celibacy meant a rejection of all sexuality in his waking life. However, a few of his dreams do have references to women and romantic situations, enough that it seems Myōe was managing to balance the conscious and unconscious dynamics of his sexual instincts, and even derive new insights from them. Here is the most remarkable of these dreams:

> I dreamed that the priest Juzo was carrying an incense burner (it was a tea bowl). I thought to myself that someone had brought this back from China and given it to Juzo. I looked at it; inside there were partitions with various Chinese objects in it. There were more than twenty kinds in it. There was something in the shape of two turtles mating, and I thought that it was a worldly, congratulatory gift. Inside there was a Chinese female doll about six inches [tall]. This was also like a tea bowl. Someone said, "This doll is very upset about being sent from China." Thereupon I asked, "Is it true that you are upset about coming to this country?" She nodded in reply. Again

I asked, "I feel for you. Do not grieve." Then she shook her head. After a while, I picked her up and looked at her; her tears were streaming down as she wept. Her eyes were filled with tears and her shoulders were soaked. She was sad for having come to Japan. Then she uttered some words and said, "If you are my prison keeper, then it will be of no use." I replied, "I am only called a priest; and that being the case, there is nothing to be concerned about. The great sages in this country think considerably of me, everyone respects me. Therefore I [can] feel for you." When the doll heard this, she flushed with great joy, nodded, [and said], "If that is so, then you can feel for me." I held her in my palms. Suddenly she turned into a living woman. Then I thought to myself, "Tomorrow I must go somewhere for a service. I want to go there to establish a spiritual connection [with someone there]. You must be with me there." The woman was happy and wanted to accompany me. I said, "There is a lady there who has some connection with you." Thus we went to that place together. Juzo was there and said, "This woman consorts with snakes." I heard his words [but knew that] she did not have sexual relations with snakes; it is just that this woman also has the body of a snake. As I was thinking about this, Juzo followed up and said, "This woman doubles up as a snake."[3]

This dream leads into quite uncanny territory, with hidden gifts, talking dolls, and sexual serpents, and yet Myōe behaves with compassion and good cheer throughout. Indeed, it is his transformative capacity for empathetic imagination that enables him to communicate with the doll, earn her trust, and thus in a sense give birth to her existence as an animate being. The dream is a microcosm of Myōe's powerful ability to sublimate his inner visions, dreams, and meditation experiences into scholarly energy, inspiring a lifetime of innovative writings and beneficial teachings for his community.

The dreams of Lucrecia de León also included beneficial teachings for her community, but in her case, they met with a severely negative reaction, ultimately prompting Philip II himself to order her arrest and imprisonment by the Inquisition. Lucrecia's dreams frequently include Philip II as a character, almost always casting him in a critical light. Some of her followers found these dreams so compelling that they actively planned for an apocalyptic war in which God would destroy the faithless king, allowing a newly purified Spain to emerge. An extremely unlikely yet historically impactful connection developed between the poor, illiterate young woman and the most powerful monarch in the world, a connection mediated by her uncannily accurate prophetic dreams. For Freud, the best way to understand this connection would be to consider its roots in Lucrecia's childhood, specifically her relationship with her father. She was the oldest child in her family by several years; a group of four siblings came later, and it seems she played a significant role in the domestic life of the family by helping her mother with the new arrivals. Her father's work at the court required him to travel frequently, which likely meant periods of expanded freedom for Lucrecia as she grew older, since her mother would always have her hands full with the younger children. It also seemed to lead to increasing conflicts with him when he was at home, leading to direct threats of physical violence.

Lucrecia's tense relationship with her father appears in a psychoanalytic view as an instance of a girl's version of the Oedipal complex, which Freud called the Electra complex. The developmental challenge for girls is different from that for boys. Girls must transform their relationships with their mothers from a source of infant nourishment to an adult role model, while also transforming their dependent relationships on their fathers into an independent readiness for future romantic partners. With Lucrecia, the first part of this process seemed to go well but not the second. Her relationship with her mother apparently remained positive through all her troubles, but she constantly struggled with her father, who eventually cut her off when the Inquisition arrested her. This kind of hostile paternal dynamic would cause lasting harm, according to psychoanalysis, especially in Lucrecia's interactions with other powerful men in her world, men like Philip II. Her criticism of him in her dreams—that he selfishly focused on his own needs, failed to uphold his duties as leader, and left the people vulnerable to attack by outside enemies—could also be directed with ample justification toward her father. Here is an example, from March 19, 1588:

> The nineteenth of March of this year at six in the morning I fell asleep and dreamt, as I had been awake all night due to a high fever I suffered. . . . I dreamt that the king was sitting down in a chair at the head of my bed and I could hear him saying: "Madam, Fray Luke [a priest who is helping record her dreams] told me that you were sick in bed and that is why I came to see you." I answered him: "Fray Luke is so afraid of you that he thought to excuse me by saying that I was sick. Now your fingernails cannot hurt me." Philip responded: "Listen, I am the king!" I answered him: "A visit from Piedrola would be nicer." And he thought that I could still not recognize him, he repeated: "Do not you see that I am the king?" I added: "Just this

year!" He said: "I came to ask what is going to happen with my son. He is sick." I answered him: "Think that he is David's son, and thank God that he is taking him away before your bad advice can damage him!" Looking down at his feet, I saw that they were bare and I asked: "How did you arrive here?" He answered that it was in a carriage. I said to him: "You are going back walking!" He replied: "I do not want anything else from you but to keep me secret." I added: "Oh, Philip, you have no idea who is in control of this dance!" I wanted to keep talking with another idea; however, I woke up because of the noise that my mother and Fray Luke made when they came into my bedroom.[4]

Some of the inquisitors who persecuted her believed that Lucrecia was fabricating her dreams to gain attention. This is plausible from a psycho-analytic view, in the sense that everyone has deep egocentric desires that seek satisfaction in conscious life. However, if everything Lucrecia did was motivated by her yearning for attention, then she must have had a virtually suicidal degree of narcissistic neediness, which does not fit with other known details about her life. In particular, it does not take account of the motives and behavior of the priests and other people who were recording, analyzing, and discussing her dreams. They told Lucrecia that she would *not* get into trouble for sharing her dreams and that by doing so, she was affirmatively helping her community during a tense and frightening time. It seems just as likely that Lucrecia's primary motivation was what she repeatedly told the inquisitors, namely, that she wanted to comply with the requests of the high-level Church officials who said her dreams had theological significance beyond her under-standing and who wanted to record them for their own purposes. The fact that those same Church officials eventually broke their promise, denounced her dreams, and abandoned Lucrecia to the Inquisition would have added them to the symbolic ranks of failed father figures in her life.

Emanuel Swedenborg's father might have felt vindicated by the psycho-analytic theory that the inner voice of moral conscience originates in the ex-ternal voice of one's father. Swedenborg's father did everything he could to instill his paternal values and ethical judgments into the minds of his chil-dren, and with Swedenborg, he succeeded to a considerable degree. From helping the Swedish king with military technology and civil engineering projects to writing treatises on mystical theology and interplanetary rela-tions, Swedenborg always behaved with a characteristic seriousness, focus, and attention to detail. He cared about other people and devoted himself to devising innovative solutions to their problems. By the end of his life, he had shown large numbers of people how to cultivate a deeper and more intimate relationship with the divine. He was not a minister, yet in many ways he acted as one. He never had a dramatic split or falling-out with his father, and the course of his life was largely consistent with his father's proud role as a religious and community leader.

In several other ways, however, Swedenborg's psychological growth and path to a mature adult identity took him in a very different direction. Because his father moved to Uppsala with the rest of the family when he received a church promotion, Swedenborg passed through his adolescence with a great degree of physical and psychological independence from his father. Instead of lectures on orthodox Protestant Christian dogma from his father, Swedenborg as a teenager spent increasing amounts of time with his uncle, a teacher at the university who encouraged his nephew's interests in philosophy and natural science. Swedenborg's unusually liberal and expansive views about sexuality may have started at this time, and insofar as he spoke openly of sexuality as a natural and healthy part of human life, he anticipated a central tenet of psychoanalysis. In the full course of his development into adulthood, Swedenborg managed to navigate his differences with his father and incorporate many of his virtues while charting an independent path toward psychological maturity.

Seen within this framework, however, the conversion experience that turned Swedenborg from science and technology to religious dreams and visions can only appear as a developmental step *backward*. Freud interpreted other mystical phenomena as psychological regressions to a state of "primary narcissism," the blissful sense of unity the infant enjoys within the mother's womb. What a spiritual seer might call an "oceanic feeling" Freud explained as the conscious ego abandoning itself to the formless expanse of the unconscious, something he would generally consider unhealthy and psychologically destabilizing.

However, as noted earlier when looking at Aristides's childlike relationship with the god Asclepius, sometimes a turn back to an earlier psychological stage is precisely what must happen before a new burst of growth can occur that enables the person to move forward in a truly new direction. It seems that Swedenborg, having reached a certain point in his life's development, realized he needed something more if he was to continue growing. Not something he could construct or engineer in the external world but something that had to emerge of its own accord within his unconscious mind, something that would help him integrate his conscious skills as a scientist with this new calling from the unconscious to explore the spiritual symbolism at the heart of the Christian faith. The criticism and abuse he received from some of his contemporaries disputed him on this exact point, arguing that his conversion was actually a step backward and not forward, a shameful retreat rather than a heroic advance, a defeat for reason and a victory of the irrational. Almost two hundred years later, Freud would make the same skeptical arguments against religious beliefs and experiences in texts such as *The Future of an Illusion* (1927) and *Civilization and Its Discontents* (1930). Yet it is the psychoanalytic concept of sublimation that suggests a different and perhaps subtler interpretation here. Swedenborg had an extraordinarily direct and open connection between the conscious and unconscious parts of his mind, with a heavy flow of traffic moving in both directions. He was a bountiful source of uncanny phenomena, an oracle of paranormal knowledge who spoke with the dead, witnessed faraway events, and traveled to otherworldly realms. After his conversion, he showed no signs of mental illness or dysfunction, so it is difficult to argue that his turn toward spiritual pursuits caused him any obvious psychological damage. On the contrary, he enjoyed tremendous energy and creative enthusiasm during this latter phase of his life. He actively wrote, taught, and corresponded with friends and foes alike until his death at the age of sixty-six. These are the marks of a successful sublimation of unconscious instinctual desires into conscious works of cultural value. Although Freud would likely disapprove of the religious content of his sublimated creativity, psychoanalytic theory can actually help us understand the powerful unconscious processes, mediated by dreams and other uncanny phenomena, that enabled Swedenborg to ascend to a new stage of psychological maturity.

Like Swedenborg, Benjamin Banneker had a tremendous capacity for creative work that extended far into the later years of his life. But Banneker was not a wealthy member of the cosmopolitan upper class who had the leisure for intellectual pursuits. He was a poor subsistence farmer and member of a brutally oppressed minority, dwelling in a rural area where hard physical labor was a pitiless necessity of life. Only after his daily toils were finished could Banneker turn to his self-motivated program in mathematics, astronomy, and mechanics, devoting countless hours to study and calculations that led eventually to the publication of his precisely detailed almanacs. This aspect of his life—the relentless power of his intellectual drive—remains something of a mystery. The truly amazing thing about Banneker's almanacs is not that he possessed the advanced skills to calculate the correct figures but that he had the ambition and singularity of purpose to make the attempt.

From the little that is known of his early life, we can see evidence that, from a Freudian view, Banneker benefited from several positive influences on his psychological development. He grew up in a large, close-knit family whose rhythms of life, although modest, were stable and rooted in their natural surroundings. He received affectionate attention from his elder relatives and enough nourishment of his mind, primarily through readings and discussions of the Bible, to give him a sense of his own intellectual potential. He seemed to have a non-problematic relationship with his father and mostly good relations with his mother and grandmother. Altogether, Banneker's family experiences seemed to have given him a healthy psychological foundation for his later life. Despite the many external social forces arrayed against a free black man in late-eighteenth-century America, Banneker entered the adult world with a relatively strong, balanced, and well-formed mind. The evident power of his self-confidence suggests that he managed to preserve a healthy degree of narcissism into adulthood, a deep feeling of goodness about his desires, and a self-reliant willingness to follow his own path in life.

And yet his dreams hint at experiences of loss and mourning, too, and a feeling of distance from other people. We do not know much about his social or romantic relationships, but as an adult, he lived and worked alone on his farm. The countless hours he spent by himself outside at night, looking up at the stars, could be interpreted as an unhealthy withdrawal from the ordinary social world. For Banneker, however, these hours of closely observing the heavens were motivated by an eminently practical and socially beneficial goal: creating an almanac to help farmers improve their crop yields. If there were interpersonal sorrows in Banneker's life, as there are in most people's lives, he managed to channel them into works of tremendous community value.

Banneker's dreams also indicate a sensitivity, and perhaps even openness, toward the uncanny. Each of his four surviving dreams has strangely unsettling contents, from ghosts and spirits to the baby with a hole in its head. In the "dream stories" he wrote earlier in life, he portrayed dreaming as a frightening portal into otherworldly realms. And there was all of that stargazing—nothing could be more "un-homely" than regularly going outside at night and projecting one's awareness as far as possible into the vast expanse of space. For many people, gazing up at the stars at night can evoke profoundly uncanny feelings, stimulating an uncomfortable consciousness of human finitude, reducing the individual ego to the merest speck in the grand scheme of the cosmos. Freud said that humanity suffered a grievous blow to our collective narcissism when the sixteenth-century astronomer Nicolaus Copernicus proved that the earth is not the center of the universe.[5] Banneker was not daunted by this narcissistic blow but seemed to embrace it and turn it to his own purposes. He stared into the heavens night after night, confident in his own intelligence, gathering knowledge that he would develop into the stuff of ancient prophecy—highly accurate predictions of the weather, the tides, and the movements of heavenly bodies.

The large and prosperous family in which Anna Kingsford grew up gave her many of these same psychological strengths Banneker had. She was the youngest of twelve children, and her conception may have been a piece of her parents' mourning the loss of their first child, a daughter named Ann, who died from consumption in 1844 at the age of seventeen. Their two-year-old daughter Alice also died in 1844, so the birth of their last child in 1846 was a cause for celebration, and they named her "Annie" in memory of their recently departed eldest. Kingsford seems to have received a great deal of positive parental attention, although as a girl, she was not allowed the same opportunities for attending school and participating in athletics as her brothers were given as a matter of course. Nevertheless, she was a precociously intelligent child with an extremely vivid imagination, uncanny dreams, and a natural talent for writing prose and poetry. The combination of Kingsford's innate mental abilities and a stable, caring family gave her a lifelong foundation of self-confidence in whatever she did.

Kingsford's relationship with her wealthy shipping-magnate father seems to have been quite positive. Paradoxically, his most beneficial and psychologically formative act toward her occurred when he died. He distributed his wealth evenly among his surviving children, not excluding Kingsford and her sister from a generous inheritance. He took the additional step of giving his daughters full legal control over their money, so that if they married, their husbands would not immediately assume control over their wives' assets, as was the general practice under British law. In essence, Kingsford's father succeeded in providing her with a safe, steady source of financial independence that would last, if prudently managed, for the rest of her life. This gave her the freedom to pursue a path of psychological development that few women of her or any era have pursued. For instance, it allowed her to choose a man for a husband who had no means of his own but would be a good father for the one child she had with him and would allow her to follow her literary, political, medical, and spiritual interests without interference.

Seen in a psychoanalytic light, it might seem that Kingsford's lifelong reliance on her father's wealth led to an unhealthy fixation on an early stage of the Electra complex. Because of an excessively long attachment to her father, she did not have enough instinctual energy left to form a normal marital relationship with another man, although she did have enough energy to form a close friendship with the father-like Edward Maitland, a man twenty-two years her senior, who became her primary companion, confidant, and chief supporter in the later years of her life. Instead of turning away from her father to bond with her husband, Kingsford held on to the image of her father, ignored her husband, and sought a father substitute in Maitland. A strict version of psychoanalysis might interpret this behavior as a dangerous deviation from the path of normal female development, likely to lead to emotional and interpersonal problems. But the actual course of Kingsford's adult life was full of vitality, social relations, and creative work. A more flexible psychoanalytic view would recognize and appreciate her powerful capacity for sublimating her instinctual energies into artistic and scientific products of immense cultural value. Rather than deviating from the female norm, Kingsford may have been charting a new course for the healthy psychological development of women, a course that does not require subsuming themselves to the control of men.

With Wolfgang Pauli, much of what we know about his life and dreams emerged in the course of his therapeutic work with Jung. For that reason, it will be easier to consider the psychoanalytic aspects of Pauli's life in the next chapter, after looking more closely at the various ways in which he interacted with Jung and other archetypal psychologists.

Before turning to that discussion, we can close here with a few Freudian observations. All of the seven dream journalists we have been examining display a high degree of self-confidence and healthy ego development. They have an unusually energetic flow between the conscious and unconscious parts of their minds, a powerful capacity for cultural work, and a keen sensitivity toward the uncanny. In terms of their instinctual economy, none of them seems primarily motivated by sexual desires, and their dreams have a relatively low proportion of sexual references and situations. Freud might say this is just the manifest content of the dreams, and the sexual themes are hidden within the underlying latent content. It is difficult, however, to find other signs of sexual problems or preoccupations in their waking lives. Rather than sexuality, these seven people seem most instinctually motivated by narcissistic desires for self-expression and public achievement. Keeping a journal of their dreams had the effect of welcoming these desires into the waking world and drawing creative strength from them.

12

Archetypal Psychology

At least as much as Sigmund Freud, Carl Jung has deeply influenced modern Western thinking about dreams. Jung was originally Freud's most promising disciple, but in 1914, he broke with psychoanalysis and set off to create his own psychological system. Although he accepted many of Freud's key concepts and incorporated them into his new approach, Jung pushed the psychoanalytic theory of dreaming into new territory. Whereas Freud viewed dreams as disguised fulfillments of repressed childhood wishes, Jung saw dreaming as a natural, undisguised expression of the psyche in relation to past, present, and future. Dreams are hard to understand not because they are intentionally masked or hidden but because they speak in a primal language of images, symbols, and emotions. For Jung, the interpretation of a dream involves a process of the conscious mind struggling to learn and make sense of that primal language. Rather than a puzzle to be solved or a lock to be picked, a dream is an invitation to a lively, open-ended dialogue between consciousness and the unconscious.

As a consequence of this fundamental difference with Freud, Jung's approach encourages attention to collections of people's dreams over time. In fact, Jung preferred having multiple dreams to analyze rather than just one. If an important meaning was emerging from a person's unconscious, Jung found it easier to identify the true nature of that meaning by tracking its various expressions through a series of dreams. Most important for Jung, interpreting dreams in a series helped give him a sense of where the dreams were *going*, where they were leading people in their further psychological development. While agreeing with Freud about the lifelong influence of past experiences from childhood, Jung emphasized that dreams look forward as well as backward, reminding us of where we have been in the past *and* where we might be heading in the future. He expanded the psychological concept of development to encompass the whole of our lives, with opportunities for new growth at every stage of the life cycle, not just in childhood and adolescence. Because these valuable opportunities for growth can arise suddenly and unexpectedly, a good way to prepare for their appearance is to pay close

The Scribes of Sleep. Kelly Bulkeley, Oxford University Press. © Oxford University Press 2023.
DOI: 10.1093/oso/9780197609606.003.0013

attention to one's dreams over time. For this reason, most Jungian analysts encourage their clients to keep a dream journal as a regular part of their therapeutic work together.

In a sense, then, archetypal psychology developed as a direct response to this aspect of dreaming, its temporal unfolding over the course of a person's life. Jung recognized from his own childhood experiences that dreaming is an ongoing process throughout the life span, a developmental dimension of human experience that can be cultivated and made more conscious *or* ignored and left unconscious. Jung devoted himself to explaining the dynamics of this deep dreaming process, and he believed his model of the mind could help in the therapeutic treatment of people suffering from various kinds of mental illness. More than that, he addressed his writings to the larger group of people who might not have a diagnosable psychological disorder but who still feel a distressing lack of meaning and purpose in their lives. He knew that in the hyper-fast, technologically dominated world of modernity, the experience of dreaming still has the capacity to remind people of the non-conscious parts of their minds, and he used the topic of dreams as an introduction to his more complex concepts about how the mind works. The basic tenets of Jung's approach are rooted in the phenomenology of dreaming, which means that a sound understanding of his ideas about dreams can provide a foundation for understanding just about everything else he wrote. Here are the four Jungian concepts that will be most helpful to our ongoing study of the historical journal keepers:

1. *Individuation.* Psychological growth does not end with the maturation of our bodies at adulthood. Our mental growth continues far beyond that, aiming at an ultimate goal, a telos toward which we are moving throughout our lives. This goal is psychological wholeness and self-actualization, the complete integration of who we are, the full manifestation of all our inner potentials. Jung calls the movement toward this goal the path of individuation.

2. *Archetypes.* Along the path of individuation, we meet a variety of constellated psychological energies known as archetypes. The archetypes arise from a level of the mind Jung called the collective unconscious, which we share with all humans. Archetypes are instinctual templates of thought. They are patterns of vivid imagery that guide us along the developmental path of human life. Archetypal symbols reflect a natural wisdom that can also be found in the world's religious

and mythological traditions. Because of these overlapping domains of archetypal symbolism, Jung applies the same basic interpretive method to dreams, myths, religious texts, works of art, and other forms of human culture.

3. *The compensatory function.* Of the various functions of dreaming, Jung gave special emphasis to its capacity to provide unconscious compensations for the imbalances of the conscious mind. Moving forward on the path of individuation requires a dynamic balance between consciousness and the unconscious, and Jung believed that dreams actively promote this kind of psychological balance by introducing into waking awareness compensatory material from the unconscious that has been ignored, devalued, and/or repressed.

4. *The prospective function.* Jung also emphasized the prospective, forward-looking function of dreaming. In dreaming, we envision our psychological future. We gain glimpses, hints, and anticipations of the developmental challenges ahead, along with possible opportunities for discovery, insight, and empowerment. Many of the most vivid and memorable dreams people ever experience, what Jung called "big dreams," have a prospective quality of future potentiality, beckoning the dreamers along the path of their unfolding individuation.

Now, instead of following the chronological order of the dream journals as in previous chapters, let's reverse the order and begin the discussion here with Wolfgang Pauli. As a patient, friend, critic, and co-theorist, Pauli had a direct impact on Jung's emerging psychological ideas, so it will help our evaluation of the other dream journals if we start with Pauli's dreams and Jung's interpretations of them. Recall that Pauli first approached Jung in 1933 for help with mental health problems following the death of his mother and his sudden marriage and equally sudden divorce from his first wife. The doctor-patient relationship began on a strangely utilitarian and disrespectful note on both sides. Jung agreed to provide treatment for Pauli but only as supervisor for a new and relatively inexperienced psychiatric trainee, Erna Rosenbaum, who would be Pauli's actual therapist. Jung arranged things in this way to preserve his own objectivity in what he immediately recognized would be an invaluable research opportunity to put his psychological theories into practice in the treatment of one of the greatest scientists of the twentieth century. Pauli's emotional problems thus served Jung as a natural experiment and testing ground for his ideas about the deepest energies and highest potentials of the unconscious mind. Pauli, for his part, decided to approach Jung not because of his therapeutic skill but because of his success with women. In his introductory letter to Rosenbaum, Pauli said:

> The background is that I consulted with Mr. Jung a week ago because of some neurotic symptoms which, among other things, have to do with the fact that it is easier to achieve success in academia than with women. Since for Mr. Jung the opposite is the case, he seemed the right person to ask for medical advice.[1]

This joking comment has a double edge to it, both belittling Jung's academic status and spotlighting his extramarital activities. It reflects some degree of Pauli's defensive insecurity and false bravado, too, as he gets ready to surrender his ego control and open himself to the honest self-scrutiny that comes with a genuinely effective analysis.

Keeping a dream journal seems to have been the easiest part of the therapeutic process for Pauli. He took to the effort with enthusiasm, recording his dreams in detail and learning how to practice Jung's method of interpretation to understand their meanings. Many of Pauli's dreams contain images and characters with no direct or obvious connection to the personal details of his waking life, which Jung regards as an indication that the dreams have arisen from the collective unconscious. The recurrent figure of the "strange woman" in his dreams suggested that Pauli's unconscious problem was not with his mother, his ex-wife, or any other actual woman but with the feminine principle as such, what Jung called the *anima* archetype. The anima is an archetypal image representing the unconscious psychological energies associated with women in a man's mind. The *animus* is the corresponding archetype representing masculine psychological energies in a woman's mind. Seen in a contemporary light, the gender essentialism of the anima and animus concepts requires immediate critique and correction to account better for the full range and variety of human sexual identity and self-expression. That said, in the early-twentieth-century context of his analytic work with Jung's trainee, Pauli found it therapeutically helpful to think of the female characters in his dreams as images of the anima archetype, whose recurrent appearances were compensating for his one-sided masculine attitude in waking life. Learning about the deepest unconscious roots of his feelings about women corresponded with an increase in his emotional stability and an improved capacity to form healthy, intimate relationships, culminating in his second marriage to a woman with whom he would remain for more than twenty years. This interpretive focus may have limited Pauli's psychological growth in other ways, but it evidently did help him with the "neurotic symptoms" that brought him to therapy in the first place.

Beyond his romantic problems in the past and present, Pauli's dreams also gazed far into the future, going beyond the here and now to explore otherworldly dimensions of time and space. This is what most excited Jung and stimulated his creative theorizing, and it is what makes Pauli's dream journal so historically significant. Illuminated by Jung's interpretive method, the dreams are full of vivid, tantalizingly abstract images that suggest an ultimate harmony of physics and psychology. As the dreams progress, Jung and Pauli begin to see the archetypal correspondences between quantum physics and depth psychology. The symmetry between subatomic particles reflects the balance between consciousness and the unconscious, a balance preserved by the compensatory function of dreams. The nucleus of an atom represents the *self*, which Jung defined as the archetype of wholeness and the ultimate goal of the individuation process. The archetypes themselves can be conceived as probabilistic fields of psychological potential, awaiting the concrete events of lived existence to collapse all their probabilities into a single determinate experience. "The archetype represents nothing else but the probability of psychic events"—that's not Jung speaking but Pauli.[2]

Along with helping Jung refine his notion of archetypes, the most consequential outgrowth of their relationship was the concept of *synchronicity*, the idea that phenomena seemingly separated in time and space are actually connected according to implicit/unconscious bonds of psychological meaning. Often occurring during times of change and transformation, synchronicities are "meaningful coincidences" that are not causally related at a physical level but have a strong emotional and symbolic connection at a psychological level. Reading the twenty-six years' worth of letters exchanged between Jung and Pauli, it becomes clear this concept was part of their joint effort to develop a kind of transcendental language to account for the fundamental interplay of psychological and physical realities in human life. Quantum physics had already disproven the classical idea of scientific objectivity. After the findings of Albert Einstein, Pauli, and others, it became clear that the observer's subjective presence can never be completely excluded from experimental procedures. Pauli and his colleagues had shown that consciousness is an indispensable element of reality, with far more impact on our perceptions and experiences than most people realize. With Jung's help, Pauli explored his dreams for archetypal insights into what he called "background physics,"[3] with synchronicity as an illustration of the new hybrid physics-psychology language. He knew from his personal experiences with the "Pauli effect" about the uncanny dynamics of synchronicities as they manifest in people's lives at psychologically significant moments, and he tried to find a new terminology to express the resonance of synchronicity and the quantum physics concept of radioactivity, both of which he felt could be accurately described as follows: "A process of transmutation of an active center, ultimately leading to a stable state, is accompanied by self-duplicating (multiplying) and expanding phenomena, associated with further transmutations that are brought about through an invisible reality."[4] Pauli said that, translated into psychological terms, the active center is Jung's archetype of the self, the transmutation is the path of individuation, the multiplying phenomena are archetypes, and the invisible reality is the collective unconscious.

Jung's approach works well with Pauli's dreams because the approach was developed and tested using his dreams. Does an archetypal approach work as well with the dreams of people from other cultures and periods of history? Maybe, maybe not. All modern psychologies are vulnerable to the critique that they reflect the implicit values and biases of their time and cannot be validly applied to people from other historical backgrounds. Skepticism is warranted in cases where a current theory overgeneralizes about human nature, positing limited cultural values as universal truths. With Jung, his universalist ideas about the collective unconscious, the archetypes, individuation, and so on, do have this potential for overgeneralization, so caution is required when applying his ideas outside their original historical and cultural context.

Having said that, it does seem that Jung's archetypal psychology has tremendous relevance and explanatory power in relation to each of the other journal keepers besides Pauli. The relatively short but spiritually intense life of Anna Kingsford, for instance, represents an accelerated process of individuation, similar to what Jung said in *Man and His Symbols* about an eight-year-old girl who would die two years later from an illness.[5] The father of the girl brought Jung a series dreams his daughter had written in a journal, and Jung was astonished at what he found:

They made up the weirdest series of dreams that I have ever seen. . . . Though childlike, they were uncanny, and they contained images whose origin was wholly incomprehensible to the father. . . . These dreams open up a new and rather terrifying aspect of life and death. One would expect to find such images in an aging person who looks back upon life, rather than to be given them by a child who would normally be looking forward.[6]

Although she lived somewhat longer than this nameless girl, Kingsford's short life was equally haunted by dark dreams and visions filled with dense networks of archetypal symbolism and existential allegory. Like the ill-fated child whose dreams Jung found so remarkable, Kingsford felt an urgent drive to express her dreams and bring them into the world, as if time were running out and everything true and meaningful in her experience had to be condensed into a form that would survive her imminent passing. She did not just follow the path of individuation, she raced along it, speeding into realms of archetypal reality that few people ever reach, no matter how long they live. She had vivid dreams of animus figures ("The Counsel of Perfection"), in which she discussed with an unknown group of sage-like men how she could be "perfect" like her Father in heaven. She had dreams of animal aggression and violence (e.g., "The Bird and the Cat," "A Lion in the Way") that corresponded to Jung's notion of the shadow archetype as symbolizing repressed or alienated instinctual energies within the unconscious that we tend to project onto other people rather than recognize in ourselves. She had dreams of ecstatic joy and cosmic beauty ("The Forest Cathedral") symbolizing the natural symmetries and harmonies that emerge with full psychological development as manifested in the archetype of the self. And she had dreams that symbolized the process of individuation itself ("The Difficult Path," "The Metempsychosis"), illuminating the way ahead and showing her what she had to learn, do, and suffer in order to reach the complete actualization of her innate potentials.

Likewise, in the few surviving dreams from Benjamin Banneker's journals, we can identify several instances of archetypal symbolism. The "infernal spirit" with whom he fights in the dream of December 13, 1797, has the half-human, half-animal attributes that Jung often associates with the shadow archetype ("some part of him in shape of a man, but hairy as a beast, his feet was circular"). In this dream, the battle with his shadow seems to be triggered by a reference to an unknown woman with the name "Beckey Freeman," who in turn appears as an anima figure, representing not an actual woman in Banneker's waking life but a constellation of feminine energies within his unconscious. From a Jungian perspective, the dream could be seen as a rough form of psychological compensation, forcing Banneker's waking consciousness to pay special attention to Beckey Freeman and whatever she unconsciously symbolizes. This is one of the many paradoxes of archetypal psychology: nightmares can be among the most positive, helpful, growth-enhancing dreams we ever experience. Jung believed that in many cases, a frightening dream is felt as frightening precisely because it brings strong compensatory energies from the unconscious into conscious awareness. The scarier the dream, the more alienated the unconscious energies have become, which suggests that an especially great potential for growth and integration exists if the energies can be brought back into relation with consciousness.

In this view, the eerie and otherworldly qualities of Banneker's dreams actually testify to his psychological healthiness. The dreams go beyond the concerns of his daily life to address questions at the core of human existence. As archetypal reflections of Banneker's development along the path of individuation, his dreams are evidence of a lively imagination, deep self-confidence, and open-minded curiosity. If, as Jung says, individuation requires a balanced actualization of all one's innate human potentials, then there can be little doubt that Banneker made unusually great progress along this path. Although his life was sharply limited in many ways, he consciously devoted himself to a wide variety of interests and activities, pushing himself forward and striving to expand his mental horizons. His impressive achievements in science and technology combined with thoughtful reflections on religion, history, and the future betterment of humankind. He dedicated his days to working the land as a farmer, with his feet and hands in the soil, and he spent his nights gazing up at the sky, casting his mind into the starry heavens. Interpreted archetypally, Banneker's almanacs have the symbolic qualities of mandalas—beautifully intricate, geometrically designed images of wholeness and integration representing the archetype of the self as a fully actualized psyche, the highest development of human consciousness, the emergence of one's natural condition as a cosmic being.

A similar individuating trajectory can be seen in the life of Emanuel Swedenborg, as he moved over time toward a yearning to create a cartography of the heavens. The two major phases of Swedenborg's life, first as a scientist and engineer and second as a visionary and theologian, offer a classic illustration of one of Jung's key points about individuation, namely, that it tends to emerge as a concern in the second half of life. Jung agreed with Freud about the importance of developing a strong, independent ego as one grows into adulthood. But whereas Freud regarded this as the end of the growth process, Jung saw it as merely the first half. Only after we put enough time and energy into building up the ego will we be ready to let go of the ego and allow the archetype of the self to emerge as the new, more holistic center of personality. Swedenborg's life story appears to be a textbook example of this process.

In light of Jung's emphasis on individuation as the appropriate developmental task for the second half of life, it makes sense that with people who die prematurely, like the eight-year-old girl he describes in *Man and His Symbols*, he would look for evidence of anticipatory dreams and archetypal experiences, dreams pushing the psychological growth process as far and as fast as possible in the shadow of looming death. Kingsford's dreams have evidence of that kind of accelerated individuation, and so do Lucrecia de León's. It is difficult to track the precise course of Lucrecia's individuation, since our knowledge of her life has been heavily filtered by religious, legal, and political authorities whose interests were not her interests. We do not even know if she survived beyond the punishment imposed on her by the Inquisition (one hundred lashes, two years' confinement in a convent devoted to the care of lepers, followed by permanent banishment from Madrid), when she was twenty-six years old. But the dreams she experienced in her late teens and early twenties have profoundly archetypal qualities, with recurrent figures who vividly symbolize the animus, the shadow, and the self. Several of the dreams portray Lucrecia herself in the symbolic form of a *trickster*, the archetype of disruption, disorder, and paradoxical transformation. Her dream interactions with Philip II have mythological resonance with stories of mighty kings and holy fools in which a temporary reversal of status—the king brought low, the fool revealing a higher truth—leads to a restoration of order at a new, healthier, more self-integrated level.

To speak in this way of Lucrecia's dreams takes seriously her claim to the inquisitors that she did not know what the dreams meant and that it was Don Alonso and the other priests who told her the dreams had relevance to political and religious matters. This cultural dimension of her dreams will be discussed further in chapter 13, but here we can observe from a Jungian perspective that Lucrecia's dreams had compensatory and prospective qualities not for her personally but for Spain. More than that, she was dreaming *as* Spain, empathetically embodying her community's concerns and conflicts and devoting her imaginal powers toward visionary anticipations of their collective future. This view helps make sense of several curious features of her dreams, for example, the prevalence of the beach and seashore as a setting. The frequency of this setting in her dreams bears no relation to her personal experiences in waking life, but it does accurately reflect the importance of the seashore as the physical boundary of the Spanish nation, its skin, if you will. Her dreams continually placed her in this location, prospectively scanning the horizon for imminent attack from the country's greatest enemies—Drake and the English, the Turks, the Moors—and compensating for Philip's feckless, myopic leadership with sharp honesty and harsh realism about the dangers facing the Spanish people.

We do not have enough information about Lucrecia's life or dreams to say more about the subsequent direction of her psychological development, Jungian or otherwise. Of all the journal keepers, only Myōe Shonin tracked his dreams from his early adulthood until the year before his death. As noted earlier, an archetypal perspective includes an emphasis on the distinctive features of dreams that accompany the final stages of life, and Myōe's last recorded dreams display many of these elements. The images that appear in these end-of-life dreams include a white light emanating from a picture of a vase (no. 175), a chick emerging from an egg he unexpectedly finds in his pocket (no. 176), a deity stepping out of a picture and giving him ritual instructions (no. 178), a dead fish somehow reviving and leading him to a large mansion (no. 181), discovering that a wooden turtle in his sleeve is actually a living being that asks him to be fed (no. 182), patiently waiting as someone is about to cut off his head (no. 183), and a round object containing an embryonic living being, like a tadpole, being tossed into a fire and transforming into a burning shrimp (no. 184). The recurrent theme in these dreams is spontaneous metamorphosis—a sudden transformation of one state into another, a blurring of the boundaries between animate and inanimate existence, an opening perhaps to a higher mode of integration that can accommodate both life and death together.

Several of Myōe's earlier dreams include female figures that have symbolic characteristics of the anima, along with shadow dreams of his struggles with his body, trickster dreams of conflicts with other Buddhist teachers, and self dreams illuminating his distinctive path of individuation. It was here, toward the end of Myōe's life, that a new factor of archetypal psychology appeared, what Jung called the *transcendent function*. Jung described it as a specific moment at the latter end of the individuation process when conscious-unconscious conflicts are finally resolved enough to allow truly new possibilities for psychological growth to emerge:

The process of coming to terms with the unconscious is a true labor, a work which involves both action and suffering. It has been named the "transcendent function" because it represents a function based on real and "imaginary," or rational and irrational, data, thus bridging the yawning gulf between conscious and unconscious. It is a natural process, a manifestation of the energy that springs from the tension of opposites, and it consists in a series of fantasy-occurrences which appear spontaneously in dreams and visions. . . . If we can successfully develop that function which I have called transcendent, the disharmony ceases and we can then enjoy the favorable side of the unconscious. The unconscious can then give us all the encouragement and help that a bountiful nature can shower upon man. It holds possibilities which are locked away from the conscious mind, for it has at its disposal all subliminal psychic contents, all those things which have been forgotten or overlooked, as well as the wisdom and experience of uncounted centuries which are laid down in its archetypal organs.[7]

This seems a fitting psychological description of Myōe's life, a life devoted to the active pursuit of transcendent dreams and visions. His identity as a monk gave him the freedom to open his conscious mind to as much of the collective unconscious as he could handle, allowing the symbol-generating energies of "bountiful nature" to fill his mind in waking and sleeping with intense, vivid, otherworldly imagery. He then used these archetypal experiences as the focus of meditation practices in which he reflected on what he had seen and what he hoped to see in future dreams and visions. Jung would agree with Myōe's emphasis on the vibrant, living power of these images arising from the unconscious, images that need to be not translated and analyzed for their messages but rather appreciated for their psychological honesty and welcomed into conscious awareness. As Myōe neared the end of his life, these images became heralds of a great impending change, the ultimate in anticipatory dreaming.

For Aelius Aristides, the path of individuation led through a long, transformational period of severe illness and bodily suffering. His dream journal chronicles the complex course of his physical ailments and his increasingly intimate relationship with the healing god Asclepius. In a Jungian context, Asclepius has a strong mythological resonance with Jesus, Osiris, Persephone, and other deities who die and are reborn and, as a result, have the power to heal suffering and restore life. Like Jesus, Asclepius offers his followers a variety of practices and rituals to relieve their pain and set them back on the course of a healthy, creative life. And also like Jesus, Asclepius made startlingly counterintuitive demands on his followers that clashed with the conventional behaviors of their society yet benefited them in the end. For Aristides, all his dreams of bizarre medical remedies gave him the confidence that the healing god was leading him toward a cure. In Jungian terms, we could say the dreams brought compensatory images and energies from his unconscious into his conscious awareness, guiding him toward greater balance and self-integration. According to Jung, "Christ himself is the perfect symbol of the hidden immortal within the mortal man. . . . Christ as an image is a symbol of the self."[8] For Aristides, the healing god Asclepius filled this archetypal role as an inspiring symbol of the actualized self.

The practice of Jungian dream interpretation involves this kind of symbolic *amplification* of the dreams, connecting their images with similar images in myths, religions, fairy tales, art, and other domains of archetypal expression (e.g., Asclepius as related to Jesus, Osiris, Persephone, etc.). Depending on the circumstances, the amplification process can lead into tremendously detailed cross-cultural and historical comparisons with these other archetypal domains. For a client in Jungian therapy, these comparisons can open new vistas of self-understanding, giving the client a reassuring sense of personal connection with the unconscious wisdom of the archetypes. In the context of our study of dream journals in history, Jung's approach has the benefit of providing a framework for identifying a psychological trajectory in dreams over time, a trajectory with several predictable stages of developmental challenge and opportunities for growth. His theories may not apply to all cultures and periods of history, and they may not apply to numerous people in contemporary society. But they do apply with great explanatory power to the lives of certain kinds of people, now and in other places and times, people who feel a strong calling for one reason or another to record their dreams, listen to them carefully, and follow them where they lead.

13

Cultural Psychology

As the study of the *psyche* (usually translated into English as "mind," although it could also be fairly rendered as "soul" or "spirit"), psychology has tended to focus on the individual, leaving the communal aspects of human life to anthropology, sociology, and history. Psychological theories like those of Sigmund Freud and Carl Jung try to explain how the mind of each individual works and what to do when the mind *doesn't* work and people need therapeutic treatment. Chapters 11 and 12 showed that dreaming offers a valuable path—a *via regia* or "royal road," in Freud's memorable phrase—into the unconscious realms of the mind. Freud focused on the personal aspects of the unconscious, and he interpreted dreams as expressions of ego-centered instinctual wishes. Even dreams with explicit references to social realities were generally treated by Freud as symbolic references to personal concerns. Going beyond a strictly psychoanalytic view, Jung recognized a collective dimension to the unconscious, which led him to interpret some dreams as expressions of archetypal symbolism having little or no personal content but conveying profound transpersonal wisdom. However, Jung's approach to dreams generally focused on universal symbolic themes, with less attention to the significance of specific cultural forms and social practices.

It may be appropriate in a therapeutic context to bracket out these cultural references in dreams, as a pragmatic decision to focus on the personal problems of the client. But that does not mean the cultural dimensions of the dreams do not exist; it just means we need different methods to explore them. What I am calling "cultural psychology" is a broad term for researchers who study dreams as they relate not only to the individual but to the broader social world as well. This approach, mostly found in anthropology but also in other social scientific disciplines, seeks to expand the notions of "psyche" and "mind" to embrace more than just what happens between an individual's ears. Cultural psychology acknowledges the dense, historically rooted relational matrix into which every human is born and within which we all live our lives. For the study of dream journals, a cultural psychology perspective

The Scribes of Sleep. Kelly Bulkeley, Oxford University Press. © Oxford University Press 2023.
DOI: 10.1093/oso/9780197609606.003.0014

can help to illuminate their potential as a valuable source of insight into the complex interplay of collective events and personal life experiences.

The most influential work in this area is Charlotte Beradt's *The Third Reich of Dreams*, which presents a collection of dreams gathered from people living in Germany between 1933 and 1939, during the rise of National Socialism and the beginning of World War II. Beradt documents in often excruciating detail how deeply the terrorizing ideology of the Nazi regime penetrated people's minds, filling their dreams with fear, aggression, and inescapable propaganda. For many researchers, her book is their first encounter with evidence demonstrating that dreams can have authentic dimensions of meaning related to culture, politics, and collective life. Beradt says very little about the personal lives of the dreamers, preferring to let the dreams speak for themselves in their natural language of vivid, emotionally complex images. Although *The Third Reich of Dreams* includes reports from several different people, Beradt singled out one of her respondents, a woman in her thirties, as having unusually potent collective dreaming capacities. This woman dreamed, for instance, that street signs had been abolished and replaced with posters on every corner, "proclaiming in white letters on black background the twenty words people were not allowed to say"[1] In another dream, she attends a performance of her favorite opera, *The Magic Flute*, and when the line is sung, "That is the devil certainly," the police suddenly march up to her and arrest her in front of the whole crowd—"a machine had registered the fact that I had thought of Hitler on hearing the word 'devil.'" Beradt marveled at the woman's special aptitude for culturally oriented dreaming:

This woman . . . experienced a whole series of such dreams between April and September 1933. Although concerned with the same basic theme, they were all quite different and not simply variations of the same dream. . . . In real life quite an ordinary person, in her dreams she proved herself of Heraclitus' Sibyl, whose "voice reached out through the millennia." In the course of only a few months, this twentieth-century Sibyl saw far into the Nazi millennium, sensing trends, recognizing correlations, shedding light on the obscure, and all the while moving to and fro between the easily exposed realities of everyday life and all that lay undisclosed beneath their surface. With extremely skillful use of tragedy as well as farce, and realistic as well as surrealistic elements, she in effect unconsciously extracted the essence of a development which was bound to lead to a national catastrophe as well as to the destruction of her own personal world. Time has proved the validity of her dream characters and sequences, her details and nuances.[2]

We do not know how many other people in the general population have oneiric capacities like this nameless woman, nor do we know if her remarkable dream sensitivity was a constant feature of her life or if it was triggered by threatening events in the social world. Further research on people like her certainly seems warranted in light of Beradt's observation that this ordinary woman's dreams "unconsciously extracted the essence" of the unfolding collective disaster. The more we can learn about this mode of unconscious intelligence as it manifests in dreams over time, the more we can understand the dynamic interplay of mind and culture as it appears in both healthy and pathological forms.

At the simplest level, a cultural psychology approach looks for dream content with literal and/or symbolic connections to collective life and interprets this content as a reflection of the dreamers' experiences within their cultural ecosystems. When people dream of public figures like politicians and celebrities, of public spaces like markets and schools, of public events like concerts and festivals, it can be worthwhile to explore these contents in relation to the dreamers' waking life experiences in society. If someone dreams of their country's president, for example, a typical Freudian view would be that the dream figure does not represent the actual president but rather symbolizes a "presidential" figure in the individual's life, probably their father at some unconscious level. A Jungian view would typically consider the archetypal meanings associated with supreme leaders like presidents. Both of those interpretive paths could lead to fruitful results, but it is also worth taking seriously the possibility raised by cultural psychology, that a dream like this represents *the actual president* and the dreamer's feelings about that specific political figure in the waking world. An especially sharp statement of the cultural psychology perspective appears in Johanna King's 1995 article "Let's Stand Up, Regain Our Balance, and Look Around," which includes a discussion of the dreams in Beradt's book, along with dreams of sexual abuse survivors and former religious cultists:

> All of these dreams, and many other less dramatic ones, make *primary* reference to the waking-life circumstances of the dreamers and illustrate, I hope, how an unbalanced or premature focus on the intrapsychic can sadly miss the dream message. In striving to understand and work with these dreams,

we must be willing to look at and engage the ugly, disturbing, dark parts of the *world*, without mislabeling them as projected shadow, repression, or any other intrapsychic construct. . . . These problems and solutions can never clearly be visualized from a purely intrapsychic perspective, which too often emphasizes *internal* changes and adjustments, not changes in the world. Insight, self-awareness, and positive affective states do not by themselves produce contextual change.[3]

It should be noted that King also believes dreaming is a powerful source of creativity, but she criticizes Western psychologists for overemphasizing the personal applications of these powers and neglecting the ways in which heightened dream awareness could be directed toward collectively beneficial goals, "enabling the dreamer to envision being in the situation, and in the world, in a different, new, enhanced, or more constructive way."[4] This expansive approach does not deny the internal psychological meanings of dreaming (King herself worked professionally as a psychotherapist on a college campus) but tries to widen our appreciation of dreams as direct calls to engage with the external realities and concerns of our communities.

Anthropology has traditionally been the field most concerned with the cultural aspects of dreaming. Ironically, many anthropologists today are criticizing earlier generations of scholars on this very point, accusing them of knowingly or unknowingly putting their cross-cultural research at the service of the violent colonial exploitation of the very people whose mental and cultural lives they were studying. It is indeed painful now to read early-twentieth-century anthropological studies of dreams, with their sweeping generalizations and facile assumptions of Western superiority. Unaware of their own cultural biases, early anthropologists vastly underestimated the limits to what they could learn from people who were being collectively traumatized and forced to endure severe disruptions to their traditional ways of life, leaving them struggling for physical and cultural survival. With dreams, the early researchers gained novel insights into cross-cultural forms of human dreaming, while overlooking the crisis conditions of their informants' lives and their personal and communal suffering.

Many anthropologists have developed research methods with more respect for the people they are studying and more self-awareness about their own cultural biases and assumptions. As mentioned in the introduction, Dorothy Eggan was the first anthropologist to recognize the potential value of exploring long series of dreams and using quantitative methods to identify meaningful patterns in the dreams. She found this approach could reveal important aspects of people's feelings about their social relations and cultural beliefs and could do so without interference from the researcher's biases and without imposing external frames of interpretation onto the dreams. Eggan observed that dreams often revolve around generally unspoken tensions between personal beliefs and behaviors on the one hand and social norms and expectations on the other. These tensions may not be obvious in people's waking-life activities, but their dreams reveal the sources of friction and conflict with remarkable clarity.[5] A good illustration is Thomas Gregor's 1981 study of the dreams of the indigenous Mehinaku people of the Amazonian river basin, which used a quantitative method very similar to Eggan's to explore cultural experiences. Gregor found a recurrent theme in Mehinaku dreams of danger and aggression involving Brazilian government officials and other outside people they encountered. Even though in waking life the Mehinaku had mostly peaceful and friendly interactions with the Brazilians, in their dreams a contrary and perhaps more honest set of feelings emerges:

> The special value of dream research is that it takes us beyond the impact of waking experiences on personality to reach conclusions we could only guess at from a knowledge of everyday life. The social anthropologist, for example, would have little basis for predicting the aggressive role played by Brazilians in the villagers' anxious dreams of assault and sexual exploitation. To be sure, the Mehinaku express concerns about the Brazilians and their intentions, but for the most part their history of contact with outsiders has been peaceful. Even today, the villagers' lands are intact and their traditional autonomy is respected by reservation authorities. The impact of the outsider on the Mehinaku is therefore easy to underestimate without the advantage of psychological data.[6]

It is this remarkable capacity of dreams to highlight hidden social conflicts that prompts the turn to cultural psychology as a resource in the study of dream journals. The following three principles can be drawn from the works of Eggan, Gregor, and others as helpful guides in exploring the social dimensions of dreaming.

1. *Personal/communal interplay.* No dreamer is an island; everyone's dreams are shaped by the cultural, social, and historical conditions of their lives, and everyone's dreams are actively responding to these

conditions. The key insight here is the dynamic interplay of the individual and the collective: dreams accurately mirror people's experiences within a community *and* honestly express their critical feelings toward those communities.

2. *Social identity.* Many dreams revolve around people's social identities and their feelings about the highly structured roles and behaviors required of them by their communities. For people who experience a sharp disjunction between who they are and who society says they must be, dreams can become a relatively free and uncensored venue for expressing aspects of one's true self that cannot be articulated in the waking social world, perhaps even in one's own conscious awareness.

3. *Power imbalances.* The mode of social intelligence that becomes active in dreaming takes a special interest in relationships with dangerously large imbalances of social power. Bad dreams and nightmares often center on the dreamer's vulnerability to specific, actual people in society—dictators, colonizers, rapists—who possess tremendous, seemingly irresistible power over their lives. Although emotionally upsetting, these dreams can reveal valuable insights and strategies for resistance. A cultural psychology approach to nightmares seeks to interpret them not just as personal symbols of inner conflict but as social references to dangerous power imbalances in the community.

Looking at our group of seven journal keepers, Lucrecia de León stands out as one of the clearest examples in all of history of a person whose dreams reflected the concerns of her community. There were certainly personal aspects of meaning in Lucrecia's dreams, too, but she had an unusually strong capacity for dreaming about collective realities, conflicts, and crises. The nightmarish cast of her dreams expressed the perilous dangers facing Spain if Philip II did not give up his grandiose imperial ambitions and focus instead on the safety of his own people at home. Her dreams also reflected, and sharply critiqued, the immense disparity in power between Philip and his subjects. What was impossible in the waking world—a poor young woman challenging the king—became possible in her dreams, a possibility she used to call him to task for the reality of his people's suffering, their faltering religious faith, and their vulnerability to external attack. A large number of people in Madrid knew of her dream predictions of the Spanish Armada's defeat in 1588, and following that devastating naval loss, even more people began turning to Lucrecia and her dreams for guidance and insight at a time of deep communal crisis. The ultimate evidence of the social impact of her dreams was the personal order by Philip to the agents of the Spanish Inquisition to arrest Lucrecia on charges of heresy and sedition. The criticism of his rule emanating from her dreams became too much for the king to abide, hence the determination of the inquisitors to compel Lucrecia to confess to making up the dreams or forming a pact with the devil or being mentally ill—anything that would diminish her dreams as a source of legitimate commentary on Philip's rule. The intense effort to force Lucrecia to change her story, the long imprisonment, the interrogations, and the torture all derived from the king's need to reassert his power over this lone rebellious dreamer. His failure was not for lack of trying but because of Lucrecia's adamant assertion that her dreams really were expressions of insight relevant to all the people of Spain during a terrible time of collective fear and confusion.

A cultural psychology perspective also sheds light on the community-themed dreams of the other journal keepers, although not quite as dramatically as with Lucrecia. Many of the dreams of Aelius Aristides, for instance, revolved around his personal health concerns, and he spent a great deal of his time at temples in geographically secluded places in the company of other religious devotees of the healing god. His dreams include a few references to interpersonal disputes and conflicts at the temple but nothing that directly challenged or questioned the basic power structures of Roman society. Aristides did, however, derive tremendous energy and inspiration from his dreams in the creation of a new social identity, as a writer and speaker teaching other people about the healing god. Similarly, the dreams of Myōe Shonin center on his religious concerns and his pursuit of new practices to stimulate his visionary imagination in both waking and sleeping. His dreams include references to disagreements with various people, especially other Buddhist teachers whose views differed from his own, and his whole life as an ascetic monk stood in sharp opposition to the conventional social behaviors of other people. That said, monks held socially acceptable identities with well-established positions in their communities, and this was true of Myōe, too, even if he pushed the ascetic aspects of monkhood to personal extremes.

Emanuel Swedenborg and Benjamin Banneker were both scientists who lent their skills and resources to their political leaders, and both made special personal contributions during times of community crisis. Swedenborg helped the king of Sweden with a variety of civil and military engineering projects, and Banneker aided the new federal government of the United States in surveying the future site of its capital city. When Sweden's navy was trapped by its enemies, Swedenborg organized the physical overland transport of the ships to a safer port several miles away. During the American Revolutionary War, when General George Washington's troops were running low on food, Banneker gave up farming tobacco and switched to wheat, a crop he had never grown before but which was desperately needed by his country's irregular military forces. Both men had strong social identities with a high degree of public acclaim and esteem, and yet they both criticized in waking and dreaming the serious moral and spiritual failings of their communities. Swedenborg's advocacy for reason and empirical science put him increasingly at odds with the theological and political authorities of Sweden, and when his dreams propelled him into the study of mystical Christianity, he became an intellectual pariah throughout Europe. For Banneker, the simple fact of his existence as a free black man caused perpetual tension with the deeply entrenched slave system of late-eighteenth- and early-nineteenth-century America. He was one of the most brilliant men of his time, and yet at any moment, a white person could seize him, transport him to a different state, and make him a slave, and he would have no legal means of regaining his freedom. This harsh social reality seemed to filter into his dreams in a pervasive sense of danger and uncertainty, although, of course, we only have a few of his dreams to study, since someone burned Banneker's cabin and its contents to ashes right after he died. In this context, it is all the more remarkable that he persevered in publishing his almanacs, which brought him widespread praise but also drew attention from unwanted quarters to his fragile social identity as a free and independent black man.

The course of Wolfgang Pauli's life was severely disrupted by the outbreak of World War II. As the clouds of war gathered in the late 1930s, Pauli realized it was possible that Switzerland, where he had lived and worked for more than ten years, would not grant him citizenship, forcing him to return to his native Austria, where anyone with a Jewish background was vulnerable to immediate arrest and imprisonment. Thus, he was very fortunate indeed to receive a surprise invitation in 1940 to come to the United States to join the faculty of the Institute for Advanced Studies at Princeton University. Here is how he described it to Carl Jung on June 3, 1940: "In the middle of May I suddenly and quite out of the blue received an invitation to be a guest professor at Princeton, where I have already been once before. I may be leaving this week; it all depends which of the two will win the race: the passport and visa bureaucracy or the war looming up in the Mediterranean."[7]

Pauli stayed in the United States until 1946, when he returned to Switzerland and resumed his academic work there. Beyond deploring the war and the deep social and cultural divisions at its roots, Pauli did not devote a great deal of attention to the present-day concerns of his community. His focus, in waking and dreaming, was on the interplay of quantum physics and the collective unconscious. He had much less interest in the intermediate realm of human social life, a point that is often made about Jung's psychology in general. Both Pauli and Jung saw the modern world as dangerously split between its dominant conscious ideals and its repressed unconscious instincts, and they agreed that only an integration of consciousness and the unconscious at the collective level could bring an end to the spiraling violence of the twentieth century.

The life and work of Anna Kingsford show how the personal-collective dreaming dynamic can lead into powerful actions aimed at solving particular problems in the community. Kingsford took an openly and resolutely oppositional stance toward the conventional power structures of her social world. She devoted herself with astonishing energy and organizational skill to four principal causes: women's rights, vegetarianism, the antivivisection movement, and occult Christianity. In the two decades of her adulthood, she was not merely active on all these fronts but a leading public figure calling for major systemic changes to ordinary British life. If Kingsford cared about it, she did something about it, always in a pragmatic spirit, guided by reason, evidence, and the actual needs of people in her community. Taken as a whole, her causes amounted to a direct assault on the upper-class male establishment of Victorian England. Not surprisingly, the establishment replied to her in kind. At every turn, she was met with scorn, mockery, and ridicule. She persevered, however, thanks to several assets: her tremendous intelligence, driving willpower, striking eloquence, radiant beauty, and, not least, financial independence. Kingsford led a remarkably busy and socially engaged life. She was a tireless writer of books, pamphlets, and articles for popular magazines. She maintained an active medical practice focusing on women's health. She traveled frequently for public lectures, organizational meetings, and private conversations with people curious to meet such a notoriously countercultural yet brilliantly charismatic figure. And wherever she was, Kingsford was paying close attention to her daughter Eadith's education and well-being.

All of these activities and concerns appear in Kingsford's dreams, from "The City of Blood" about the horrors of vivisection to "The Enchanted

Woman" referring to social injustices against women. One of her dreams, "The Square in the Hand," involves her being arrested in France because of her political struggles "for liberty and the people's rights."[8] Throughout her life, she focused on power imbalances not only in metaphysical terms but in concrete, tangible forms in her contemporary society. She opposed materialism, atheism, dogmatism, misogyny, and cruelty to animals not just in the abstract but in every instance where she found them to be causing actual harm. If she was riding in a carriage and saw a boy in the street mistreating a dog, she would stop the carriage to chastise the boy—much to the consternation of her companions. Realizing that male physicians took no interest in women's personal grooming, exercise, and dietary practices, Kingsford wrote a short book, *Health, Beauty, and the Toilet: Letters to Ladies from a Lady Doctor*, in 1886, addressed to ordinary women who could benefit practically from accurate scientific information about how best to take care of themselves. Her mystical and theosophical pursuits never supplanted her community activities but rather infused them with greater energy.

It is possible to explore the cultural and social references in people's dreams in much greater depth than this, leading to new opportunities for meaningful insights about collective beliefs and concerns that cannot be easily recognized from a waking-world perspective alone—Eggan's key insight. This chapter's excursion into cultural psychology has tried to demonstrate some of the specific ways in which dream journals can be remarkably fruitful sources of information about collective behaviors and attitudes. For two members of our group of journal keepers—Lucrecia and Kingsford—the collective themes appeared in the vivid foreground of their dreaming. For the others, cultural references appeared in their dreams, too, less centrally and overtly but still easily identified and connected with the concerns of their communities. The presence of this aspect of dreaming in so many people across so many different places and times suggests that there is a deep unconscious potential for socially attuned dreaming that can be actualized and brought to the fore of consciousness when the right circumstances come together.

PART IV

EXPLORING DIMENSIONS OF RELIGIOSITY

The findings presented so far reveal a wide range of meanings in the dreams of these seven remarkable people. But we have not yet discussed the meanings they themselves felt were the most important and worthy of deeper exploration.

Consistently recording one's dreams in a journal seems to correlate with greater awareness of the religious, spiritual, and existential insights that emerge in the dreams over time. This is not true for absolutely everyone, but it is true for many, and there are good reasons to believe the practice of keeping a dream journal itself cultivates an increasing interest in that direction. There are, of course, multiple ways of being religious, practicing religion, and experiencing religion, and the following three chapters will use a broad and inclusive definition of "religious concerns." Many people disavow formal religious institutions and dogmas, yet they still hold personal beliefs (e.g., about the essence of human nature, what happens after death, good and evil, the origins of the world, how to lead a good life) that can be fairly referred to as religious. However, to emphasize the distinction from organized forms of religion, other terms can also be used—"spiritual," "existential," "metaphysical"—to characterize these perennial human concerns about the ultimate nature of reality and our place within it.

The chapters in this part will examine the dream-infused religiosity of this small but historically significant group of people as expressions of individualism (chapter 14), mysticism (chapter 15), and pluralism (chapter 16). These three characteristics of religious life derive from the early-twentieth-century research of William James, whose *The Varieties of Religious Experience* has been a uniquely influential text in the psychology of religion for more than one hundred years. James was one of the first to define these important concepts for the scientific study of religion, and they can help us clarify what the journal keepers found so spiritually compelling about their dreams. With the help of James plus contemporary religious studies researchers, we will look at the dynamic interplay between the dreams of our seven journal keepers and their spiritually individualist, mystical, and pluralist approaches to the world.

It should be noted at the outset that each of these three concepts represents one end of a spectrum of religiosity, with its conceptual opposite at the other end. Thus, individualism will be contrasted with communalism, the mystical with the mundane, and pluralism with monism. For each pair of conceptual opposites, there is a broad spectrum with intermediate and mixed positions between the two endpoints. In most people's lives, we can usually find a combination of elements from both sides of the spectrum. The exact midpoint between the two is not necessarily the best or healthiest place to be, nor is an optimum to be found at one or the other of the endpoints. It does seem, however, that for each of the three polarities, people who keep dream journals tend to cluster at one of the far ends—more individualist than communalist, more mystical than mundane, and more pluralist than monist. These spiritual tendencies are what the following three chapters will explore.

14

Individualism

The English word "religion" has its linguistic roots in the Latin word *religare*, which means "to bind." This suggests that an essential element of religion is to be bound to something of great importance—to a group, a faith, a God. The word gained currency in medieval Europe in reference to the practices of Christian monks, whose lifelong vows of obedience bound them to a monastic order. Since then, the term has expanded its range of usage beyond Christianity to encompass other cultures and traditions in which people bind themselves to groups, faiths, and gods. In the modern academic field of religious studies, debate continues over the best definition of the term, but many researchers agree that religion is fundamentally about people's close, committed involvement with a community of shared faith. Hence, we find textbook definitions like the following, which appeared in *The Psychology of Religious Belief, Behavior, and Experience*, by Benjamin Beit-Hallahmi and Michael Argyle (1997): "Religion is a system of beliefs in divine or superhuman power, and practices of worship or other rituals directed towards such a power."[1]

The present chapter looks at dream journals in relation to the twin concepts of religious individualism and religious communalism. As a way of beginning, I would note that a definition of religion like the one above presumes communalism as the norm and casts individualism as something of a problem. A social context is required for systems of belief, practices of worship, and rituals to emerge, which implies that a social group is the necessary predicate for authentic religion. A person who is *not* bound to the systematic beliefs, practices, and rituals of a faith community necessarily falls outside this definition of religion. It seems an individualist cannot also be religious, if being religious means yielding to the centripetal pull of the group. The individualist resists that pull. Can this resistance itself be a form of religion? According to an exclusively communalist definition of religion, no. But if we look beyond this element of social binding, we are free to consider alternative definitions of religion—even alternatives that hark back to much earlier times in religious studies. Here is how William James put

The Scribes of Sleep. Kelly Bulkeley, Oxford University Press. © Oxford University Press 2023.
DOI: 10.1093/oso/9780197609606.003.0015

it in *The Varieties of Religious Experience*, from 1902: "Religion, therefore, as I now ask you arbitrarily to take it, shall mean for us *the feelings, acts, and experiences of individual men in their solitude, so far as they apprehend themselves to stand in relation to whatever they may consider the divine*."[2] Setting aside the gender exclusivity, this is obviously a much more individualist view of religion than the Beit-Hallahmi and Argyle definition. James has been criticized by later generations of scholars on this very issue, saying that his approach is too individualist, too Protestant, too Western. But that criticism misses the important benefits that come from conceiving religion in Jamesian terms. First, it can be applied to people who do not belong to or participate in a formal religious tradition but who still have a strong sense of connection to whatever they consider to be the ultimate powers of the universe. In present-day American society, the rising percentage of people who are "nones," that is, who do not explicitly affiliate with any particular religious group or creed, has prompted concerns about religion's declining influence and worsening conflicts with secular culture. James's approach to religion enables us to dispel these concerns and recognize the authentically religious lives of many of the nones, despite their unconventional ways of relating to the divine.

Second, this definition justifies James's turn to a psychological approach to religion, with a specific focus on what he called the *subconscious* regions of the mind, or what we are calling the *unconscious*. Sigmund Freud and Carl Jung are rightly considered pioneers in developing the concept of the unconscious, but James recognized even earlier than they did the potential for applying this concept to the study of religion. In *Varieties*, he describes how the most intensely religious people tend to have the strongest flow of unconscious material into their conscious minds:

> Let me then propose, as an hypothesis, that whatever it may be on its farther side, the "more" with which in religious experience we feel ourselves connected is on its hither side the subconscious continuation of our conscious life. . . . In the religious life the control is felt as "higher"; but since on our hypothesis it is primarily the higher faculties of our own hidden mind which are controlling, the sense of union with the power beyond us is a sense of something, not merely apparently, but literally true.[3]

This hypothesis implies that a psychological focus on the dynamics of the unconscious can be a helpful way of illuminating the essence of religion.

As already mentioned, people in their actual religious lives tend to embody elements from both sides of a polarity such as individualism and communalism. It is rarely all one or all the other or a perfect balance between. In that context, it is even more remarkable how strongly the qualities of individualist religiosity emerge in the lives of the seven people whose dream journals we have been exploring. This can be seen most easily in its negative form, in their anti-communal behaviors and convictions. To take the most vivid example from chapter 13, Anna Kingsford was effectively a one-woman army battling against the dominant collective values of Victorian England. As an expression of her deepest religious beliefs, she felt called to fight her community and its traditions, not bind herself to them. In her relatively brief life, Kingsford attacked British culture on multiple fronts, sharply questioning long-hallowed beliefs about gender, health, medicine, animals, literature, and religion. She was involved in countless public debates that played out in the London newspapers, where her opponents mocked her arguments and repeatedly emphasized the fact of her being a woman as an obvious disqualification for even participating in such discussions, let alone having the audacity to call for a fundamental transformation of their cultural traditions. At a time when the British Empire had reached perhaps the zenith of its global power and preeminence, Kingsford deliberately set herself apart from her community's reigning spiritual values and moral principles. She was not an extreme individualist, however. She held to an abiding hope that her community could learn, grow, and become better in the future. That ultimately religious hope motivated her to stay engaged with her community and continue struggling rather than withdraw into a simpler life of morally pure isolation.

A similar dynamic can be seen in the life and dreams of Lucrecia de León. She had virtually none of the freedoms that Kingsford enjoyed, but by sharing her dreams, she found an unusual opportunity to articulate anti-communal feelings and ideas, far beyond what one would expect from a young servant-class woman in her place and time. Indeed, it is hard to exaggerate the magnitude of Lucrecia's defiance against Philip II, the hereditary sovereign of Spain, "the most Catholic king," the supreme ruler of the greatest empire the world had ever known. Her status was near the bottom of society, his at the very top. Yet in her dreams, she held a morally and religiously superior position to him. Lucrecia was not an individualist in the sense of rejecting her Catholic faith or her devotion to Spain, but in her dreams, she expressed a strongly anti-communal tone toward the king and his current policies, specifically his failure to protect the Spanish people. Like Kingsford's, Lucrecia's harsh criticism of her community was motivated by a hope for a better future for everyone, a future that could only be reached if the terrible problems and injustices of the present were finally overcome.

Both Aelius Aristides and Myōe Shonin pursued anti-communal religious paths that involved explicit rejections of conventional social behaviors. Aristides turned away from his traditional education and devoted himself instead to the dreams and visions he received while sleeping at the temples of the healing god Asclepius. Myōe was an ascetic monk who deliberately practiced a way of life that dismissed conventional social activities as irrelevant distractions from higher religious concerns. However, as much as Aristides and Myōe set themselves apart from the mainstream of their communities, they still held on to recognizable, well-established social identities—as a religious devotee, as a monk—that connected their individualist pursuits to the greater sphere of their present-day communities. They were socially rebellious but in socially acceptable ways. Kingsford and Lucrecia did not have the benefit of this cultural option for religious individualism. Their unorthodox social identities were continually challenged and attacked, and their anti-communal dreams and visions looked beyond the corruption of the present toward a more just community in the future.

The anti-communal activities of Emanuel Swedenborg, Benjamin Banneker, and Wolfgang Pauli took forms that were less explicitly confrontational but just as directly aimed at collective transformation. Swedenborg's turn from the Swedish king's favorite engineer to mystical outcast and intellectual laughingstock was not simply a social withdrawal; it was an effort to stimulate a radical change in the conventional religious beliefs of his community, by teaching them a new way to read and understand the Bible.

Banneker lived under a constantly threatening shadow of racial violence, so his anti-communal energies had to be exercised with the greatest caution. And yet, within these strict limits, he found in the study of the heavens a means to access higher truths and realities that transcended the ignorant boundaries of his community, enabling him to establish a new, revolutionary kind of social identity in America—a free black intellectual.

The external circumstances of Pauli's life had little drama or action and no anti-communal activism. Other than fleeing from a Swiss university to an American university during World War II, he had a fairly conventional existence, working as a teacher in socially prestigious institutions. And yet his research helped lead a seismic change in our understanding of the fundamental nature of reality. Along with Albert Einstein, Werner Heisenberg, Niels Bohr, and other pioneers of quantum physics, Pauli overthrew the common-sense view of how the world works and revolutionized our most basic conceptions of matter, causality, time, and energy. Crucially, he and his colleagues proved that human consciousness is inseparable from the external world. The world manifests not as a separate, objective reality but as it relates to our consciousness and its intentions. A more successful anti-communal assault on conventional Western metaphysics could hardly be imagined. (Pauli foresaw even bigger changes to come: "Indeed I myself even conjecture that the observer in present-day physics *is still too completely detached*, and that physics will depart still further from the classical example.")[4]

An individualistic religiosity shows itself in other ways, too, beyond the negative work of critique and analysis. A more positive aspect is having a high degree of trust in one's own reason, experience, and intuition. On the spectrum of trusting oneself versus trusting external authorities, all seven members of our group of dream journalists stand at the farthest reaches of the individualist pole. Aristides put so much trust in his inner resources that when he became sick with a potentially life-threatening illness, he defied the urgent advice of the best human physicians available and did everything his dreams and visions told him to do, no matter how strange or irrational. Myōe oriented his monastic activities around his lifelong yearning for experiential encounters with the living Buddha; no group rituals or traditional teachings could provide him with this, only a deep immersion in the visionary realities that spontaneously emerged while he was dreaming or meditating. Lucrecia endured years of persecution, imprisonment, and abuse rather than deny the authenticity of her dreams. The key feature of Swedenborg's personal transformation in midlife was a vigorous turn inward, during which he cultivated maximal openness toward the world of his dreams, visions, and other internal manifestations of spiritual insight. Banneker's strong trust in his own judgment and intellect can be seen in many aspects of his life, from his determination to build a working clock out of wood and scrap metal, to his self-education in mathematics and engineering, to his lifelong practice of personally tracking the movements of the stars and planets and carefully recording his observations for further analysis. The Bible always remained a sacred text for him, but Banneker's primary means of worshipping the divine was by discerning the grand rhythms of the cosmos. His almanacs are remarkable testaments of individualist religiosity.

Kingsford followed her own personal intuitions, although she was clear that she did not consider them authoritative for other people. By the same token, she refused to consider other people's personal intuitions as authoritative for her. During the nineteenth century, the spiritualist movement was rising in popularity in Europe and America, with increasing interest in seances at which the spirits of the dead were summoned forth to speak to the living. Also popular was theosophy, a blend of Western esotericism and anglicized Hindu teachings, with Helena Blavatsky as a leading figure who relayed the ethereal teachings of a spirit guide from India who spoke only to her. Although she admired theosophy, Kingsford tried to distance herself from these practices. She appreciated Blavatsky's ideas about non-Christian traditions, occult spirituality, and alternative health practices, but she ultimately saw them as equally as dogmatic as the Church of England or the Catholic Church in terms of asking the followers to trust an external authority rather than their own inner judgment. In response to a controversy over the discovery that Blavatsky's ancient Hindu spirit guide had apparently plagiarized teachings from a book recently published in America, Kingsford said she was glad the incident occurred:

[I]t gives me a good occasion of expressing my mistrust of all appeal to authority, and my conviction that no system having historical data and persons as its nuclei will ever successfully contend with time and criticism. I look with sorrow and concern on the growing tendency of the Theosophical Society to introduce into its method the superstitions; the exaggerated veneration for persons and for personal authority; an element which has been the ruin of every other religious system in the past, and the inevitable outcome of which is a mere servile hero-worship, degenerating into the substitution of events for processes; of personalities for principles; of authority for reason; of history for experience.[5]

This is the spirit of a religious individualist, expressed in Kingsford's forceful prose. The sorrow she felt stemmed from her disappointment that even the Theosophical Society, with its high moral aspirations, could not escape this temptation. She had come to expect the Church of England and the Catholic Church to maintain their power by using authority to cow people into submission. There was nothing surprising or disappointing about that. But she had greater hopes for theosophy, and when those hopes were dashed, her distress was especially acute.

In his final writings, Pauli turned increasingly to philosophical questions of mind and consciousness, searching for a transcendent language to account for the integrated nature of reality. Dissatisfied with conventional concepts in physics and psychology and trusting his own intellectual ability to do better, Pauli followed the individualist's path and tried (with Jung's active encouragement) to forge something entirely new, something no one had been able to do before. Earlier in his career, he displayed a remarkable ability to generate major scientific discoveries based purely on internal reasoning and insight, when in 1930, he postulated the existence of a third subatomic particle besides the proton and the electron, which he called the "neutron." More than twenty years later, experimental physicists confirmed the existence of what we now call neutrinos, thus validating Pauli's determination to trust his own personal powers of reasoning over what conventional authorities told him.

A widely used method that researchers have developed to examine these aspects of religion is to distinguish between *extrinsic* and *intrinsic* religiosity.[6] These terms refer to two different understandings of religion, two different ways religion manifests in people's lives. According to studies of survey data from tens of thousands of participants, some people primarily view religion in utilitarian terms, as something *useful*, as a means to an end such as higher social status, moral self-control, comfort in suffering, and protection from danger. For them, religion is important not in itself but insofar as it can help them succeed in life and accomplish their nonreligious goals. This is extrinsic religiosity, and many of its characteristics correspond to the communalist end of the spectrum we have been considering in this chapter. By contrast, other people regard religion as an *end in itself*, not a means. Religion for them is something that permeates their whole life and centers on an inner awareness of the presence of the divine. In terms of religious practice, they are less likely to find group rituals meaningful and are more likely to pray, meditate, and reflect in private. This is intrinsic religiosity, and its characteristics have especially strong connections to religious individualism as is being discussing here.

Although we cannot here make use of the survey methods employed in the development of the extrinsic/intrinsic scale, we can still observe and appreciate how closely the religious beliefs, experiences, and practices of the seven dream journalists map onto the intrinsic end of the scale. *Is religion an all-embracing way of life?* Certainly yes for Aristides and Myōe and yes for Lucrecia, too; the inquisitors accused her of many heretical and traitorous acts, but they never questioned the depth of her personal piety. Religion was definitely all-embracing for Swedenborg and Kingsford and for Banneker and Pauli, too, if an expanded sense of religion can include innovative scientific explorations into the fundamental workings of the cosmos. *Do they have an inner sense of the divine?* Yes, they all do, in their dreams and in various aspects of their waking lives. *Do they gravitate away from group rituals and toward private reflections?* Mostly, yes. Myōe, Swedenborg, Banneker, Kingsford, and Pauli had many connections with social groups in their communities, but they all sought long and frequent opportunities for reflective solitude. An exception might be Aristides, who participated in public ceremonies and dream incubation rites with the other people at the Asclepian temples, although these practices were aimed at eliciting a powerful inner experience that prompted a great deal of private reflection. Similarly, Lucrecia and her mother visited numerous churches and cathedrals throughout Madrid, sometimes participating in several masses every week. And yet what Lucrecia seemed to learn from these experiences, and what manifested within the internally reflective space of her dreams, was a deeply skeptical view of the king and the church and their capacity to help the people of Spain during a time of national crisis. For her, the collective rituals had the paradoxically antisocial effect of stimulating highly critical dreams of the alarming vulnerability of her present-day community.

The extrinsic/intrinsic dichotomy, despite its limits as a general measure, does help to clarify one specific and widely recognized aspect of religion, namely, how it orients people toward their social groups. For many, if not most, people, religion is one interest among many, and it is communally practiced and experienced. For other people, probably the minority in most societies, religion is the central interest of their lives, which they pursue less in collective rituals and more in practices of individualist spirituality. From our perspective, the polarity of extrinsic versus intrinsic religiosity illuminates an important shared tendency among the seven dream journalists. The behaviors attributed to extrinsically religious people are almost entirely absent in the lives of these dream journalists, while the behaviors of the intrinsically religious can be found in abundance.

Some of the criticism of the original extrinsic/intrinsic research involved offering alternative models to account for a wider range of religious behavior observed around the world. The most frequently used of these alternatives offered a third category of religiosity; in addition to religion as a *means* (extrinsic) and religion as an *end* (intrinsic), there is religion as a *quest*.

According to Gregory Bateson's initial formulation of the quest scale, it was designed to measure "the degree to which an individual's religion involves an open-ended, responsive dialogue with existential questions raised by the contradictions and tragedies of life."[7] The new scale served as a way of distinguishing between two significantly different types of intrinsic religiosity: one that settles on a single source of religious truth and another that actively seeks new and better ways of accessing religiously meaningful insights. Bateson emphasizes the active energy inherent in the quest type of religiosity and its distinctive openness to change and transformation. This resonates strongly with the lives of the seven dream journalists, who certainly did not rest content with their religious and spiritual beliefs but continually tested them against new experiential insights, always pushing themselves toward greater understanding and awareness of divine presence in human life. It is no coincidence that four of the dream journalists were accomplished scientists who applied the experimental method to aspects of their own lives in waking and dreaming—closely observing and documenting their experiences, identifying spiritually significant patterns, testing possible interpretations, and reflecting on the practical results. This unfolding cycle of active dialogical engagement with one's dreams over time is the hallmark of keeping a dream journal. Indeed, we could propose that dream journalists are representatives par excellence of the quest type of religiosity. To make a regular practice of recording one's dreams in a journal and tracking their meanings over time is almost by definition a commitment to "an open-ended, responsive dialogue with existential questions raised by the contradictions and tragedies of life."

The dynamic energies of quest religiosity make it difficult to become too attached or bound to a traditional religious community. These restless spiritual yearnings inevitably propel a person of the quest type in an individualist direction, motivating strenuous activities to bring their personal religious intuitions into the world. In a similar vein, James spoke admiringly of a "heroic" quality in the religious lives of some people, whom he described as "saintly" in their radical selflessness, passionate devotion to worshipping the divine, and boundless concern for the well-being of others.[8] However, James also lamented the limited methods for cultivating these supreme fruits of religious experience. Extreme asceticism and self-mortification can be effective means of developing saintly qualities, but they are grisly in practice and just as likely to coarsen one's consciousness as to elevate it. War and military training can stimulate saintly levels of passionate activity and disregard for personal welfare but only at the cost of turning all that energy toward destruction and death. This prompts James to ask:

> Is it not possible for us to discard most of these older forms of mortification, and yet find saner channels for the heroism which inspired them? . . . What we now need to discover in the social realm is the moral equivalent of war: something heroic that will speak to men as universally as war does, and yet will be as compatible with their spiritual selves as war has proved itself to be incompatible.[9]

The seven dream journalists considered here were not saints in James's definition, but they certainly led spiritually heroic and strenuous lives. A few of them (Aristides, Myōe, Kingsford) developed bodily regimes and dietary practices with varying degrees of self-control and ascetic intensity. Lucrecia did not ask to spend five years imprisoned by the Inquisition, but she was willing to endure the severe privations of her captive condition rather than repudiate the authenticity of her dreams. Swedenborg, Banneker, and Pauli all faced numerous challenges to their beliefs and their ways of making sense of the world, and they responded vigorously to these challenges by trying to explain their admittedly unorthodox ideas in terms that others could understand. All seven of them found in their dreams an individualized path toward spiritual growth and insight, a path that ultimately transformed into a lifelong journey of religious discovery.

15

Mysticism

Chapter 14 showed that the practice of keeping a dream journal is closely correlated with individualist types of religion and spirituality. We cannot say for sure whether the causal influence moves in one direction or the other— whether recording dreams in a journal makes people more inclined toward individualist religiosity or people who are already religious individualists find it especially interesting to keep a dream journal or, as seems most likely, a mutual dynamic emerges between the types of people who are drawn to dream journals and the spiritual impact of tracking one's dreams over time. Research in this area is too limited to determine the exact causal relations between individualist religiosity and dream-journaling practice. What we can do, however, is identify and describe more precisely the distinctive qualities of each side of the relationship. This will not settle the ultimate question of causality (if it can ever be settled), but it will enhance our understanding of the spiritually transformative powers that can be generated when certain types of people turn their energies toward keeping a dream journal. This chapter considers our group of seven dream journalists as religious individualists who are also mystics.

Mysticism is a general term used in religious studies to designate practices and experiences involving extreme alterations of consciousness, leading to otherworldly visions, secret revelations, and absorption into the divine. Forms of mystical religiosity can be found in cultures all over the world, although always as a relatively rare and intensified form of spiritual life. Most people, communalists and individualists alike, tend *not* to be mystical in their religiosity. They do not have visions, receive revelations, or strive to disrupt, decenter, or overthrow their ordinary state of consciousness. Their spiritual lives can be active and fulfilling in many other ways—through moral causes, group ceremonies, caregiving practices, family traditions, quiet prayer—but they are grounded in the world of ordinary here-and-now reality. If mystical religiosity is placed at one end of a spectrum, we can refer to the other end, with no disrespect, as *mundane* religiosity. And we can immediately add that although the lives of most people are spent on the mundane side of the

The Scribes of Sleep. Kelly Bulkeley, Oxford University Press. © Oxford University Press 2023.
DOI: 10.1093/oso/9780197609606.003.0016

spectrum, few people are entirely, absolutely, 100 percent mundane in their spiritual lives. In other words, some degree of mystical experience occurs to many people whose religious behaviors are otherwise quite ordinary and this-worldly.[1]

William James considered himself a religiously mundane person, not prone to mystical flights of ecstasy and enlightenment. However, in *The Varieties of Religious Experience*, he described his experiments with the mental and spiritual effects of inhaling nitrous oxide, "which stimulate[s] the mystical consciousness in an extraordinary degree."[2] These experiments also gave him a sense of the limits and potential deceptiveness of mystical consciousness. When under the influence of nitrous oxide,

> Depth beyond depth of truth seems revealed to the inhaler. This truth fades out, however, or escapes, at the moment of coming to; and if any words remain over in which it seemed to clothe itself, they prove to be the veriest nonsense. Nevertheless, the sense of a profound meaning having been there persists. . . . One conclusion was forced upon my mind at that time [of these experiments], and my impression of its truth has ever since remained unshaken. It is that our normal waking consciousness, rational consciousness as we call it, is but one special type of consciousness, whilst all about it, parted from it by the filmiest of screens, there lie potential forms of consciousness entirely different.[3]

James's experiences with nitrous oxide provided him with a psychological template for identifying mystical types of religiosity. In a mystical experience, the influence of ordinary consciousness is suspended or reduced to a minimum, and other, usually hidden dimensions of consciousness emerge. Although this can become an extreme form of religiosity cultivated and pursued by relatively few people, James believed that it provided a special window into the basic nature and transformative value of religion in human life. To help identify instances of mysticism in various cultural and historical settings, he offered the following four descriptive characteristics, or *marks*, of mystical experience.

1. *Ineffability*. People often find it difficult or impossible to describe in ordinary language what transpired during a mystical state. This can lead to expressive efforts that sound, to non-mystical ears, completely bizarre and deranged. James was puzzled by his own linguistic

"nonsense" following his nitrous experiments, but he attributed this to an overwhelming surplus of meaning and insight, not to a degraded functioning of his language abilities.

2. *Noetic quality.* Mystical experiences convey a kind of knowledge, or *gnosis*, about alternative realities, transpersonal beings, secret truths, and future potentials. This knowledge is felt to be extremely important, valuable, and relevant to the concerns of ordinary reality—so important that the ineffability of the insights can be painful, prompting urgently creative efforts to communicate the mystical discoveries in terms that others in the community can understand and put into practice in their own lives.

3. *Transiency.* This mark refers to the inevitability of a shift out of the mystical mode back into an ordinary mode of consciousness. However long the mystical experience may last in chronological time, there is always a return to the non-mystical world and thus a loss of that state of knowledge and insight—another source of emotional pain and distress for those who are mystically inclined. James does acknowledge the possibility that someone could cultivate a series of mystical experiences and through a process of "continuous development" enhance their "inner richness and importance."[4]

4. *Passivity.* Even if elaborate preparations have been made to elicit a mystical state, the experience itself is felt to be passive in the sense of an acute awareness of powers vastly greater than oneself. It involves a temporary suspension of the ordinary concerns, intentions, and defenses of the waking ego, as the deepest energies of the unconscious rise like a tidal wave and, for a few moments, at least, completely overwhelm the mystic with surging, swirling currents of cosmic awareness and existential insight.

Viewed in the light of these Jamesian marks, the seven dream journalists appear to be mystics of a rather unusual kind. To begin with, they were all skilled communicators who showed little indication of struggling with the ineffability of their experiences. On the contrary, they all devoted tremendous amounts of time and energy to bringing their dreams, visions, and other mystical insights into a language that other people could understand. There is, of course, an inevitable gap between the immediate experience of a dream and the later recollection of it, which means there is always some degree of ineffability in a dream report. But for people with frequent and vivid dream recall, like our seven dream journalists, this gap is much narrower than for most people. This enables much more detailed descriptions of mystically charged dream experiences than what James found with his nitrous oxide episodes.

As an ongoing literary practice, keeping a dream journal seems to enhance the "effability" of precious mystical insights that would otherwise be lost to the inadequacy of language. It certainly helps to have innate talent and a good education, too. Aelius Aristides, for instance, received extensive training in rhetoric and oratory in his youth, and this made it easier to comply when Asclepius first beckoned him to record his dreams and write a book in praise of the god's oneiric powers. It also helped that the Asclepian temples had a long tradition of encouraging grateful patients to inscribe their stories of illness and dream-mediated cures on stone markers and marble plaques scattered around the temple grounds. For Aristides, a vivid dreamer with an excellent literary education, the cultural environment of the temples enabled him to articulate depths of mystical experience that might not have been capable of expression in any other setting. Much the same could be said of Myōe Shonin, a naturally vivid, high-recall dreamer with literary training who immersed himself in a religious tradition that especially prized the experience of visionary dreams and tried to communicate their value and importance to others in the community. Myōe spent much of his time in solitary monastic pursuits, but he was also an active writer and teacher trying to share his spiritual insights with others, and he turned more in this direction as he grew older. His life in waking and dreaming was filled with otherworldly dreams and visions, and he had the literary skill to describe these mystical experiences with precisely detailed language.

Lucrecia de León did not receive a formal education comparable to what Aristides or Myōe received, but she had an extremely high frequency of intense dreams from an early age and a well-developed verbal fluency, especially on the topics of religious prophecy and spiritual visions. Although she could not write down her own dreams, she was able to record them over time with the help of a church-appointed scribe. The free-flowing abundance of her mystical dreams was precisely what Don Alonso found so compelling about her. Unlike the "street prophets" and their unpredictable, elusive, and ambiguously expressed visions, Lucrecia provided Don Alonso and his priestly colleagues with a consistent stream of vividly detailed mystical dreamscapes. Her dream experiences were strange and otherworldly, but they were not ineffable.

The same dynamic can be observed among the other dream journalists. Emanuel Swedenborg maintained a careful record of his dreams during the crucial period of 1743–1745, when he made his pivot from scientist-engineer to mystical theologian, and he expressed no special anxiety about his capacity to document these experiences in a reasonably full and accurate fashion. On the contrary, the dreams seemed to stimulate him to go beyond simply recording them to elaborating at great length on their spiritual significance. Swedenborg wrote several massive tomes in the later part of his life, explaining in systematic terms how the insights from his dreams correlated with the hidden symbolic meanings of the Bible and current knowledge about the nature of the solar system and the universe as a whole. Again, ineffability was not a problem for Swedenborg. Nor was it for Benjamin Banneker, although fewer written texts of his survive to indicate how far he went in articulating the mystical insights of his dreams. The "dream-story" he wrote, about seeing people condemned to eternity in hell while others ascend to heaven, gives evidence of his literary capacity to convey the essential qualities of an experience from a radically altered state of consciousness. Anna Kingsford was prolific dream recaller, a skilled writer, and a charismatic speaker; her mystical dreams took her to realms far beyond the reach of ordinary language, but she still found literary methods enabling her to successfully communicate the spiritual insights of these experiences. Wolfgang Pauli went perhaps the farthest in seeking a new, transcendent language that would overcome the limits of ordinary words and concepts, enabling people to communicate truths that derive equally from physical and psychological realities. In his own dreams, he found evidence of integrative symbolic images that could serve as the building blocks of this new language. Pauli did not concede the ineffability of his experiences; on the contrary, he felt it his scientific responsibility to communicate them to others as clearly as he could.

All in all, the experiences of this group do not fit well with the first Jamesian mark of mysticism. If anything, their dream journals display the opposite tendency, toward what we might call "hyper-effability," a sustained and highly energetic impulse to express their experiences in a linguistic form that others can understand.

The dream journalists *do* fit closely with the second Jamesian mark, insofar as their dreams revealed various kinds of extraordinary knowledge that could not be accessed in ordinary states of consciousness. Everything that James said about the noetic qualities of mystical insights is directly applicable to their dream experiences. Turning the point around, the special kinds of knowledge gained by the dream journalists can illuminate what James meant by this second mark. Mystically inspired noetic insights can stimulate scientific knowledge about the fundamental workings of the universe (Swedenborg, Banneker, and Pauli), therapeutic knowledge about healing and spiritual growth (Aristides, Myōe), and cultural knowledge about the practical concerns and looming dangers facing one's local community (Lucrecia, Kingsford). Considering the visionary power of these people's dreams and their many impressive accomplishments in waking life (scientific, technological, artistic, political), we can appreciate how their dream journal practices stand forth as a remarkably accessible, powerful, and multifaceted source of mystical gnosis.

The third mark that James associated with mysticism, transiency, can be applied to every dream as its own limited, time-bound, self-contained experience. When we wake up from sleep, dreaming ceases. The inevitability of the fact that every dream, no matter how spiritually ecstatic and illuminating, must end with waking resonates with what James meant by the transiency of mystical experiences, as evidenced by his own brief moments of noetic insight under the influence of nitrous oxide. However, if we consider dreams not in isolation but in relation to other dreams, as an unfolding series over time, then the mark of transiency has less applicability. The process of keeping a dream journal defies mystical transiency and cultivates an ongoing awareness of dreaming experience through the course of one's life, an awareness that can grow and develop if additional efforts are made. The dream incubation practices at the Asclepian temples strongly supported those kinds of amplifying efforts for Aristides, and so did the monastic practices of medieval Buddhism for Myōe. The Catholic priests of Madrid helped Lucrecia nurture and expand her dreaming abilities (until suddenly they didn't). The scientific training of Swedenborg, Banneker, Kingsford, and Pauli gave them an appreciation for a longitudinal perspective, for observing phenomena as they unfold over time, carefully analyzing their patterns, and identifying the deeper principles that emerge.

Here again, James's paradigmatic case of inhaling nitrous oxide seems misleading as a way of characterizing all mystical experiences. With dream journals, the quality of mystical transience can be overcome by the consistency and longevity of the practice. A more enduring awareness of the noetic insights from all the dreams in a series can be developed and maintained in this way. As I noted when introducing the four marks, James recognized that mystical experiences are capable, through a process of "continuous development," of being enhanced in their "inner richness and importance."[5] He never specified what such a process of long-term mystical amplification would look like, but everything discussed in this book suggests that keeping a dream journal fits the bill.

The passivity of mystical experience as conceived by James is, in one sense, definitional of dreaming. When we go to sleep and dream, we withdraw our senses from the external world, yield to the muscle-relaxing atonia that prevents us from physically moving (except for the eyes under closed lids), and surrender our waking ego as the energetic processes of the unconscious mind come to the fore. Both physically and psychologically, dreaming is a condition of extreme passivity. If, as James argued, religious experiences emerge from a suspension of ordinary waking consciousness and an opening to the imaginal dynamism of the unconscious, then dreaming seems to provide optimal conditions for mystical receptivity.

And yet within its own sphere, dreaming can be extremely active, involving vigorous bodily movements, purposeful actions, and high-level cognitive functions (such as self-awareness or lucidity). Some of the most spiritually powerful dreams experienced by this group of dream journalists— Kingsford's runaway train, Myōe's mating turtles, Banneker's "infernal Spirit"—are full of self-directed action and movement. It may be accurate to characterize the *process* of dreaming as "passive" but not the *experience* of dreaming. The seven journalists are also active, not passive, in regard to their *preparations* for dreaming. They put tremendous effort into recording their dreams, preserving them, studying their meanings, enacting their insights in waking life, and trying various ways of stimulating new ones. These practices enhance their receptivity not just for one night's dream but for a lifetime of dreaming. We might call this a kind of "active passivity" in which a maximally inviting space is created for the autonomous emergence of mystical dreams.

What can emerge in these dreams is, by definition, not caused by the waking ego and thus is likely to appear surprising, startling, and incomprehensible ("the veriest nonsense"). James argued that in these moments, the virtues of radical humility and open-mindedness are crucial. Without them, people can turn their mystical insights into ego-driven fantasies that have the potential to do enormous damage to themselves and others. This is not an issue with the seven dream journalists, however, none of whom showed any signs of confusing themselves with the divine powers that manifested in their dreams. Aristides formed a very close relationship in his dreams with the god

Asclepius, and he did have dreams in which he felt a divine transcendence, but he never completely lost himself in the experience, nor did he awaken with the belief that he had become a god himself. Myōe also had numerous interactions in his dreams with divine beings, and in some of these dreams, he acquired seemingly magical powers, but he always awakened from these dreams with a grounded sense of himself as Myōe the monk. With Lucrecia, there was no evidence in her waking life that she was conflating herself with the divine beings she encountered in her dreams, even though the inquisitors tried their hardest to prove otherwise. Although Swedenborg and Kingsford had impressively far-flung adventures and memorable encounters with numinous beings in their dreams, they maintained their personal sense of human identity when they awoke. More than that, they treated their dreams as scientific data from which they could gain important new insights. This was the approach of Banneker and Pauli toward their dreams, too. They were open to whatever came and willing to be surprised, constantly. The practice of recording their dreams over time made it clear that whatever the ultimate source of their nocturnal visions, it was *not* the waking ego. This point is worth underscoring. Keeping a dream journal strongly encourages a more tangible and immediate awareness of the living reality of the unconscious, non-ego parts of the mind. It is fair to say that this group of dream journalists generally maintained a sense of well-grounded humility in relation to the transcendent powers and mystical insights of their dreams.

The Jamesian approach suggests that the seven dream journalists were mystics of a somewhat unusual kind. Their religious dream experiences were filled with noetic insights, but they were not ineffable, transient, or passive in the exact sense in which James used the terms. Dreams themselves can have qualities of ineffability, transience, and passivity, but as we have seen, the practice of keeping a journal seems to have the effect of helping people more fully articulate their mystical dream experiences, extend their memorability, and stimulate more active engagement with these extraordinary dimensions of consciousness.

A more contemporary approach to the study of religion can help clarify further what exactly distinguishes dream journals from other sources of mystical experience. The "modes of religiosity" theory of anthropologist Harvey Whitehouse proposes two fundamentally different ways in which people act, think, and behave religiously.[6] The more common of these two ways Whitehouse calls the *doctrinal mode*. Doctrinal religiosity involves relatively minimal commitment and low emotional arousal, centering on regular gatherings of large groups of people, with a focus on traditional teachings and systems of belief. Religion becomes bigger and more formalized in the doctrinal mode, with weaker social bonds between individual members but more institutional resilience and consistency over time. According to Whitehouse, doctrinal religiosity depends on the mind's capacity for *procedural memory*, which enables us to remember how to perform specific actions and sequences of behavior—for example, opening a door, brushing your teeth, or performing in a group ritual. The less common approach Whitehouse calls the *imagistic mode* of religiosity, which involves groups that are smaller and more intense, with unorthodox beliefs and minimally structured practices that generate high degrees of emotional arousal and spontaneous behavior. Imagistic religiosity depends on the cognitive system responsible for *episodic memory*, which becomes active when we have especially impactful experiences with ongoing relevance for our lives—for example, a first kiss, the death of a loved one, a spiritual revelation.

The doctrinal/imagistic dichotomy highlights a key element in the experiences of the dream journalists, one that I have not yet discussed: their emotionally arousing imagery. James's approach to mysticism tends to emphasize the contemplative, transcendent, emotionally detached aspects of mysticism. Some religiously significant dreams have those aspects, too, with a sense of boundless serenity and peace. However, many other revelatory dreams are overflowing with intense characters, lively settings, and emotionally stimulating actions, more like what Whitehouse describes as the realm of imagistic religiosity. The seven journalists provide many examples of dreams with clear qualities of the imagistic mode—Aristides's visions of the goddess Athena, Lucrecia's nightmares of the streets of Madrid flowing with blood, Swedenborg's mysterious stream of holy water from above. Viewing these powerful dreams in light of Whitehouse's modes of religiosity theory enables us to add another layer of precision to our understanding of their mystical qualities. For these seven people, keeping a dream journal became a practice of documenting their visually intense and emotionally arousing mystical experiences.

Two other concepts from Whitehouse's theory also apply here, what I would define as the urge with imagistic religiosity to *share* and *interpret* one's experiences. In contrast to the doctrinal mode's large, long-term groups with weak social bonds, the imagistic mode involves the creation of small, intimate groups with intense social bonds. Rather than performing traditional rituals, people in the imagistic mode gather closely with a few people to share their unorthodox but highly impactful religious experiences. Whitehouse talks of an innate cognitive impulse toward "spontaneous exegetical reflection" that arises immediately after a mystical experience, which is an awkward phrase that gets at something very important with religiously significant dreams. All of the dream journalists were individualist mystics, and yet they all had a very close companion or small group of intimates—human and otherwise—who helped them interpret their vividly imagistic dream experiences and make sense of what they were learning. Aristides had Asclepius, Myōe had the Buddha, Lucrecia had Don Alonso, Swedenborg had God, Banneker had the stars, Kingsford had Maitland, and Pauli had Jung. This was a very different kind of sociality from what typically occurs in doctrinal religiosity but almost identical to what Whitehouse says is characteristic of imagistic religiosity. The dream journalists had relationships that were fewer in number but closer and more intimate in quality. They relied on these few intense relationships to help them complete the process of bringing their powerfully imagistic dreams into the world and actualizing their insights. A deeper appreciation of the mystical qualities of keeping a dream journal thus leads to the surprising recognition of relational intimacy—of close, trusted friends—as a necessary element in fully manifesting the religious potentials of dreaming.

16

Pluralism

Now that the mystical qualities present in the dreams of the seven dream journalists have been highlighted, we can look more closely at the mystical qualities that seem *absent* from their experiences. The dreams of this group of people rarely involved feelings of total union with God and absorption in the divine, nor did they include a disembodied state of emotion-free detachment and emptiness. In that sense, these were not "classic" mystical experiences, such as might be experienced at the height of meditation or prayer. The seven journalists remained themselves in their dreams, more or less; they had strong emotions and clear thoughts, they acted and reacted, they encountered a variety of intelligent and autonomous characters, and they strove for deeper truths about themselves and the world. Although they were asleep in bed at the time, motionless and unconscious, their dreams involved a colorful array of feelings, thoughts, images, movements, and social interactions. These qualities distinguish their dreams from other kinds of mystical experiences involving an all-encompassing sense of union or oneness with the divine. Hence the need for a third way of conceptualizing the religiosity of the dream journalists: they were religious *pluralists*.

This is another idea drawn from William James, in this case from his philosophical work *The Pragmatic Method* (1977), where he gave a bold introduction to the two terms: "If you know whether a man is a decided *monist* or a decided *pluralist*, you perhaps know more about the rest of his opinions than if you give him any other name ending in *ist*. To believe in the one or in the many, that is the classification with the maximum number of consequences."[1] This chapter will look at several ways in which keeping a dream journal seems to have the effect of inclining people away from a monist view of the world and toward a pluralistic perspective. We will also consider how people who already have a pluralistic worldview can find it especially compelling to keep a dream journal.

At first sight, this correlation between pluralism and dream journals seems like a poor fit with our group. Several of the dream journalists were Christians of one form or another and thus presumably committed to a monotheistic

The Scribes of Sleep. Kelly Bulkeley, Oxford University Press. © Oxford University Press 2023.
DOI: 10.1093/oso/9780197609606.003.0017

outlook in which one God rules over all. We cannot claim that these people were polytheists, that much is clear. However, we can say they were pluralistic in the sense of an unusual openness to alternative perspectives, new ideas, and different voices. In general, they took more interest in exploring multiplicities than in defining unities; they favored the complex over the simple, the anomalous over the expected, the dynamic over the static. What follows will consider three specific ways in which the dream journalists can be understood and appreciated as religious pluralists: in relation to other parts of their minds, to other ways of being religious, and to otherworldly beings.

The psychological study of religious experience often considers the possibility that certain aspects of religion overlap with mental illness. It would be too reductionistic to explain everything about religion as symptomatic of psychopathology (what James condemned as "medical materialism"). But if religious experience involves an unusually intense and open interaction with the unconscious portions of the mind and a corresponding alteration of ordinary consciousness, it should not be surprising that people who regularly have these experiences are also prone to painful disruptions of mental functioning in normal life. The group of seven dream journalists include several people who suffered from periods of mental illness. Aelius Aristides had numerous psychosomatic maladies that drove him to seek help at the Asclepian temples, while Myōe Shonin engaged in masochistic/self-harming behaviors that he felt demonstrated the strength of his spiritual devotion. Lucrecia de León and Benjamin Banneker both suffered long periods of social withdrawal and apparent depression. The course of Emanuel Swedenborg's conversion process took him through several phases of painful confusion and uncertainty about his life. Wolfgang Pauli had his "Dr. Jekyll and Mr. Hyde" era of erratic, self-destructive behavior that led him to seek psychotherapeutic help from Carl Jung. Of all the group, only Anna Kingsford seemed to be relatively free from mental health problems, even though she regularly conversed with ancient spirits in her dreams and visions and even though many people publicly questioned her sanity in fighting so hard against the power structures of nineteenth-century English society.

Whatever else we could say about these instances of mental illness, the point here is that all of the dream journalists recognized a multiplicity within their own minds. They were not inner monists. They knew from often painful personal experience that the conscious ego is not the sum total of the mind but only one element among many and not remotely the strongest of them all. The dream journalists had constant interaction with the unconscious powers of the psyche, powers that often conflicted with one another in unpredictable ways. Indeed, by keeping track of their dreams over time, they welcomed a constant stream of surprising, complex, and contentious energies into their conscious awareness. The practice itself seemed naturally to elicit a more pluralistic view of the range, complexity, and richness of their inner world.

The dream-journaling practice also seemed to cultivate a more pluralistic outlook toward being religious and experiencing the divine. Lucrecia may have been the most conventionally religious person among our group of seven dream journalists, in the sense of accepting and practicing the predominant Catholic faith of her community, but her dreams were filled with a variety of vibrant characters who criticized that community from within (e.g., the street-prophet Piedrola), threatened it from without (e.g., English Protestants, Ottoman Turks, North African Muslims), and transcended it entirely (e.g., The Ordinary Man). In waking life, Lucrecia was extremely limited in her agency and actions, thanks to the Church's strict teachings about women's proper behavior. In dreaming, however, she gained the freedom to go beyond those limits and explore a wide variety of other ways of looking at the community and her role within it. Something similar occurred with Pauli, although he started as perhaps the most conventionally *non*-religious person among the seven journalists. He boasted to Jung of being baptized as an "anti-metaphysician," and he always self-identified as a rational scientist with the reputation as "the conscience of physics." Yet in his dreams, Pauli discovered strange new aspects of reality that blurred the boundaries between psychology and physics, mind and matter, self and other. He developed a deep appreciation for Jung's psychospiritual notions of archetypes, as constellations of autonomous energy in the unconscious, and synchronicity, as an acausal principle of meaningful coincidence. His own voluminous experiences of dreaming gave Pauli a more personally nuanced understanding of religion and spirituality than he otherwise would have had based solely on his scientific training.

For both Aristides and Myōe, dreaming provided a powerful and virtually endless source of ideas for innovative religious practice. Within the socially sanctioned context of their respective traditions, Aristides and Myōe did everything they could to infuse their lives with the unpredictable, unorthodox, iconoclastic energies of their dreams. Aristides interacted with several different gods and goddesses in addition to Asclepius, along with a variety of priests, creatures, and spirit guides. According to one of his biographers, "far from being a monotheist, Aristides was a devotee of a variety of deities found in the Greek and Egyptian pantheons."[2] Likewise with Myōe, the "upholder of the tradition of being open to all traditions," who had dreams that included many different deities and supernatural beings, some of which were familiar in Buddhist teachings and some of which were making novel appearances in his dreaming: "Myōe, then, had his own answer for the new age. His approach was pluralistic, and included an easy practice that relied upon the natural benevolence of the deities without sacrificing self-assertion."[3] The pluralistic quality of keeping a dream journal emerged very clearly with Aristides and Myōe, both of whom engaged in regular efforts at dream incubation with an openness toward whatever, or whoever, might appear in response to their pre-sleep invitation. Perhaps the fact that they were the only two people in our group not raised in a Christian society meant that Aristides and Myōe could freely explore the multiplicities of their dreams without having to worry about running afoul of monotheistic authorities.

Swedenborg's dreams and visions expanded his sense of religious possibility and opened alternative paths of spiritual insight and discovery, far beyond what his Christian cultural upbringing anticipated or allowed. In comparison with his contemporaries—Church of Sweden theologians, rationalist philosophers, scientist-engineers—Swedenborg was a pioneer of pluralism who actively sought hyperrealistic encounters in both waking and dreaming with new spiritual beings, leading him on journeys to new celestial realms. He was not a polytheist, in that he always remained oriented toward the one supreme God. Indeed, through his dreams, Swedenborg became increasingly open to the deeper meanings and secret complexities of the Christian tradition. This seems true of Banneker, too, insofar as he was raised with the Bible and remained a lifelong Christian but also explored unconventional dimensions of the tradition. His friendship with Andrew Ellicott and other members of the Society of Friends in the Baltimore region opened him to radical new ways of experiencing the divine in prayer and worship. The Society of Friends, or Quakers, were notorious among traditionalist Christians for their extreme behavior in ritual settings (trembling, crying out, fainting) and for emphasizing the equality of all people before God, regardless of rank or status in the church hierarchy (one of the reasons they fled England for the Americas). Banneker did not become a Quaker himself, but he had long, close relationships with several members of the group, and he clearly admired their openness to science and reason, their respect for individual conscience and faith, and their acceptance of people from different racial and ethnic backgrounds. In addition to these pluralizing influences, he undoubtedly carried with him countless family stories and teachings drawing on his grandfather's cultural memory from Africa, all of which connected Banneker to an entirely different religious system and metaphysical outlook from the one predominant in late-eighteenth-century Christian America.

Given that she was married her whole adult life to an Anglican priest, Kingsford might be considered the most conventionally monotheistic person of all the dream journalists. She did regard herself as Christian, it is true, but *not* as a practicing member of either the Anglican or the Catholic Church. As we have seen, she followed her own distinctive spiritual path of dreams and visions, and she argued tirelessly in favor of other people's right to do as she had done and develop their own ways of worshipping the divine. Much more than the dream journalists from earlier eras, Kingsford knew about the variety of religious traditions around the world, and she found them illuminating and potentially helpful in improving her own practices, not threatening to her unitary vision of what true religion is and must be. She was active at a time when many other spiritualists, theosophists, and spiritual seekers were trying to combine classic Western religious beliefs and a variety of esoteric traditions with the teachings of Hindu, Buddhist, and Taoist sages. There were limits, of course, to what someone in nineteenth-century England could know about the actual lives and spiritual practices of people in other parts of the world, and gaps in knowledge were often filled with fanciful conjecture. To her credit, Kingsford avoided the worst of these crowd-pleasing confabulations. Her insistence on the authority of her own inner spiritual light and her refusal to abide by the authority of anyone else's inner light enabled her to remain open, curious, and clear-eyed toward other religious and spiritual traditions, without ever falling prey to either naive acceptance or naive rejection of their teachings.

Another way of identifying and appreciating the pluralistic tendencies of the dream journalists is to apply a recently developed concept in the psychology of religion, namely, that of *supernatural agents*. This concept draws on recent findings in cognitive science showing that humans have built-in, highly refined mental capacities to identify and think about animate beings, or agents. These capacities have deep roots in the evolutionary history of our brains, reflecting the development of a cognitive function with a high degree of survival value. We are quick to distinguish between things that are living and things that are inanimate matter, and based on this distinction, we instinctively make a series of additional inferences about their basic properties and behaviors. For instance, we assume that living agents have autonomous intentions, independent mobility, and internal self-awareness. Inanimate objects do not have these qualities, but agents do. Evidence of this agent-detecting module in the mind is the visceral shock and alarm we feel when we realize we have mistaken an agent for an object, as when a stick on the path turns out to be a snake. Since there is so much more danger in mistaking a snake for a stick than in mistaking a stick for a snake, the agent-detecting part of the mind is "tuned" to be highly sensitive to the appearance of agents in the environment.

Religions typically involve the belief in and worship of a special class of agents that possess powers beyond those available to ordinary living beings—for instance, they can read minds, look forward in time, and travel instantly from one place to another. These are not natural agents but *supernatural* agents, who combine extraordinary powers with many other features commonly found among all agents, such as having intentions, self-awareness, and responsiveness to stimuli in the environment. Because of their supernatural powers, such agents make a strong and lasting impression on people's minds. Contemporary researchers suggest that the supernatural agents featured in the most successful religions (successful in the sense of spreading the widest and lasting the longest) are *minimally counterintuitive*, meaning that they represent an optimal cognitive balance between expectation and surprise. Minimally counterintuitive supernatural agents have abilities that violate a few, but not all, of our natural assumptions about what agents can and cannot do. They are sufficiently counterintuitive to attract our attention and engage our minds but not so wildly counterintuitive that we feel overwhelmed and cannot process the bizarre perceptions into long-term memory.

This concept from the psychology of religion has direct relevance to our exploration of the relationship between dream journals and religious pluralism. Dreaming provides an arena for the appearance of a seemingly infinite variety of supernatural agents with minimally counterintuitive powers, as evidenced in the cross-cultural phenomenon of highly memorable dreams (Jung's "big dreams") influencing people's religious beliefs and practices. This was certainly the case with the seven dream journalists, whose dreams were filled with an abundance of these kinds of supernatural agents. Lucrecia offers an especially clear case with her dreams of the Ordinary Man, a figure who mixed conventional behaviors with mysterious, trans-human knowledge and powers. We can say the same of the various part-human, part-divine figures who appeared in the dreams of Aristides and Myōe, the ghostly spirits of Swedenborg's and Banneker's dreams, the angelic beings and numinous animals of Kingsford's dreams, and the otherworldly women visiting Pauli in his dreams. The vivid, dynamic presence of these figures triggers the immediate recognition that they are agents, not things. Their supernatural qualities stimulate interest, attention, and enhanced memory processing, making it more likely that these particular agents will be remembered and shared with others. These effects are enhanced and intensified by the practice of keeping a dream journal, which promotes the memorability of the supernatural agents and strengthens their overall impact on the individual's waking mind.

We are only considering these seven dream journalists, but the prospect of this being a more widespread phenomenon (as it is hoped future research will consider) suggests intriguing possibilities. If, as claimed by some researchers, the memorability of a religious idea is key to its long-term transmission and survival—whether it lives and spreads or withers and dies—then keeping a carefully recorded journal of one's most intense, dramatic, and supernaturally populous dreams can be seen as a kind of spiritual technology for stimulating and preserving cognitively optimal religious insights. We have been following a group of seven people with unusual aptitude for such dreams, but "big dreaming" is a pan-human experience that represents perhaps the most widely accessible source of memorable encounters with supernatural agents. This means that *everyone* has the potential for these kinds of experiences, regularly, all the way through their lives. Simply by virtue of having a brain that goes to sleep each night and dreams, every human has access to an inner wellspring of pluralistic religiosity.

Where might it lead if more people developed a dream-journaling practice and cultivated an openness toward the full range and variety of what they discovered in their oneiric experiences over time? Toward a more pluralistic world? At the end of *The Varieties of Religious Experience*, James observed that all religious and spiritual traditions do not necessarily seek the same ultimate goal, and there are no empirical facts compelling us to accept the monist's claim that all the different paths lead to a single final destination. There are, however, several empirical facts of psychology, specifically in our knowledge about the unconscious, that compel us at least to entertain an alternative possibility:

> Meanwhile the practical needs and experiences of religion seem to me sufficiently met by the belief that beyond each man and in a fashion continuous

with him there exists a larger power which is friendly to him and to his ideals. All that the facts require is that the power should be both other and larger than our conscious selves. Anything larger will do, if only it be large enough to trust for the next step. It need not be infinite, it need not be solitary. It might conceivably even be only a larger and more godlike self, of which the present self would then be but the mutilated expression, and the universe might conceivably be a collection of such selves, of different degrees of inclusiveness, with no absolute unity realized in it at all. Thus would a new polytheism return upon us. . . . I think, in fact, that a final philosophy of religion will have to consider the pluralistic hypothesis more seriously than it has hitherto been willing to consider it.[4]

This might seem like an extremely negative trend in religion, as people spin off into their own private spiritual worlds, lost in aimless, solipsistic fantasies of cosmic narcissism. To the extent that religion involves a passionately devoted binding to something greater than oneself, the pluralistic religiosity foreseen by James has the appearance of doing the very opposite and transforming the individual self into something greater than it truly is. That does not need to be the outcome, however, as illustrated by the religious lives of the seven dream journalists, none of whom could be fairly described as lost in a personal fantasy world. It is true that they all dove deeply into the unconscious depths of their own minds, more deeply than most people are accustomed to doing, but they also maintained a clear sense of social reality and acted in various ways to help others and improve human life in this world. In fact, they were all unusually curious and perceptive people with an eagerness to explore, experiment, and experience. Their pluralistic outlook led them to be *more* engaged with the world, not less so. Contrast this with the personal impact of monistic religious traditions, which researchers have found to be consistently associated with close-mindedness, intolerance of outsiders, and cognitive biases favoring the interests of the insider group.[5] In practice, the monist assumption of ultimate unity often discourages the recognition of distinctions, respect for differences, and the ability to imagine alternative possibilities. Before we worry too much about the possible risks of growing religious pluralism, we should account more fully for the actual, concrete problems associated with religious monism.

More positively, we can appreciate the efforts of the seven dream journalists to listen closely to their inner guides and find creative ways of connecting their personal spiritual insights with their cultures' religious traditions. They are dreamers calling for a religiosity that is more engaged with the world, less self-centered, and less tightly bound to the narrow concerns of an in-group. The radically open-ended experience of dreaming naturally challenges the horizon-limiting, inward-turning tendencies of monistic religiosity.

Before closing the chapter, I would like to raise a question that has puzzled me for a long time. Why are there so few references to dreams in *The Varieties of Religious Experience*? Other than a quote near the end referencing revelatory dreams in Islam and a footnote with a quote about revelatory dreams in the Church of Jesus Christ of Latter-day Saints, the *Varieties* says nothing about dreaming.[6] And yet, as we have just seen in the three chapters of part IV of this book, James's ideas are perfectly suited to explain the distinctive spirituality of our group of dream journalists. I have been wondering about this since I first read the *Varieties*, many years ago in a college class that I attended just a few months after my Hawaiian encounter with Ann Faraday's *Dream Power* (described in the introduction) and the beginning of my dream-journaling practice. The class was a graduate-level seminar on James and religion, with just four students who met once a week in a small, legendarily obscure room on the top floor of the religious studies department. As a sophomore, I was only allowed in because I persuaded the professor that I really, really wanted to learn about James's psychological approach to religious experience. It was an excellent class, one of the best I took in college, and it gave me a very encouraging introduction to graduate studies.[7] And yet I couldn't help being disappointed that James said practically nothing about dreaming, despite talking about religious and psychological phenomena that I knew from personal experience applied to dreams as much as to any of the other types of religiosity he described. Paradoxically, this disappointment revealed both the future path of my research and the strange challenges that would occur along the way. I realized that the fact that the *Varieties* said so little about dreaming actually created an interesting opportunity to make an original contribution to the psychology of religion. If no one else was interested in exploring this realm of experience as an intersection of religious and psychological dynamics, maybe that was what I could do. And away I went.

Still, the question lingered. Why didn't James include more discussion of dreaming in the *Varieties*? At first, it made me wonder if I was missing something. Was there a problem with dreaming that I hadn't seen yet? If so, why wasn't it stated openly, rather than leaving it to be inferred by the topic's absence? How could he devote so much respectful analytic attention to his experiences with nitrous oxide, using them as a model for mystical experience, and never say anything significant about dreams? I admit to having once experimented with nitrous oxide, late on a Saturday night between rounds of poker with a group of high school friends. For me, at least, the effects on consciousness were mildly amusing but not nearly as powerful or spiritually illuminating as my most vivid dreams. I found it hard to imagine someone thinking a nitrous experience was more psychologically revealing or religiously illuminating than a "big dream." Perhaps James didn't have any dreams of his own with special significance? Still, he talked at length about many other forms of religiosity that he had not personally experienced, so that could not be the answer. Nor could he have been unfamiliar with reports of religiously significant dreams in the same sacred texts and myths (e.g., the Bible, the Upanishads, the Qur'an) that he was using to illustrate other points in the *Varieties*. What was it, then? The absence of dreaming in the *Varieties*, despite how perfectly dreams exemplify James's key concepts about the psychological roots of religious experience, became more mysterious and perplexing the more I thought about it. Alas, I still do not understand this omission in James's approach. But now I realize that by pondering the question for so long and so hard, I have in effect been creating my *own* answer. As a personal counterfactual, had James devoted one of his lectures in the *Varieties* to dreams and discussed them in thorough and exhaustive detail, it's entirely possible I would not have made a lifelong pursuit of their study. Instead, for whatever reason, James's famous and highly influential work had virtually nothing to say on this topic, which presented an open chance for novel research in an area I already found personally compelling. Forty years later, that path remains as compelling as it was in the beginning.

Conclusion

Not everyone who keeps a dream journal is a religiously active person or develops in a more spiritually intense direction. That would be too strong a claim. For instance, the "Engine Man," an early-twentieth-century scientist whose journal of 234 dreams featured prominently in J. Allan Hobson's 1988 book *The Dreaming Brain*, had no apparent interest in religion, and he recorded his dreams for a few months simply for his own curiosity. The individual known as "Pegasus," whose 1,093 dreams have been archived on G. William Domhoff and Adam Schneider's Dreambank.net website, was a gambler who tracked his dreams because he thought they could give him tips for winning horses at the racetrack. Santiago Ramón y Cajal, the Nobel Prize–winning neurologist from Spain, kept a journal of his dreams for the specific purpose of disproving the theories of Sigmund Freud, his biggest contemporary rival as the world's leading scientist of the mind.[1] Perhaps a more detailed biographical study of their lives would reveal that each of these nonreligious dreamers actually did become more individualist, mystical, and/or pluralist in the course of recording their dreams over time. But the more limited goal of this book has been to highlight a *strong tendency*—not an automatic effect but a strong tendency—of keeping a dream journal to enhance several specific qualities of religiosity. We can acknowledge that this may not be true for everyone while also recognizing that it *is* true for many people in various cultures and periods of history.

To help understand the spiritually stimulating quality of the practice of dream journaling, I have drawn on the resources of digital analysis, depth psychology, and religious studies. Research from these three fields has yielded a host of valuable insights into the lives and works of our group of seven dream journalists. At the same time, the study of dream journals has shed new light on each of these three fields of scholarship. In digital analysis, dream journals represent a richly meaningful form of human self-expression with multiple layers of significance. As shown in part II, standard methods of big-data analysis can reveal some of these layers, but any system originally

The Scribes of Sleep. Kelly Bulkeley, Oxford University Press. © Oxford University Press 2023.
DOI: 10.1093/oso/9780197609606.003.0018

designed to work with texts from the waking world will struggle with the complex ambiguities that characterize dream texts. Until new systems are designed with specific attention to the peculiar features of dream language, a great deal of potential in this field will be left unrealized.

In depth psychology, dream journals offer ideal illustrations of key theoretical insights, such as Freud's concept of sublimation, Carl Jung's archetypes, and the social embeddedness of individual dreaming posited by cultural psychologists. However, as shown in part III, the study of dream journals goes beyond providing supportive examples to push depth psychologists into new territory in their explorations of the unconscious. Can Freudian psychoanalysis accommodate the multidimensional patterns of meaning in the manifest content of a series of dreams? Can Jungian archetypal psychology account for "little dreams," for all the dreams in a journal that do not have an obvious connection to the process of individuation? Can cultural psychologists help us understand why certain elements from collective life do and do *not* enter people's dreams over time? Focusing more attention on dream journals is not just a matter of learning more about dreams but also a way of developing better overall theories of how the mind works, awake and asleep.

For religious studies, a close examination of the practice of keeping a dream journal reveals a distinctive type of religiosity that, while rare in most populations, seems to exist in potentia in virtually everyone. Drawing on William James and *The Varieties of Religious Experience*, three qualities of this religiosity were identified in part IV, looking at the conceptual polarities of individualist/communalist, mystical/mundane, and monist/pluralist. Here we can step back and locate the dream journalists in relation to other ways people make existential sense of their lives. The three polarities produce eight possible combinations of these qualities (with an ideal-typical example of each combination in parentheses):

1. Communalist/mundane/monist (e.g., theocracy)
2. Communalist/mystical/monist (e.g., cult)
3. Communalist/mundane/pluralist (e.g., democracy)
4. Communalist/mystical/pluralist (e.g., globalism)
5. Individualist/mundane/monist (e.g., rational actor)
6. Individualist/mystical/monist (e.g., monk)
7. Individualist/mundane/pluralist (e.g., scientist)
8. Individualist/mystical/pluralist (e.g., dreamer)

Like any abstract framework, this one is simplistic and overly generalized. But I hope that thinking about the dream journalists in this broader context will make it easier to see what is truly distinctive about their religiosity. With each of the three polarities, the journalists tend to gather at the less populated end of the spectrum. They are strongly drawn toward an individualist path, with less interest in communal norms of behavior. They are especially active in seeking mystical insights, even if they also remain engaged in mundane pursuits. They have a curious open-mindedness toward the variety of phenomena in the world, with less focus on making everything conform to a single unitary perspective. In their unusual combination of these three religious attributes, I believe our seven dream journalists can best be characterized as *free spirits*. Independent, energetic, curious, playful, and courageously creative in their idiosyncrasies, each followed a special path that unfolded in and was illuminated by their dreams. Other people in their societies might not have been able to perceive or appreciate those paths, but this group of journal keepers was remarkable for their unshakable faith in the spiritual guidance emerging through their dreams. Their dreams became primal wellsprings of religious experience and metaphysical insight that inspired their lives in countless ways. In turn, their lives increasingly became attuned to the rhythms of their dreaming and the optimal methods for stimulating and amplifying their power. They had many of the qualities Friedrich Nietzsche associated with "the free spirit" as he described it in aphorism 44 of his *Beyond Good and Evil* (1886):

At home in many countries of the spirit, or at least having been guests there . . ., grateful to the god, devil, sheep, and worm in us, curious to the point of vice . . ., with fore- and back-souls into whose ultimate intentions no one can easily see, with fore- and backgrounds to whose end no foot may go, hidden under mantles of light, conquerors even though we look like heirs and prodigals, collectors and arrangers from morn till night.[2]

And from night till morn, too, we might add. The free spirits who are drawn to and created by the practice of keeping a dream journal develop a dynamic combination of openness and conscientiousness, of adventurous curiosity and systematic analysis. Over time, they cultivate an emergent nocturnal awareness, a kind of night vision of the soul that enables them to see within the dynamic darkness of sleep and move with purpose and intentionality through the manifold dimensions of their unconscious mind and through whatever other worlds and realms of reality they discover in the process. In the course of tracking their long-term patterns of dreaming, these free spirits become more fully who they already are as big dreamers, natural visionaries, cosmic thinkers, and compassionate humans. They learn that enhancing their awareness of meaningful patterns in dreaming can enhance their awareness of meaningful patterns in waking reality, too. Their journals became a personalized portal of deepening self-knowledge and sensitivity to the wonders of the world, enabling them to see beyond the daunting limits of the present to envision new possibilities ahead and better paths forward for themselves and others.

Further Reading

To enhance and deepen your own dream-journaling practice, the best book to read is . . . your own journal. Going back through your previous dreams from the vantage of different points of time in life is always a thought-provoking and imaginatively stimulating experience. Along with regularly reviewing your past dreams, it can also be helpful to read a few different books on the study of dreams. The following are some suggestions of books about dreams in general and dream journals in particular. Try the ones that immediately strike your interest, of course, but also consider looking into some of the other books that do not seem at first sight relevant to you and your dreams. You might find alternative perspectives you had not considered before, opening up new possibilities for understanding the patterns of your dreams. You might also find your dreams give you critical leverage to challenge researchers whose claims do not account for experiences like yours, revealing where the study of dreams needs to grow and where you perhaps can make a new contribution.

The modern psychology of dreams began with Sigmund Freud, and for that reason alone, it is helpful to become familiar with his *The Interpretation of Dreams* (1965). It's a fascinating text on many levels, with many of Freud's own dreams along with those of his patients and other sources from history and mythology. He kept adding new material to the text over the years, so it has a strangely organic quality in places, as his ideas grow and expand in various directions over the years. (The first time you read it, you might want to skip chapter 1, the long literature review of dream research in the nineteenth century, and start with chapter 2 and his famous "Dream of Irma's Injection.") Along with Freud's basic dream theories, I suggest getting to know Carl Jung's life and works, starting with the memoir he dictated near the end of his life, *Memories, Dreams, Reflections* (1965). One of his last writings, "Approaching the Unconscious," which appeared in the unfortunately titled *Man and His Symbols* (1964), offers an excellent introduction in his own words to the basic ideas of archetypal psychology and the role of dreams in human life. Jung wrote several other short papers on dreams, which have been collected in a volume titled *Dreams* (1974) (his primary analysis of Wolfgang Pauli's dreams appears in this text).

Beyond Freud and Jung, several other books discuss new developments in the study of dreaming. G. William Domhoff's *Finding Meaning in Dreams* (1996) is a useful compendium of research using Hall and Van de Castle's content analysis method. *Dream Research: Contributions to Clinical Practice* (2015), edited by Milton Kramer and Myron Glucksman, covers new developments in therapeutic practices involving dreams and nightmares. Rosalind Cartwright's *The Twenty-Four Hour Mind: The Role of Sleep and Dreaming in Our Emotional Lives* (2010) explains how sleep laboratory technologies have helped us understand new dimensions of our experiences in sleep and dreaming. Edward Bruce Bynum's *Families and the Interpretation of Dreams* (1993) draws on both contemporary psychology and African healing traditions to highlight the value of dreams for understanding the interpersonal dynamics among members of a family. Michael Schredl's *Researching Dreams: The Fundamentals* (2018) offers an overview of methodological issues in the study of dreams. An excellent short introductory text is Josie Malinowski's *The Psychology of Dreaming* (2021). I am partial, of course, to Kelly Bulkeley, *An Introduction to the Psychology of Dreaming* (2017), but Malinowski's work is better in many ways and highly recommended.

Paying attention to dreams usually means paying attention to sleep, too, so it can be helpful to explore sleep research as well. The collection *Sleep around the World: Anthropological Perspectives* (2013), edited by Katie Glaskin and Richard Chenhall, offers a fascinating panorama of the variety of sleep practices in different cultures. David Hufford's *The Terror That Comes in the Night: An Experience-Centered Study of Supernatural Assault Traditions* (1982) is a classic work of cultural psychology focusing on experiences of sleep paralysis and the uncanny myths and legends they have spawned. A more recent work on this topic is Ryan Hurd's *Sleep Paralysis: A Guide to Hypnagogic Visions and Visitors of the Night* (2010), which explores both the psychological and the spiritual dimensions of sleep paralysis experiences.

Several books about long-term dream series were noted in passing: J. W. Dunne's *An Experiment with Time* (1927), Vladimir Nabokov's *Insomniac Dreams* (2018), and Benjamin Ehrlich's *The Dreams of Santiago Ramón y Cajal* (2017). To these I would add William Burroughs's *My Education: A Book of Dreams* (1995), Jack Kerouac's *Book of Dreams* (2001), Graham Greene's *A World of My Own: A Dream Diary* (1993), and Henry Rollins's *Black Coffee*

Blues (1992). These are all books about the dreams of twentieth-century literate men, so the demographic variety is not great, but the descriptive eloquence and depth of self-observation make any one of these a worthy read.

Women's dream memoirs have not received as much attention, but they exist. *Acquainted with the Night: A Book of Dreams* by Nancy Price (1949) is an early instance. Michelle Herman's *Stories We Tell Ourselves* (2013) includes a lengthy "Dream Life," with many subtle and intriguing comments along the way. Nori Muster's *Betrayal of the Spirit: My Life behind the Headlines of the Hare Krishna Movement* (1996) includes reflections on a long series of her dreams during and after her involvement with a violent and secretive religious group. Helene Cixous's *Dream I Tell You* (2006) is more elusive and playful, infused with French-inflected psychoanalysis. Similar in theoretical background but different in tone is Sharon Sliwinski's *Dreaming in Dark Times: Six Exercises in Political Thought* (2017), a powerful and haunting work that highlights the deep intertwining of psyche, culture, and history. It is also worth noting that Mary Whiton Calkins's article "Statistics of Dreams" (1893) initiated the modern empirical study of dream content by analyzing a series of her own dreams and another series from a colleague.

For those who want to pursue even further the implications and potentials in this practice, I highly recommend Dennis Schmidt's article "Stretched Dream Science: The Essential Contribution of Long-Term Naturalistic Studies" (1999), which appeared in a special issue of the journal *Dreaming*. His concluding words, about a future in which dream journals will be respected as valuable sources of primary data, are worth repeating:

> An integrated field of dream study would be a new fusion of disciplines, in which scientists appreciate open-eyed straining to see everything that there is to see, and explorers appreciate scientific striving for clarity and sureness. We would manifest in a new way this fundamental attitude of science: Look to nature, not to received wisdom or other preconceptions, to learn how nature works. Look through eyes both creative and discriminating, and use imagination in your seeing. In fact, use every way of looking that you can. (67)

Summary of Word-Search Results

	Baselines Females N=3,110 mean 100	Baselines Males N=2,135 mean 105	Aelius Aristides N=121 mean 89, median 42	7-898	Myōe Shonin N=170 mean 88, median 65	4-431	Lucrecia de León N=45 mean 874, median 842	265-1698
	Percent	Percent	Percent	Most-used words	Percent	Most-used words	Percent	Most-used words
Perception								
Vision	37	29	19	saw, see	25	saw, see	100	saw, see, eyes, vision
Hearing	10	9	12	heard, ears	7	hear	82	heard, listen, noise, loudly
Touch	12	12	14	hand, hands, held	14	hand, hands, held	84	hand, hands, holding
Smell and Taste	2	1	2	sweet	2	sweet	31	nose, tongue, smell
Color	17	12	5	white	10	white, black, blue	69	white, black, red, brown, green
Emotion								
Fear	23	15	3	afraid	9	afraid, fear	58	scared, afraid
Anger	8	5	4	angry	1	disgusted	22	anger, angry
Sadness	5	3	2	distressed	2	depressed	18	sad, disappointed
Wonder	18	18	4	wondered	11	wondered, suddenly	13	suddenly, surprised
Happiness	9	6	6	pleased, glad	8	happy, pleased	36	happy, glad, pleased
Characters								
Family	40	27	12	father, son, brother, mother	6	mother, son	53	son, wife, father, mother
Animals	13	12	10	horse	22	horse, fish, bird, dog, snake	89	lion, crows, lions, turkey
Fantastic Beings	2	2	0		3	dragon, spirit	24	spirit, devil, demon, dragon
Male References	47	40	65	he, him, his, man	48	he, his, him	100	he, him, man, his, men
Female References	44	35	6	her, mother, she, woman	13	she, her, ladies, lady	80	her, she, woman, women

Social Interactions								
Friendliness	46	34	26	friends, praise, honor	27	visit, friend, honored, visited	76	help, friend, warn love
Physical Aggression	12	19	2	attack, enemies	5	killed	69	enemies, war, fight, battle, killed
Sexuality	4	6	2	kiss, lover	1	sexual	20	naked
Movement								
Walking/Running	27	27	5	walking, run	11	stepped, walked, walking	60	walking, walked, running
Flying	4	6	0		3	flew, flying	16	flying, flew, floating
Falling	7	8	1	fell	8	fell, fall, falling	42	fell, fall, falling
Death	9	7	4	dead, death	6	dead, die	62	dead, die, death
Cognition								
Thinking	39	38	27	thought, think, in-tended, prepared	51	thought, think, thinking	87	think, thought, aware, pray
Speech	35	32	55	said, say, spoke, called	37	said, saying, called	100	said, saying, say, called, talk
Reading/Writing	6	5	14	written, letter, read, wrote	15	letter, written, wrote, book	51	read, letter, letters, write
Culture								
Architecture	47	41	9	home, house, room	20	house, hall, room	73	house, room, door, floor, home
Food and Drink	14	12	14	eat, drink, wine, bread, eggs	12	ate, eat, food, rice	56	bread, drink, fruits, wheat
Clothing	14	11	3	wore	11	wearing, robes, clothes	73	dressed, clothes, clothing
School	17	13	5	teacher	1	teacher	2	educate
Transportation	24	28	4	road, ship, path	8	road, boat, avenue, path	58	street, ships, streets, cart

(continued)

	Baselines Females N = 3,110 mean 100	Baselines Males N = 2,135 mean 105	Aelius Aristides N = 121 mean 89, median 42	7-898	Myōe Shonin N = 170 mean 88, median 65	4-431	Lucrecia de León N = 45 mean 874, median 842	265-1698
	Percent	Percent	Percent	Most-used words	Percent	Most-used words	Percent	Most-used words
Technology	7	8	0		0		0	
Money and Work	18	22	4	bought, coins, rich, work	4	wealth, work	49	work, money, business, rich
Weapons	3	5	1	daggers	2	arrow, sword	44	weapons, sword, knife, spear
Sports	4	4	3	athlete, gymnasium	0		0	
Art	10	7	8	drawing, poet, sang, theater	2	drawing, poem	22	paintings, painting
Religion	7	6	50	god, temple, Zeus, priest, sacred	54	priest, meditation, Buddha, priests, nun	91	God, church, saint, priests, prophet
Elements								
Fire	4	4	8	sun, burn, fire, star	5	fire, burn, burning, star	47	fire, burning, star, flames, sun
Air	4	5	2	air	2	air	24	air, blowing, breath
Water	13	12	12	water, river, sea	18	water, pond, ocean, river, sea	56	water, sea, river
Earth	10	10	8	mud, earth, land	15	mountain, rock, landed	60	land, earth, lands, stone, rock

	Emanuel Swedenborg N = 120 mean 86, median 61		Anna Kingsford N = 24 mean 709, median 607		Wolfgang Pauli N = 58 mean 48, median 22		Author 2019–2021 N = 1,095 mean 88, median 69	
	7-287		123-2055		5-550		10-456	
	Percent	Most-used words	Percent	Most-used words	Percent	Most-used Words	Percent	Most-used words
Perception								
Vision	41	saw, see	84	saw, eyes, see	7	see	47	see, watching, watch
Hearing	8	heard	72	heard, sound, hearing	3	hear, heard	5	hear, listening
Touch	23	hand, hold, hands, held, holding	80	hand, hands, holding, touch	5	hand	10	hand, holding, hold, hands, touch
Smell and Taste	5	tongue	8	bitter, delicious	0		1	nose, disgusting, smell
Color	19	white, black, brown, green	68	white, grey, black, red, green	16	green, red, yellow, blue	46	white, black, green, blue, brown, red
Emotion								
Fear	10	afraid, frightened	36	anxiety, fearful, guilty, nervous	1	regrets	18	worried, worry, scared, upset, anxious
Anger	2	angry	16	furious, mad	0		5	angry, mad, annoying
Sadness	0		24	distress, hopeless, miserable	0		3	disappointed, sad
Wonder	9	wondered, wondering	52	suddenly, sudden, confusion, wondered	3	suddenly	37	wonder, surprised, suddenly, confused
Happiness	2	glad	12	happy, cheerful	2	cheerful	13	happy, relieved, pleased, glad

(*continued*)

| | Emanuel Swedenborg N = 120 mean 86, median 61 | | Anna Kingsford N = 24 mean 709, median 607 | | Wolfgang Pauli N = 58 mean 48, median 22 | | Author 2019–2021 N = 1,095 mean 88, median 69 | |
| | 7-287 | | 123-2055 | | 5-550 | | 10-456 | |
	Percent	Most-used words	Percent	Most-used words	Percent	Most-used Words	Percent	Most-used words
Characters								
Family	13	father, brother, married, sister	28	brother, father, husband, mother	12	father, mother	18	wife, mom, family, dad
Animals	19	dog, horse, animal, bear	48	animals, bear, horse	9	animal, dogs, foxes	17	cat, dog, cats, birds
Fantastic Beings	6	spirit, dragons	36	spirit, monster, spirits, devil, dragon	0		1	alien, monster
Male References	56	he, him, his, man	88	him, he, his, man, men	48	he, his, him, man, father	41	he, guy, him, his, guys
Female References	23	she, woman, her	48	her, she, woman, women	33	woman, mother, she	51	woman, she, her, wife, women
Social Interactions								
Friendliness	24	love, help, friend, helped	60	friend, help, save, social, visited	10	friend, party	40	help, helping, party
Physical Aggression	13	bite, attacked, hit	40	shot, hurl, killed, pursuing	17	battle, war, attacked	12	hit, fight, shoot
Sexuality	5	kissed	8	naked	0		7	naked, sex, sexual

Movement								
Walking/ Running	14	walked, walking, ran, walk	48	ran, step, run, walk	19	running, run, walk, runs	19	walking, walk, running, run
Flying	4	flying, flew	20	floating, flying, fly	2	glide	5	flying, floating, fly
Falling	11	fell, dropped	24	fell, dropping	3	falls	6	fall, falling, drop
Death	6	dead, died	36	death, dead, die	0		2	dead, dies
Cognition								
Thinking	30	thought, thoughts, noticed, intended	80	aware, thought, sense, effort	9	concentrate, discover, notice	45	realize, think, decide, sense
Speech	43	said, spoke, saying	80	said, called, speak, spoke	26	says, say, said	21	say, says, talking, talk
Reading/ Writing	12	book, written, letter	44	read, written, book, scroll	7	letter, reads, writes	5	book, books, letters, write
Culture								
Architecture	18	room, house, home, door	56	room, door, house, apartment	9	room, door, house	37	house, room, building, door, floor
Food and Drink	13	bread, wine, dinner	24	wine, bread, eaten	5	nuts, drunk, wine	9	food, eat, drink, bread
Clothing	9	dressed, clothes, wearing	48	dress, wore, attire, robe	3	hat	16	clothes, wearing, shirt, shoes
School	1	library	8	education, school, student	2	students	4	school, test
Transportation	10	road, ship, stairway	32	path, cart, street, train	7	airplane, car, ship, train	25	car, road, street

(continued)

	Emanuel Swedenborg N = 120 mean 86, median 61 7-287		Anna Kingsford N = 24 mean 709, median 607 123-2055		Wolfgang Pauli N = 58 mean 48, median 22 5-550		Author 2019-2021 N = 1,095 mean 88, median 69 10-456	
	Percent	Most-used words	Percent	Most-used words	Percent	Most-used Words	Percent	Most-used words
Technology	1	machine	8	engine, scientific	0		9	television, phone, TV, computer
Money and Work	15	money, work, buy, costly	24	work, bought	5	business, coins, work	15	work, working, job, company
Weapons	5	sword, cannons	16	arrow, bullets, knives, spear	2	guns	4	gun, guns, knife
Sports	0		0		0		7	basketball, baseball, football
Art	3	drawing, sang	24	drawing, art, artistic, dancing	12	drawing, actor, dance, music	9	theater, music, artists, movie
Religion	24	God, holy, Christ, church	72	spirit, heaven, Christ, God, religious	9	ascetic, Catholic, Christ, church	2	church, divinity
Elements								
Fire	2	fire, sun	48	fire, flame, stars, sun	10	star, burning, fire	3	fire, sun, star
Air	3	air, blows	36	air, wind	0		4	air, wind
Water	8	water, ice, lake	56	sea, mist, snow, water	12	water, fog, river, sea	11	water, ocean, creek, wet
Earth	5	earth, hills	52	earth, crag, mountain, stone, crystal	10	cave, diamond, crystals, mountain	11	dirt, hill, land, rocks

Notes

Introduction

1. Jung, "Individual Dream Symbolism," 119–120.
2. Hall, "Diagnosing Personality," 69.
3. Eggan, "Manifest Content," 470.
4. See Kryger, Roth, and Dement, *Principles and Practices*; Maquet, Smith, and Stickgold, *Sleep*; Jouvet, *Paradox*.
5. Pagel, "Non-Dreamers."
6. Borges, "Nightmares," 27.
7. Nabokov, *Insomniac Dreams*.
8. See Bulkeley, *Dreaming*.

Part 1

1. sleepanddreamdatabase.org.

Chapter 1

1. The following texts have been used in developing this portrait of Aristides's life and dreams: Aristides, *Complete Works*; Edelstein and Edelstein, *Asclepius*; Meier, *Healing Dream*; Stephens, *Dreams and Visions*; Mitchell-Boyask, *Plague*; Tick, *Practice*; Pedley, *Sanctuaries*; Jayne, *Healing Gods*; Harris, *Dreams and Experience*.
2. Aristides, *Complete Works*, 292.
3. Stephens, *Dreams and Visions*, 13.
4. Meier, *Healing Dream*, 9, 19.
5. Aristides, *Complete Works*, 293.
6. Ibid., 299.
7. Ibid., 322–323.
8. Ibid., 329–330.
9. Ibid.
10. Ibid.
11. Ibid.

Chapter 2

1. The following texts have been used in developing this portrait of the life and dreams of Myōe Shonin: Kawai, *Dreams, Myths*; Kawai, *Buddhist Priest Myōe*; Tanabe, *Myōe the Dreamkeeper*.
2. Tanabe, *Myōe the Dreamkeeper*, 50.
3. Kawai, *Dreams, Myths*, 43.
4. Ibid., 47.
5. Tanabe, *Myōe the Dreamkeeper*, 177.
6. Ibid., 188.
7. Ibid., 182–183.
8. Ibid., 176.
9. Ibid., 158.

Chapter 3

1. The following texts have been used in developing this portrait of the life and dreams of Lucrecia de León: Kagan, *Lucrecia's Dreams*; Jordán, "Competition and Confirmation"; Zambrano, Simons, and Miguel, *Sueños y procesos*; Bulkeley, *Lucrecia the Dreamer*.
2. Bulkeley, *Lucrecia the Dreamer*, 57.
3. Ibid., 70.
4. Ibid., 61.

Chapter 4

1. The following texts have been used in developing this portrait of the life and dreams of Emanuel Swedenborg: Van Dusen, *Emanuel Swedenborg's Journal*; Toksvig, *Emanuel Swedenborg*; Cassirer, *Kant's Life*; Johnson, *Kant on Swedenborg*; Lachman, *Swedenborg*.
2. Lachman, *Swedenborg*, 8.
3. Toksvig, *Emmanuel Swedenborg*, 63.
4. Van Dusen, *Emanuel Swedenborg's Journal*, 15.
5. Ibid., 21.
6. Ibid., 22.
7. Ibid.
8. Ibid., 69.
9. Ibid., 189.
10. Cassirer, *Kant's Life*, 77–92.
11. Johnson, *Kant on Swedenborg*, xi–xii.

Chapter 5

1. The following texts have been used in developing this portrait of the life and dreams of Benjamin Banneker: Banneker, *Dreams*; Tyson, *Sketch*; Bedini, *Life*; Cerami, *Benjamin Banneker*.
2. Bedini, *Life*, 39.
3. Cerami, *Benjamin Banneker*, 59–61.
4. Banneker, *Dreams*.

Chapter 6

1. The following texts have been used in developing this portrait of the life and dreams of Anna Kingsford: Kingsford, *Dreams and Dream-Stories*; Ashe, *Hermetic Kabbalah*; Maitland, *Story*; Hart, *Clothed*; Pert, *Red Cactus*.
2. Kingsford, *Dreams and Dream-Stories*, 7.
3. Lectures originally published in 1929 as Woolf, *A Room*, 3.
4. Pert, *Red Cactus*, 172.
5. Kingsford, *Dreams and Dream-Stories*, 17.
6. Ibid., 8.
7. Ibid., 19.
8. Ibid.
9. Ibid.
10. Ibid., 18–19.
11. Ibid., 28–29; emphasis in original.
12. Ibid., 30.
13. Ibid.
14. Ibid.
15. Ibid., 31.
16. Ibid., 39–40.

Chapter 7

1. The following texts have been used in developing this portrait of the life and dreams of Wolfgang Pauli: Meier, *Atom and Archetype*; Gieser, *Dream Symbols*; Pauli, *Writings*; Miller, *Deciphering*; Jung, "Individual Dream Symbolism."
2. Pauli, *Writings*, 13–14.
3. Jung, "Individual Dream Symbolism," 116.
4. Meier, *Atom and Archetype*, 4.
5. Ibid., 18.
6. Ibid., 121–123.
7. Ibid., 50.

8. Ibid., 27.
9. Ibid., 175.
10. Pauli, *Writings*, 17.
11. Meier, *Atom and Archetype*, 33.

Chapter 8

1. The following texts have been used in developing this methodological over-view: Freud, *Interpretation of Dreams*; Hall and Van de Castle, *Content Analysis*; Domhoff, *Finding Meaning*; Windt, *Dreaming*; Domhoff and Schneider, "*Studying Dream Content*"; Bulkeley, *Big Dreams*.
2. Wilson, *Consilience*.
3. Damasio, *The Feeling*, 83.
4. Freud, *Interpretation of Dreams*, 136.
5. Ibid., 274n2.
6. Ibid., 275.
7. Jung, "On the Nature, 76–77.
8. See Tedlock, *Dreaming*; Mageo and Sheriff, *New Directions*.

Chapter 9

1. Bulkeley, *Wilderness of Dreams*, 107.
2. Domhoff, *Finding Meaning*.

Chapter 10

1. Bulkeley, "Religious Content."
2. Bulkeley, *Big Dreams*.
3. Ibid.
4. The night after I wrote this paragraph, I had a dream in which I was working on this book, moving paragraphs and pages around, and I suddenly realized in the dream, *Hey, here I am, writing in a dream!*

Chapter 11

1. Freud, *Interpretation of Dreams*, 143n2.
2. Aristides, *Complete Works*.
3. Tanabe, *Myōe the Dreamkeeper*, 178–179.

4. Bulkeley, *Lucrecia the Dreamer*, 77–78.

5. Freud, *Introductory Lectures*, 284–285.

Chapter 12

1. Gieser, *Dream Symbols*, 25.

2. Meier, *Atom and Archetype*, 69.

3. Pauli, *Writings*.

4. Meier, *Atom and Archetype*, 66–67.

5. Jung, "Approaching the Unconscious," 58–64.

6. Ibid., 59, 63.

7. Jung, "On the Psychology," 80, 116.

8. Jung, *The Archetypes*, 121, 367.

Chapter 13

1. Beradt, *Third Reich*, 23.

2. Ibid., 24–25.

3. King, "Let's Stand Up," 234–235; emphasis in original.

4. Ibid., 235.

5. Eggan, "Manifest Content."

6. Gregor, "Content Analysis," 164.

7. Meier, *Atom and Archetype*, 28.

8. Kingsford, *Dreams and Dream-Stories*, 88.

Chapter 14

1. Beit-Hallahmi and Argyle, *Psychology*, 6.

2. James, *Varieties*, 42.

3. Ibid., 386–387.

4. Pauli, *Writings*, 132; emphasis added.

5. Pert, *Red Cactus*, 117.

6. Allport and Ross, "Personal Religious Orientation"; see also Wulff, *Psychology of Religion*, 231ff.; Beit-Hallahmi and Argyle, *Psychology*, 173ff.

7. Wulff, *Psychology of Religion*, 238.

8. James, *Varieties*, 282–285.

9. Ibid., 282, 284.

Chapter 15

1. Beit-Hallahmi and Argyle, *Psychology*, 73.
2. James, *Varieties*, 298.
3. Ibid.
4. Ibid., 293.
5. Ibid.
6. Whitehouse, *Modes of Religiosity*.

Chapter 16

1. James, "The One," 405–406.
2. Stephens, *Dreams and Visions*, 11.
3. Tanabe, *Myōe the Dreamkeeper*, 116.
4. James, *Varieties*, 396.
5. Wulff, *Psychology of Religion*, 223–243; Beit-Hallahmi and Argyle, *Psychology*, 218–228.
6. James, *Varieties*, 365.
7. The guiding text of the class was Levinson, *Religious Investigations*.

Conclusion

1. Ehrlich, *Dreams*.
2. Nietzsche, *Beyond*, 54–55.

Bibliography

Allport, G. E., and J. M. Ross. "Personal Religious Orientation and Prejudice." *Journal of Personality and Social Psychology* 5, no. 4 (1967): 432.

Aristides, Aelius. *The Complete Works*. Translated by Charles Behr. Leiden: Brill, 1981.

Ashe, Emma, ed. *The Hermetic Kabbalah of Anna Kingsford*. Glastonbery: Glastonbury Books (2006).

Banneker, Benjamin. *The Dreams of Benjamin Banneker*. Maryland Center for Culture and History, 2022.

Bedini, Silvio. *The Life of Benjamin Banneker*. New York: Charles Scribner's Sons, 1972.

Beit-Hallahmi, Benjamin, and Michael Argyle. *The Psychology of Religious Belief, Behavior, and Experience*. New York: Routledge, 1997.

Beradt, Charlotte. *The Third Reich of Dreams*. Translated by A. Gottwald. Chicago: Quadrangle, 1966.

Borges, Jorge Luis. "Nightmares." In Jorge Luis Borges, *Seven Nights*, translated by Eliot Weinberger, 26–41. New York: New Directions, 1984.

Bulkeley, Kelly. "Dreaming in Adolescence: A 'Blind' Word Search of a Teenage Girl's Dream Series." *Dreaming* 22 (2012): 240–252.

Bulkeley, Kelly. *Dreaming in the World's Religions: A Comparative History*. New York: New York University Press, 2008.

Bulkeley, Kelly. "The Religious Content of Dreams: A New Scientific Foundation." *Pastoral Psychology* 58 (2009): 93–101.

Bulkeley, Kelly. *The Wondering Brain: Thinking About Religion with and beyond Cognitive Neuroscience*. New York: Routledge, 2005.

Bulkeley, Kelly. *Big Dreams: The Science of Dreaming and the Origins of Religion*. New York: Oxford University Press, 2016.

Bulkeley, Kelly. *An Introduction to the Psychology of Dreaming* (Second edition). Westport, CT: Praeger, 2017.

Bulkeley, Kelly. *Lucrecia the Dreamer: Prophecy, Cognitive Science, and the Spanish Inquisition*. Stanford, CA: Stanford University Press, 2018.

Bulkeley, Kelly. *The Wilderness of Dreams*. Albany: SUNY Press, 1994.

Bulkeley, Kelly, and G. William Domhoff. "Detecting Meaning in Dream Reports: An Extension of a Word Search Approach." *Dreaming* 20 (2010): 77–95.

Burroughs, William. *My Education: A Book of Dreams*. New York: Viking, 1995.

Bynum, Edward Bruce. *Families and the Interpretation of Dreams: Awakening the Intimate Web*. New York: Harrington Park, 1993.

Calkins, Mary. "Statistics of Dreams." *American Journal of Psychology* 5 (1893): 311–343.

Cartwright, Rosalind. *The Twenty-Four Hour Mind: The Role of Sleep and Dreaming in Our Emotional Lives*. New York: Oxford University Press, 2010.

Cassirer, Ernst. *Kant's Life and Thought*. New Haven, CT: Yale University Press, 1981.

Cerami, Charles A. *Benjamin Banneker: Surveyor, Astronomer, Publisher, Patriot*. New York: John Wiley, 2002.

Cixous, Helene. *Dream I Tell You*. New York: Columbia University Press, 2006.

Damasio, Antonio. *The Feeling of What Happens: Body and Emotion in the Making of Consciousness*. San Diego: Harcourt, 1999.

Domhoff, G. William. *Finding Meaning in Dreams: A Quantitative Approach*. New York: Plenum, 1996.

Domhoff, G. William, and Adam Schneider. "Studying Dream Content Using the Archive and Search Engine on DreamBank.net." *Consciousness and Cognition* 17 (2008): 1238–1247.

Dunne, J. W. *An Experiment with Time*. Charlottesville, VA: Hampton Roads, 1927.

Edelstein, Emma, and Ludwig Edelstein. *Asclepius: Collection and Interpretation of the Testimonies*. Baltimore: Johns Hopkins University Press, 1945.

Eggan, Dorothy. "The Manifest Content of Dreams: A Challenge to Social Science." *American Anthropologist* 54 (1952): 469–485.

Ehrlich, Benjamin. *The Dreams of Santiago Ramón y Cajal*. New York: Oxford University Press, 2017.

Faraday, Ann. *Dream Power*. New York: Berkley, 1972.

Freud, Sigmund. *The Interpretation of Dreams* [1900]. Translated by James Strachey. New York: Avon, 1965.

Freud, Sigmund. *Introductory Lectures on Psychoanalysis*. Translated by J. Strachey. New York: W.W. Norton, 1966.

Gieser, Suzanne, ed. *Dream Symbols of the Individuation Process: Notes of C. G. Jung's Seminars on Wolfgang Pauli's Dreams*. Princeton, NJ: Princeton University Press, 2019.

Glaskin, Katie, and Richard Chenhall, eds. *Sleep around the World: Anthropological Perspectives*. New York: Palgrave Macmillan, 2013.

Greene, Graham. *A World of My Own: A Dream Diary*. New York: Viking, 1993.

Gregor, Thomas. "Content Analysis of Mehinaku Dreams." *Ethos* 9, no. 4 (1981): 353–390.

Hall, Calvin. *The Meaning of Dreams*. New York: McGraw-Hill, 1966.

Hall, Calvin. "Diagnosing Personality by the Analysis of Dreams." *Journal of Abnormal and Social Psychology* 4, no. 1 (1947): 68–79.

Hall, Calvin, and Robert Van de Castle. *The Content Analysis of Dreams*. New York: Appleton-Century-Crofts, 1966.

Harris, William V. *Dreams and Experience in Classical Antiquity*. Cambridge, MA: Harvard University Press, 2009.

Hart, Samuel Hopgood, ed. *Clothed with the Sun: Being the Book of the Illuminations of Anna Kingsford*. 2nd ed. London: John M. Watkins, 1906.

Herman, Michelle. *Stories We Tell Ourselves*. Iowa City, IA: University of Iowa Press, 2013.

Hobson, J. Allan. *The Dreaming Brain*. New York: Basic Books, 1988.

Hufford, David. *The Terror That Comes in the Night: An Experience-Centered Study of Supernatural Assault Traditions*. Philadelphia: University of Pennsylvania Press, 1982.

Hurd, Ryan. *Sleep Paralysis: A Guide to Hypnagogic Visions and Visitors of the Night*. Los Altos, CA: Hyena, 2010.

James, William. "The One and the Many." In William James, *The Pragmatic Method*, 405–417. Chicago: University of Chicago Press, 1977.

James, William. *The Varieties of Religious Experience*. New York: Mentor, 1958.

Jayne, Walter Addison. *The Healing Gods of Ancient Civilizations*. New York: University Books, 1925.

Johnson, Gregory R. *Kant on Swedenborg: Dreams of a Spirit-Seer and Other Writings*. New York: Swedenborg Foundation, 2002.

Jordán, María V. "Competition and Confirmation in the Iberian Prophetic Community: The 1589 Invasion of Portugal in the Dreams of Lucrecia de León," in *Dreams, Dreamers, and Visions: The Early Modern Atlantic World*, edited by Ann Marie Plane and Leslie Tuttle, 72–87. Philadelphia: University of Pennsylvania Press, 2013.

Jouvet, Michel. *The Paradox of Sleep: The Story of Dreaming*. Translated by Laurence Garey. Cambridge, MA: MIT Press, 1999.

Jung, Carl. "Approaching the Unconscious." In Carl Jung, *Man and His Symbols*, 18–103. New York: Doubleday, 1964.

Jung, Carl. *The Archetypes and the Collective Unconscious*. Translated by R. Hull. Princeton: Princeton University Press, 1969.

Jung, Carl. *Dreams*. Translated by R. Hull. Princeton, NJ: Princeton University Press, 1974.

Jung, Carl. "Individual Dream Symbolism in Relation to Alchemy." In Carl Jung, *Dreams*, translated by R. Hull, 111–298. Princeton, NJ: Princeton University Press, 1974.

Jung, Carl. *Memories, Dreams, Reflections*. Translated by R. and C. Winston. New York: Vintage, 1965.

Jung, Carl. "On the Nature of Dreams" [1945]. In Carl Jung, *Dreams*, translated by R. Hull, 67–83. Princeton, NJ: Princeton University Press, 1974.

Jung, Carl. "On the Psychology of the Unconscious." In Carl Jung, *Two Essays on Analytical Psychology*, translated by R. Hull, 1–119. Princeton: Princeton University Press, 1966.

Kagan, Richard L. *Lucrecia's Dreams: Politics and Prophecy in Sixteenth-Century Spain*. Baltimore: Johns Hopkins University Press, 1990.

Kawai, Hayao. *The Buddhist Priest Myōe: A Life of Dreams*. Venice: Lapis, 1992.

Kawai, Hayao. *Dreams, Myths, and Fairy Tales in Japan*. Einsiedeln, Switzerland: Daimon, 1995.

Kerouac, Jack. *Book of Dreams*. San Francisco, CA: City Lights Books, 2001.

King, Johanna. "Let's Stand Up, Regain Our Balance, and Look Around." In *Among All These Dreamers: Essays on Dreaming and Modern Society*, edited by Kelly Bulkeley, 225–236. Albany: SUNY Press, 1996.

Kingsford, Anna Bonus. *Dreams and Dream-Stories*. London: John M. Watkins, 1908.

Kramer, Milton, and Myron Glucksman, eds. *Dream Research: Contributions to Clinical Practice*. New York: Routledge, 2015.

Kryger, Meir H., Thomas Roth, and William C. Dement, eds. *Principles and Practices of Sleep Medicine*. 4th ed. Philadelphia: Elsevier Saunders, 2005.

Lachman, Gary. *Swedenborg: An Introduction to His Life and Ideas*. New York: Jeremy Tarcher, 2009.

Levinson, Henry Samuel. *The Religious Investigations of William James*. Chapel Hill: University of North Carolina Press, 1981.

Mageo, Jeannette, and Robin Sheriff, eds. *New Directions in the Anthropology of Dreaming*. New York: Routledge, 2021.

Maitland, Edward. *The Story of Anna Kingsford and Edward Maitland and of the New Gospel of Interpretation*. London: John M. Watkins, 1893.

Malinowski, Josie. *The Psychology of Dreaming*. London: Routledge, 2021.

Maquet, Pierre, Carlyle Smith, and Robert Stickgold, eds. *Sleep and Brain Plasticity*. New York: Oxford University Press, 2003.

Meier, C. A., ed. *Atom and Archetype: The Pauli/Jung Letters 1932–1958*. Princeton, NJ: Princeton University Press, 2001.

Meier, C. A. *Healing Dream and Ritual: Ancient Incubation and Modern Psychotherapy*. Einsiedeln, Switzerland: Daimon Verlag, 1989.

Miller, Arthur I. *Deciphering the Cosmic Number: The Strange Friendship of Wolfgang Pauli and Carl Jung*. New York: W. W. Norton, 2009.

Mitchell-Boyask, Robin. *Plague and the Athenian Imagination: Drama, History, and the Cult of Asclepius*. New York: Cambridge University Press, 2008.

Muster, Nori. *Betrayal of the Spirit: My Life behind the Headlines of the Hare Krishna Movement*. Champaign, IL: University of Illinois Press, 1996.

Nabokov, Vladimir. *Insomniac Dreams*. Princeton, NJ: Princeton University Press, 2017.

Nietzsche, Friedrich. *Beyond Good and Evil*. Translated by R. J. Hollingdale. New York: Penguin Classics, 1973.

Pagel, James F. "Non-Dreamers." *Sleep Medicine* 4, no. 3 (2003): 235–241.

Pauli, Wolfgang. *Writings on Physics and Philosophy*. Leiden: Springer-Verlag, 1994.

Pedley, John. *Sanctuaries and the Sacred in the Ancient Greek World*. New York: Cambridge University Press, 2006.

Pert, Alan. *Red Cactus: The Life of Anna Kingsford*. Watson's Bay, Australia: Books & Writers, 2006.

Price, Nancy. *Acquainted with the Night: A Book of Dreams*. Oxford: George Ronald, 1949.

Rollins, Henry. *Black Coffee Blues*. Los Angeles: 2.13.61, 1992.

Schmidt, Dennis. "Stretched Dream Science: The Essential Contribution of Long-Term Naturalistic Studies." *Dreaming* 9 (1999): 43–69.

Schredl, Michael. *Researching Dreams: The Fundamentals*. Leiden: Springer, 2018.

Sliwinski, Sharon. *Dreaming in Dark Times: Six Exercises in Political Thought*. Minneapolis: University of Minnesota Press, 2017.

Stephens, John. *The Dreams and Visions of Aelius Aristides: A Case-Study in the History of Religions*. Piscataway, NJ: Gorgias, 2013.

Tanabe, George, Jr. *Myōe the Dreamkeeper: Fantasy and Knowledge in Early Kamakura Buddhism*. Cambridge, MA: Harvard University Press, 1992.

Tedlock, Barbara, ed. *Dreaming: Anthropological and Psychological Perspectives*. New York: Cambridge University Press, 1987.

Tick, Edward. *The Practice of Dream Healing: Bringing Ancient Greek Mysteries into Modern Medicine*. Wheaton, IL: Quest, 2001.

Toksvig, Signe. *Emanuel Swedenborg: Scientist and Mystic*. New York: Swedenborg Foundation, 1948.

Tyson, Martha. *Sketch of the Life of Benjamin Banneker: From Notes Taken in 1836*. Maryland Historical Society, 1854.

Van Dusen, William. *Emanuel Swedenborg's Journal of Dreams*. New York: Swedenborg Foundation, 1986.

Whitehouse, Harvey. *Modes of Religiosity: A Cognitive Theory of Religious Transmission*. Walnut Creek, CA: Altamira, 2004.

Wilson, E.O. *Consilience: The Unity of Knowledge*. New York: Alfred A. Knopf, 1998.

Wilson, E. O. *Sociobiology: The New Synthesis*. 25th anniversary ed. Cambridge, MA: Belknap Press, 2000.

Windt, Jennifer. *Dreaming: A Conceptual Framework for Philosophy of Mind and Empirical Research*. Cambridge, MA: MIT Press, 2015.

Woolf, Virginia. *A Room of One's Own*. London: Penguin UK, 2021.

Wulff, David. *Psychology of Religion: Classic and Contemporary*. New York: John Wiley, 1996.

Zambrano, María, Edison Simons, and Juan Bázquez Miguel, eds. *Sueños y procesos de Lucrecia de León*. Madrid: Tecnos, 1987.

Index